Frontiers of Artificial Intelligence, Ethics and Multidisciplinary Applications

Artificial Intelligence is now present in numerous spheres of our everyday lives. It is poised to lead new and efficient business models for effective and user-centric services in the private and public sectors. Advances in AI in deep learning, (deep) reinforcement learning, and neuroevolutionary techniques can pave the way forward for artificial general intelligence (AGI). However, the development and use of AI also present challenges. Inherent biases prevalent within data corpora used to train AI and machine learning systems attribute to most of these challenges. In addition, multiple instances have highlighted the need for privacy, fairness, and transparency in AI-powered decision-making. This book series will provide an avenue for researchers, leaders, decision-makers, and policymakers to share research and insights on the forefronts of AI, including its use in an Ethical, Explainable, Privacy-Preserving, Trustworthy, and Sustainable manner.

The series has relevance across disciplines and be multi-disciplinary. Advances in AI, explainability AI, privacy-preserving AI, and ethical AI explored in this book series are unexplored areas for research and competence building. Such developments can reduce hesitancy for AI integration in many domains. The book series thus fits in well as an essential and growing need among those who work on artificial intelligence in academia, business and industry, and the public sector to exploit the opportunities in the constantly evolving field of AI.

The series publishes research monographs, authored works by practitioners and case studies to highlight innovative and best practices, and edited volumes putting together varied perspectives.

Sachin Kumar · Ajit Kumar Verma · Amna Mirza

Digital Transformation, Artificial Intelligence and Society

Opportunities and Challenges

Springer

Sachin Kumar
Cluster Innovation Centre
University of Delhi
New Delhi, Delhi, India

Amna Mirza
Department of Political Science
Shyama Prasad Mukherji College for Women
University of Delhi
New Delhi, Delhi, India

Ajit Kumar Verma
Faculty of Technology
Environmental and Social Sciences
Western Norway University of Applied Sciences
Haugesund, Norway

ISSN 2731-8125 ISSN 2731-8133 (electronic)
Frontiers of Artificial Intelligence, Ethics and Multidisciplinary Applications
ISBN 978-981-97-5655-1 ISBN 978-981-97-5656-8 (eBook)
https://doi.org/10.1007/978-981-97-5656-8

This Springer imprint is published by the registered company Springer Nature Singapore Pte Ltd.
The registered company address is: 152 Beach Road, #21-01/04 Gateway East, Singapore 189721, Singapore

"To Almighty"—Dr. Sachin Kumar

"To My Loving Deities, Gurus, Parents, Family and Friends in India and Norway"—Prof. Ajit Kumar Verma

"To my family who always motivated me to keep up the stride"—Dr. Amna Mirza

Foreword

In the landscape of technological advancement, digital transformation and artificial intelligence (AI) have not only reshaped businesses and industries but have also left an indelible mark on individuals and the fabric of society itself. As we stand on the precipice of a new era defined by innovation and connectivity, we must explore both the opportunities and challenges that accompany this profound shift.

This book, *Digital Transformation, Artificial Intelligence, and Society: Opportunities and Challenges*, serves as a beacon amid the complexities of our rapidly evolving digital age. Within its pages, readers will embark on a journey that delves into the multifaceted intersections of technology and society from several dimensions. Through a very fact and research-based topic introduction, insightful analysis, and thought-provoking discourse based on real-world scenarios, this book offers a comprehensive exploration of the myriad ways in which digital transformation and AI are shaping our world, personal or professional.

From the realms of business and economics to healthcare, education, information ecosystem, knowledge economy, climate actions, global affairs, and governance, the impact of digital transformation and AI knows no bounds. While these technologies hold immense promise for enhancing efficiency, driving innovation, and improving quality of life, they also present profound challenges. Concerns surrounding privacy, ethics, biases, equity, fairness, and the future of work loom large demanding careful consideration and strategic action from stakeholders specifically from policymakers and governments.

Yet, amidst these challenges lie unparalleled opportunities for progress and prosperity. By harnessing the power of digital transformation and AI responsibly and inclusively, we have the potential to build a future that is more equitable, sustainable, and resilient. This book serves as a vital resource for policymakers, industry leaders, academics, and concerned citizens alike, offering insights and guidance to navigate the complexities of our digital landscape.

This book serves as a roadmap for navigating the complex terrain of our digital future, offering insights, perspectives, and strategies to harness the transformative potential of digital transformation and AI while mitigating the associated risks and pitfalls. It is a call to action for policymakers, industry leaders, scholars, and citizens alike to come together in pursuit of a shared vision of a future where technology catalyses positive change and collective flourishing.

As we embark on this journey of exploration and discovery, I hope that this book will inspire meaningful dialogue, foster collaboration, and catalyse positive change. Together, let us embrace the opportunities before us, confront the challenges that lie ahead, and chart a course towards a future where technology serves as a force for good, enriching the lives of all members of society.

Venu Govindaraju, Ph.D.
SUNY Distinguished Professor
of Computer Science
and Engineering & Vice President for
Research and Economic Development
University at Buffalo, The State
University of New York
New York, USA

Preface

In today's rapidly evolving world, the convergence of digital transformation, artificial intelligence, and societal dynamics has become a focal point for both scholars and practitioners alike. The integration of these technologies into our daily lives has brought about unprecedented opportunities along with profound challenges to all stakeholders such as general public, researchers, public policy experts, administrators, governments, and private institutions. As we navigate this intricate landscape, it becomes imperative to comprehensively understand the interplay between technology and society.

This book, titled *Digital Transformation, Artificial Intelligence, and Society: Opportunities and Challenges*, delves deep into this dynamic relationship, exploring the multifaceted impacts of digitalisation, artificial intelligence (AI), and their intersection with societal structures and systems. This book aims to provide a holistic understanding of the complex interdependencies shaping our present and future from the point of view of opportunities and challenges.

The journey begins with an exploration of the foundational elements underpinning digital transformation and its profound impact on society. From the advent of computing technologies to the rise of the Internet age, this chapter sets the stage for a deeper understanding of the transformative forces at play. Building upon the groundwork laid in the preceding chapter, Chapter 2 delves into the historical antecedents of societal transformation due to technological revolutions. By tracing the evolution of human civilisation alongside technological advancements, we gain invaluable insights into the cyclical nature of societal change and innovation.

The convergence of digitalisation, AI, IoT, and Industry 4.0 marks a pivotal moment in human history. Chapter 3 examines the synergistic effects of these technologies on shaping the contours of a digital society, offering a glimpse into the transformative potential of interconnected systems. As we transition towards a knowledge-based economy, the role of digital transformation becomes increasingly pronounced. This section explores the interplay between technology, knowledge creation, and economic growth, shedding light on the opportunities and challenges inherent in this paradigm shift. The emergence of AI-driven governance systems heralds a new era of efficiency and innovation in public administration. Through case studies and theoretical frameworks, this chapter elucidates the transformative impact of smart cities and governance on urban development.

In the realm of industry, AI holds the promise of revolutionising traditional manufacturing processes. By harnessing the power of intelligent automation, this section explores the transition towards smart factories and its implications for future industrial landscapes. The concept of a data-driven circular economy offers a novel approach to sustainable development and resource management. This chapter investigates the potential benefits and challenges associated with leveraging data analytics to promote circularity and environmental stewardship.

In an increasingly interconnected world, Industry 4.0 serves as a catalyst for global economic integration and collaboration. Through an examination of international relations theory and geopolitical dynamics, this section explores the transformative effects of Industry 4.0 on shaping a new era of globalisation. The proliferation of misinformation poses a significant threat to the fabric of society. By analysing information consumption patterns and the rise of deep fake technology, this chapter unpacks the challenges associated with combating fake news in the digital age. As humanity grapples with the existential threat of climate change, AI emerges as a powerful tool for mitigation and adaptation. This section explores the intersection of artificial intelligence and environmental sustainability, highlighting innovative approaches to addressing climate-related challenges. Amidst the rapid pace of technological innovation, ethical considerations loom large on the horizon. From algorithmic biases to privacy concerns, this chapter confronts the ethical dilemmas inherent in the digital revolution, urging stakeholders to prioritise responsible AI development. In conclusion, the book outlines a roadmap for navigating the complex terrain of digital transformation and artificial intelligence. By advocating for responsible and ethical AI practices, the authors articulate a vision for a future where technology serves as a force for positive societal change.

As we embark on this intellectual journey, we invite readers to critically engage with the themes presented within these pages. It is our sincere hope that this book serves as a catalyst for dialogue, innovation, and collective action towards harnessing the transformative potential of digitalisation and AI for the betterment of society.

New Delhi, India — Dr. Sachin Kumar
Haugesund, Norway — Prof. Ajit Kumar Verma
New Delhi, India — Dr. Amna Mirza

Acknowledgements

We would like to express our deep gratitude for the blessings of the Almighty for making us successful in writing this book.

Writing a book is never a solitary endeavour; it is the culmination of the collective efforts, support, and inspiration of many individuals and institutions. As we reflect on the completion of "Digital Transformation, Artificial Intelligence, and Society: Opportunities and Challenges", We are humbled and deeply grateful for the contributions of those who have accompanied us on this journey.

We extend our heartfelt gratitude to all our research collaborators and students whose expertise, insights, and dedication have enriched the content of this book and guided us to have a book at the emerging technological landscape and its impact on society. Your willingness to share your knowledge and perspectives has been instrumental in providing a comprehensive exploration of the complex intersections of technology and society.

We are indebted to the reviewers and editors whose meticulous attention to detail and constructive feedback have been invaluable in refining the ideas and arguments presented in this book. Your expertise and guidance have played a pivotal role in shaping the final manuscript.

We extend my appreciation to the publishers and production team for their professionalism, expertise, and support throughout the publication process. Your commitment to excellence and attention to detail have ensured the quality and integrity of this book, and I am grateful for your hard work and dedication.

We are deeply thankful to our colleagues, mentors, and advisors for their encouragement, support, and scholarly insights. I would like to express my deep gratitude to my doctoral Supervisor Dr. Saibal K. Pal for motivating me to write the book. His guidance and mentorship have been instrumental in shaping my understanding of the complex technological and socio-economic issues addressed in this book, and We are grateful for your wisdom and encouragement.

To our friends and family, We extend our heartfelt thanks for your unwavering support, encouragement, and understanding throughout the writing process. Your love, patience, and encouragement have been a constant source of inspiration and motivation, and I am grateful for your presence in my life.

Finally, We express my gratitude to the readers of this book for your interest, engagement, and curiosity. It is my sincere hope that "Digital Transformation, Artificial Intelligence, and Society: Opportunities and Challenges" will serve as a catalyst for meaningful dialogue, critical reflection, and positive change in our rapidly evolving digital world.

Contents

About the Authors

Dr. Sachin Kumar is Assistant Professor of Computer Science at Cluster Innovation Centre (CIC), University of Delhi (UoD), Delhi, India. He is also an executive officer of the University of Delhi Foundation, an endowment fund section 8, not-for-profit company of UoD. He has been awarded a Ph.D. degree from the Department of Computer Science, University of Delhi (UoD) on a thesis titled "Modeling and Prediction of Building Energy Performance Using Machine Learning Approaches". His research work has been published in the domain of intelligent information systems, urban computing and smart systems reputed international high-impact factor SCI/SCIE/Scopus journals and conferences such as Energy and Buildings (Elsevier, IF = 7.6), Sustainable Cities and Societies (Elsevier, IF = 11.5), Sustainable Energy, Grids and Networks (Elsevier, IF = 5.6). His thesis primarily focuses on developing models for energy performance optimization through modelling and prediction of energy usage toimprove energy conservation in residential and commercial buildings in order to achieve the goal of sustainable cities and societies to contribute to Sustainable Development Goals (SDGs). He secured several placement offers during MCA and after completion served as a software development engineer (SDE) with IHS Markit Information Mosaic, United Kingdom (UK). He is offering courses and supervising research and development in the area of Artificial Intelligence/Machine Learning/Deep Learning, Industry 4.0, Digital Transformation and Governance, Smart Cities, Urban Computing, Information Systems and Computational Social Systems. He has published more than 25 peer review research publications in high-impact factor SCI/SCIE/Scopus-indexed journals and conferences. He has also written a book on operating systems titled "Operating Systems: Concept Building and Problem Solving Approach" published by Cengage Publication, USA. He has participated in and demonstrated his research works at domain-specific several highly reputed international conferences such as IEEE-ELM, ISTA, ISDA, IEEE-WCCI, IEEE-IJCNN, ACM-ICEGOV, etc. He has been invited as a resource person to many conferences, faculty development programs (FDPs), refresher courses, and workshops to share his knowledge and expertise. His main thrust is to develop technological artefacts to solve societal problems with the application of technology and specifically Artificial Intelligence/Machine Learning, Big data analytics and their deployment in a real-world environment. He also writes on technology and social issues in national newspapers and news web portals and creates digital content for creating awareness about technology and social issues on the youtube channel "Professor and Mentor". He has been continuously providing his consultations to corporations and startups. He is also promoting interdisciplinary research, innovation, and entrepreneurship, through project-driven pedagogy, research publication outputs, and startup promotion.

Prof. Ajit Kumar Verma is a Professor in the Faculty of Technology, Environmental and Social Sciences, Western Norway University of Applied Sciences, Haugesund, Norway (since 2012) and was a Professor/Senior (HAG) scale Professor for around 15 years with the Reliability Engineering/Department of Electrical Engineering at IIT Bombay with a research focus in RAMS, Risk and Safety Engineering, Computational Intelligence applications in various domains. He was awarded (2017) 'Honorary Professor' at Amity University, India and also a Life Time Achievement award at IIT Madras by SRESA. He has supervised/co-supervised 39 Ph.D.s and over 100 Masters theses (IITB; HVL, Norway; University of Gåvle, Sweden; LJM Univ, UK; WMG, Warwick Univ, UK) in the area of Electronic Systems Reliability, Software Reliability, Reliable Computing, Power Systems Reliability, Reliability Centred Maintenance, Soft Computing in RAMS for Complex Engineering Systems and Probabilistic Safety/Risk Assessment in power plants and Computational Intelligence Applications in multiple domains. He has executed various research projects in India to promote industry interface and has been the course co-ordinator for industry CEPs like Reliability Engineering, Six Sigma, Software Inspections, Competency Tracking System and Software Reliability for IT industries. He is also a Guest Professor at Lulea University of Technology, Sweden and was an adjunct at the University of Stavanger. He has several publications to his credit. He was the Editor-in-Chief of OPSEARCH published by Springer (January 2008–January 2011). He is currently the Patron and Founder Editor-in-Chief of the International Journal of Systems Assurance Engineering and Management (IJSA) published by Springer and is the Editor-in-Chief of the journal of Life Cycle Reliability and Safety Engineering published by Springer. He has been a Guest Editor of Special Issues of various journals. He has been an author/editor in over a dozen books and is also a series editor in several book series including the 'Frontiers of Artificial intelligence, Ethics and Multidisciplinary Applications'.

Dr. Amna Mirza is an Academician, Author, Social Entrepreneur, and Curator of Ideas on technology and society. She is Associate Professor in the Department of Political Science at Shyama Prasad Mukherji College for Women, University of Delhi and former Associate Professor at Sarojini Naidu Centre for Women Studies, Jamia Millia Islamia, Delhi, India. She has done Masters's Degree in Political Science from Hindu College, University of Delhi and M.Phil. and Ph.D. from the Department of Political Science, University of Delhi. She has eight books to her credit, which were well-received by academia, media and others alike. She has more than 20 research papers in reputed peer-reviewed journals and has participated in more than 100 conferences at the national and international level for paper presentations and as a resource person to deliver invited lectures, amongst others. She has patents awarded by the governments of Australia and India, supervised two Ph.D. candidates, pursued two research projects, and contributed towards MOOCs, among others. She has also pursued additional coursework from HarvardX, amongst others. Her research areas include Digital transformation, Industry 4.0, Foreign Affairs, Digital Society, International Political Economy, Globalization, and International Relations. An avid traveller, voracious reader and vegan, her academic initiatives took her to the University of Duisburg Essen (Germany) and the University of Fribourg (Switzerland), amongst others. She is a recipient of 'The Godfray Philips Golden Ovary Award', the St. Stephens College Centenary Medal for 'character combined with learning', the Bharat Nirman Award for Women Entrepreneurship, the Mook-Nayak National Award, and the Business Rankers Women Achievement Award, amongst others. She has been associated with art and culture festivals and regularly contributes columns to several newspapers in multiple languages.

Abbreviations

4G	Fourth Generation
5G	Fifth Generation
ACLU	American Civil Liberties Union
ADAS	Advanced Driver Assistance Systems
AI HLEG	European Commission's High-Level Expert Group on Artificial Intelligence
AI	Artificial Intelligence
AMRs	Autonomous Mobile Robots
APIs	Application Programming Interface
ARPANET	Advanced Research Projects Agency Network
AWS	Amazon Web Services
BCE	Before Christ Era
BDA	Big Data Analytics
CAGR	Compound Annual Growth Rate
CH_4	Methane (CH_4)
CNC	Computer Numerical Control
CO_2	Carbon dioxide
COMPAS	Correctional Offender Management Profiling for Alternative Sanctions
CPS	Cyber-Physical Systems
DAS	Domain Awareness System
DFRLab	Atlantic Council's Digital Forensic Research Lab
DPI	Digital Public Infrastructure
DSM	Demand-Side Management
DVD	Digital Versatile Disc
ENIAC	Electronic Numerical Integrator and Computer
EPR	Extended Producer Responsibility
ERP	Enterprise Resource Planning
EVs	Electric Vehicles
FDM	Fused Deposition Modelling
FSD	Full Self-Driving

FTC	Federal Trade Commission
GANs	Generative Adversarial Networks
GDP	Growth Domestic Product
GDPR	European Union's General Data Protection Regulation
GHGs	Greenhouse Gases
GPS	Global Positioning System
IC	Integrated Circuits
ICT	Information and Communication Technology
IIoT	Industrial IoT
IoT	Internet of Things
IPCC	Intergovernmental Panel on Climate Change (IPCC)
IT	Information Technology
ITS	Intelligent Transportation Systems
ITU	International Telecommunication Union
KPIs	Key Performance Indicators
LAWs	Lethal Autonomous Weapons (LAWs)
LoRaWAN	Long-Range Wide Area Network
LTA	Land Transport Authority
LTE	Long-Term Evolution
ML	Machine Learning
MOOCs	Massive Open Online Courses
N_2O	Nitrous Oxide
NIST	National Institute of Standards and Technology
NLP	Natural Language Processing
NPCI	National Payments Corporation of India
PC	Personal Computer
R&D	Research and Development
RFID	Radio Frequency Identification
RPA	Robotic Process Automation
SDG	Sustainable Development Goals
SLS	Selective Laser Sintering
UBI	Universal Basic Income
UPI	Unified Payments Interface (UPI)
WCAG	Web Content Accessibility Guidelines
WEF	World Economic Forum
WHO	World Health Organisation
WWW	World Wide Web
XAI	Explainable AI (XAI)

List of Figures

Chapter 1
Background of Digital Transformation and Society

Abstract This chapter introduces and prepares the background to understand recent technological advancements and their impact on society. The chapter temporally and spatially highlights significant events and innovations which have led to the emergence of digital transformation and emerging technologies such as artificial intelligence (AI). The chapter provides a brief journey of information and communication technology (ICT) along with the development of products and services and emerging trends impacting our daily lives and transforming the socio-economic systems starting from home to business and economy, educational systems, governance systems, political systems, entertainment, and sports. However, Digital Transformation and AI have also posed certain challenges in front of society. There are issues related to job losses, misinformation, fake news, deep fakes, change in cultural value systems, embedding discrimination, amplification of biases, cultural shifts, propaganda, and loss of democratic value systems. This chapter provides a comprehensive background to guide readers through the intricate interplay between digital transformation, artificial intelligence, and society and explore opportunities and challenges.

Keywords Artificial intelligence · Digital transformation · Information and communication technology · Internet and connectivity · Society · Opportunities and challenges

1.1 Background

Starting from the twentieth century, Information and communication technology (ICT) and its offerings have defined how we live and interact with the socio-economic ecosystem around us. ICT has improved access to people, products, and services. ICT provides affordable, efficient, and effective means of communication to express our feelings, emotions, information, and exchange of ideas to a particular person or people on a large scale instantly (Palvia et al. 2018). Present-day digital revolution results in digital platforms and social media platforms running on the foundation of

S. Kumar et al., *Digital Transformation, Artificial Intelligence and Society*, Frontiers of Artificial Intelligence, Ethics and Multidisciplinary Applications,
https://doi.org/10.1007/978-981-97-5656-8_1

ICT and its applications. ICT brought novel and exciting upgrades/improvements to interact and utilise previously available systems according to human and societal requirements. ICT has its offerings in each dimension of life such as entertainment and leisure, delivering education remotely, providing universal access to information resources, procuring services, and goods from suppliers, online purchases and payments, and interacting with governance systems as citizens (Choudrie et al. 2018). ICT has transformed every professional or personal domain and revolutionised how we utilise and use services and products in economic systems, financial systems, governance systems, social systems, education systems, and personal life (Legner et al. 2017). It has completely redefined how humans interact with humans and how humans interact with social groups. A very relevant and revolutionary example of how ICTs have transformed access to services is "Aadhaar" and the Unified Payments Interface (UPI) in India. Aadhaar is a 12-digit unique identity number that can be obtained voluntarily by all residents of India from Indian authorities (Bhatia and Bhabha 2017). It is based on their biometrics and demographic data validated by the Indian government. UPI is an Indian instant payment system developed by the National Payments Corporation of India (NCPI) to facilitate inter-bank peer-to-peer and person-to-merchant transactions (Fuloria 2023). "Aadhaar" and UPI together and the mobile revolution have completely changed the way people and their identity is recognised and validated and make payments and purchases (Fig. 1.1). Such innovative products and services providing services to a huge number of citizens are appreciated across the globe. With the Industrial Revolution, the function of work was taken over by machines and devices, which also produced products and services on a large scale. But now in the twenty-first century, developed over the foundation of ICT, the technological revolution has transformed our machines, devices, and software products with advanced capabilities. This transformation is bringing autonomy and decision-making into machines, software, devices, etc.

Digital transformation and associated technologies such as AI aim to assist human capabilities and systems. Hence they are forcing our systems in the direction of replacing human decision-making. All this is being developed as one of the factors based on data collected from softwares, systems, and machines in several domains on the advancements made due to ICT. More advances in technology and the Internet led to the digital transformation of business and governance processes and systems which created the foundation for data generation and collection (Mergel et al. 2019). This collected data has a wealth of information about the transactions between customers and businesses with a history of purchases, customer or citizen behaviour, socio-economic backgrounds, etc. AI, machine learning, big data analytics, and advanced analytics techniques can help in the extraction of useful information and make better choices for governments, businesses, and customers for more value creation to stakeholders (Sarker 2021). In government systems citizens, government, and business interaction started more efficiently due to the deployment of digital platforms such as websites/web portals and software (Fig. 1.2). Earlier citizens were coming to government institutes and now the government is reaching out to citizens through digital technologies and its products and services (West 2004).

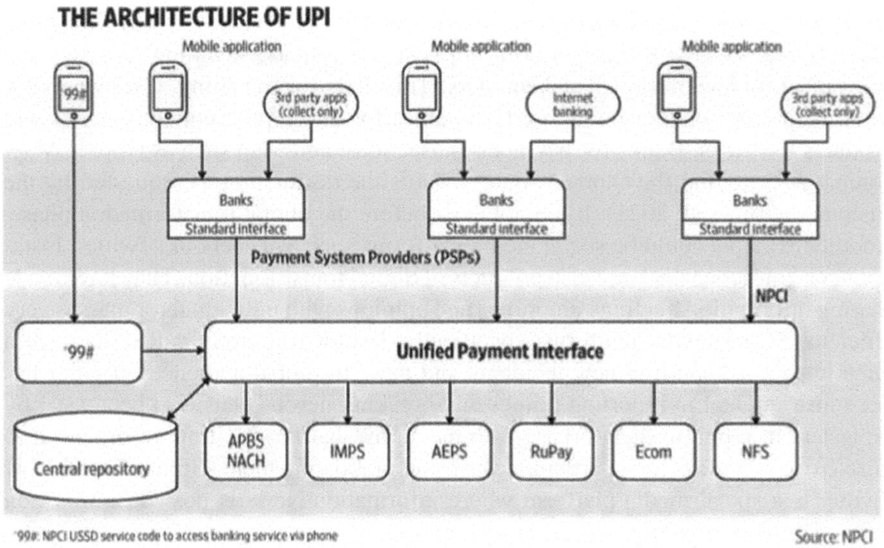

Fig. 1.1 UPI payment system and its fundamental components (https://www.livemint.com/Industry/bTGwxmykXhSKX5Vf8050NI/How-UPI-works.html)

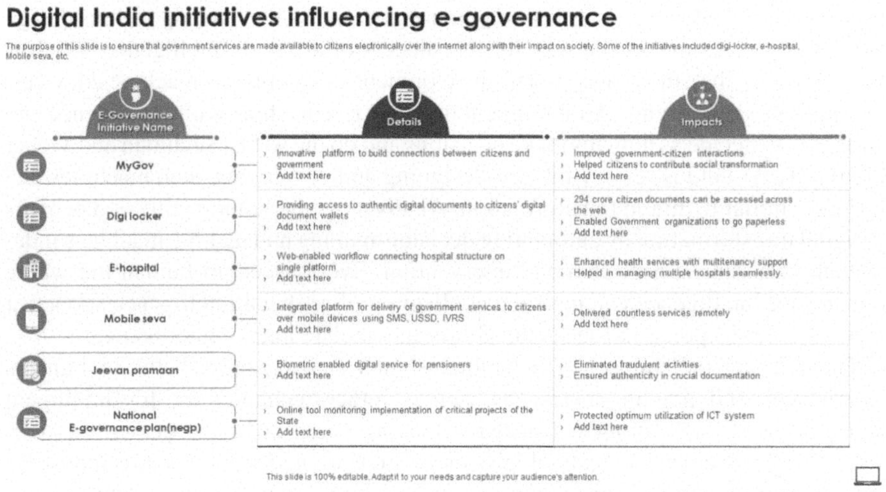

Fig. 1.2 Digital products and services for citizens by the Government of India (https://www.slideteam.net/digital-india-initiatives-influencing-e-governance.html)

Digital transformation is the adoption of digital technology and its products and services by an organisation to create new or modify existing products, services, and operations by translating business processes into a digital format and entities (Gong and Ribiere 2021). These new business or governance products and services or processes deliver more value to customers or citizens both accurately and efficiently. For example, the UBER transportation application has made travelling very easy and convenient by integrating all stakeholders: Travellers for travelling, Car owners for using their cars for transportation, Companies for developing new businesses and products for travel, Banks for payment transactions, and Map such as Google Map/ company for telling the shortest route towards the destination as requested by the customer (Min et al. 2021). It did not exist before the digital transformation phase. Another example could be social media platforms such as Facebook, Twitter, Instagram, or YouTube which are also products of digital transformation. They have made sharing information, feelings/emotions, and opinions with individuals or masses very efficient. Social media platforms specifically Twitter (presently called X) have a huge impact in reporting new incidents and news to global audiences. Twitter has been instrumental in reporting crimes and breaking news. It has also been used by protesters in toppling dictatorial governments by sharing real-time information to raise citizens' voices for a particular cause and mobilising them (Breuer 2016). Now Twitter is a social media platform where information/News is posted first, not on news platforms anymore.

The capabilities of these digital technologies and ICT-driven systems/platforms/ software/tools are to generate huge amounts of diverse data over a long period due to large numbers of user traction and interaction with systems which have substantial knowledge that can be extracted and used in decision-making. Such data having huge information and advancements in computational power with novel algorithms design and developments makes the way for the success of artificial intelligence which is the domain of the study, design and development of intelligent machines/devices/ systems/softwares/agents. An Intelligent machine is a machine with intelligence and autonomy to decide as humans make decisions and do the work (Suchman and Weber 2016). The AI field is responsible for designing and developing such machines and devices. Similar to digital transformation, AI advances the functionality and benefits of digital transformation by automating decision-making and making machines independent of human supervision and intervention. Every aspect of human life where humans use intelligence can have the application of artificial intelligence sooner or later. AI, with its potential, seeks the ability to simulate human intelligence.

The Internet of Things (IoT) facilitates interconnectedness between humans and devices and among devices as well as other technologies, for intelligent data processing and automated decision-making (Tien 2017). Together, AI, IoT, Blockchain, and emerging technologies drive innovation, disrupt business industries and governance systems, and fundamentally reshape socio-economic and cultural landscapes of society. All these emerging technologies have huge potential for heightened efficiency, productivity, and competitiveness of governance, Industries, businesses, and individuals (Faboye 2024). There is a need for a comprehensive exploration of the dynamic interplay between technology-driven transformations and their profound impact on human life and societies from several perspectives around the world (Fig. 1.3).

In addition to the huge benefits and opportunities for individuals and society, Digital Transformation and the emerging technological landscape driven by AI also

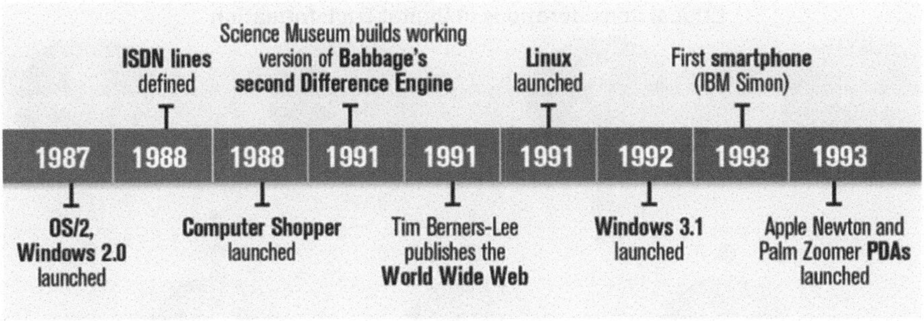

Fig. 1.3 A brief history of the computer (https://www.expertreviews.co.uk/technology/7885/a-brief-history-of-the-computer/7)

pose some serious threats and challenges to human life and the functions of society (Siebel 2019). For example, there is a genuine threat to existing jobs in a few sectors. Few types of jobs may disappear and few may emerge as well. This leads to the challenges of reskilling the public and citizens. AI as a transformative technology will completely change society and will have an impact as created by electricity as said by Prof. Andrew NG, Stanford (Sharma 2018).

Digital products and services and digital transformation also witness socio-ethical issues. Information ecosystems are also facing issues of misinformation, Fake news and Deep Fake being used in propaganda and creating threats to democratic institutions and information decentralization (Whyte 2020). There are cyber security threats as well due to the channels of interconnected billions of devices due to the adoption of the IoT domain (Tyagi and Nair 2020). Moreover, there are serious concerns for individuals, social groups, and social fabric. Digital technology and AI products and services have resulted in gender discrimination for example discriminating against women in the hiring process in companies and amplifying biases in the allocation of welfare and health benefits to certain sections of citizens (Belenguer 2022). Such application of AI if implemented on a large scale can amplify the injustice in society against disadvantaged groups such as women, black people, elderly, and people coming from diverse socio-economic, cultural, and linguistic backgrounds. There are social issues as well such as critical issues of digital exclusion and the digital divide (Fig. 1.4).

Digital transformation and AI must underscore and ensure equal access to information and opportunities, welfare, and justice for all members of society, emphasising the imperative to bridge the digital gap and provide solutions that are equal and just. As technology becomes an enabler of progress, these disparities must be addressed as a moral and societal obligation. The narrative emphasises the need for ethical considerations to be at the forefront, ensuring that technology is harnessed responsibly for the betterment of society (Jain 2021).

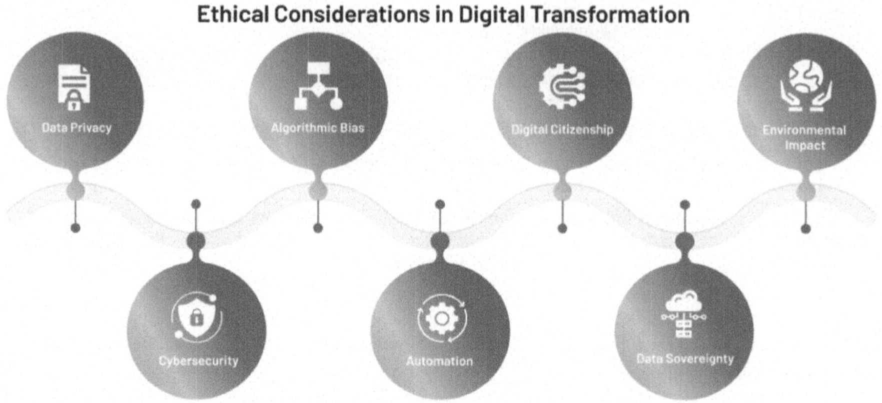

Fig. 1.4 Ethical considerations in digital environments (https://copperdigital.com/blog/ethics-of-digital-transformation/)

1.2 Historical Evolution of Digital Transformation

The digital age was expanded and fueled by innovations in microelectronics and telecommunications. It led to the development of electric devices which form the foundation of communication and information storage, information processing, and information exchanging for future requirements (Alberts et al. 1997). The initial stage was digitisation which was to store information from analogue format to digital format. The next phase was digitalisation using computers and software to solve stand-alone problems of organisations/systems so that business processes can become efficient and more effective in silos. Later on, it led to digital transformation which is a modification of existing processes or the creation of new processes for better service delivery and value creation in any sphere of society (Hanelt et al. 2021). In the phase of digital transformation, we are witnessing new entities, new processes, and new systems emerging and transforming our interaction, processing, and service delivery, majorly different from existing systems. That is why we see new entities, and new processes, emerging and changing our experience in society (Auriga 2016).

The early promise of interconnectedness and information access laid the foundation for what we now recognise as digital transformation. The genesis of digital transformation can be traced to the convergence of several technological threads. Starting from the proliferation of personal computing devices, the advent of the Internet and connectivity, and the rise of mobile technologies collectively set the stage for the complete transformation of society and its systems. Organisations, governments, and individuals found themselves in a landscape where data became the lifeblood of connectivity. From the realm of commerce to governance, the transformative potential of digitisation became increasingly evident (Helal et al. 1999).

Early computing systems were large mainframes with limited processing power that laid the groundwork for the gradual transition from analogue information processing to digital processing. In the 1960s and 1970s, businesses embraced mainframe computers to automate tasks like accounting, inventory management, and payroll. This marked the dawn of the digitisation era, where analogue information was meticulously converted into digital form. In this journey, the development of electronic computers in the 1940s, Electronic Numerical Integrator and Computer (ENIAC) have a significant role in causing the paradigm shift in information processing capabilities. Later on, computing technologies evolved in the form of the invention of transistors, integrated circuits (ICs), and microprocessors. These advancements paved the way for the democratisation of computation in the form of personal computers. The invention of microchips and semiconductors laid the foundation for the digital revolution by enabling the development of computers, capable of processing information at unimaginable speeds. The invention of the personal computer (PC) in the 1970s democratised access to computing power to individuals. Businesses and individuals alike could now leverage a wider range of software applications, such as word processing and spreadsheets to graphic design and communication tools. From the 1980s and 1990s onwards, the technological landscape saw the rise of personal computers in the form of several types of products coming from several companies such as Microsoft and Apple emerging and leading the personal computer revolution (O'Regan and O'Regan 2008) (Fig. 1.5).

The 1990s witnessed the explosive growth of the Internet, fundamentally changing how businesses and consumers interacted. The Internet is an interconnection of devices to share information. It allowed several applications such as sending emails, logging into remote systems, file transfers, and downloading web pages. Websites became the new storefronts which led to online sales booming, and communication channels diversified, fostering deeper customer connections (Leiner et al. 1997). The 2000s saw the rise of micro-level computing which was portable led by mobile technologies like smartphones and tablets. It empowered users with on-the-go access to computation, information processing, communication, and other related services transforming businesses through mobile commerce and mobile marketing

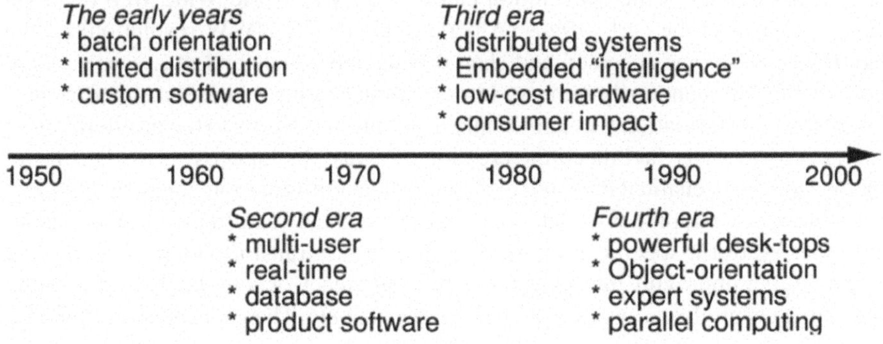

Fig. 1.5 Computing evolution (https://www.researchgate.net/figure/Computing-Evolution-PRES96_fig5_342883350)

and engaging their audiences (Thalanany 2015). Social media platforms like Facebook, Twitter, and LinkedIn gained immense popularity, offering businesses novel avenues for customer engagement and brand building (Macarthy 2021).

In 2005 and more aggressively after 2010, the focus shifted towards developing products and services on the foundation of so many years of adoption of digital technology and its success in terms of offering useful products and services. In this phase, new products and services emerge with the integration of multiple independent systems to completely transform that sector and invent new entities' products and services. For example, In India, "Aadhaar," the largest biometric identity system in the world, and DigiLocker, a secure platform for storing digital documents, are prime examples of Digital transformation (Verma and Kumaran 2021). More than a billion people may now take part in the digital economy because of the Aadhaar being used as a unique identification of their identity. The price dropped from \$20 to \$1 with the implementation of Aadhaar-based authentication. Just this one change has completely disrupted the commercial/banking landscape in India and increased the use of Online Payment Methods developed on the foundation of UPI. UPI has become a game-changer since it facilitates frictionless Person-to-person (P2P) and Person-to-Merchant (P2M) transactions. Now people access services and make payments through UPI (Desk 2023). This has reached almost the last man in the row of society such as small vendors in vegetables and bookstores. The effectiveness, efficiency, and low cost of UPI have put India at the forefront of real-time payment transactions worldwide and accrued around 260 million users to date. Countries around the world are surprised with the scale and adoption in society making it a true example of digital empowerment of citizens.

1.3 Rise of the Internet and Connectivity

The Internet emerged as a transformative force, connecting people, information, and devices on a global scale. Revolution came when The World Wide Web (WWW) was introduced in the early 1990s (Alberts et al. 1997). WWW revolutionised the way information was accessed and shared with individuals and masses on a large scale. WWW tremendously improved information sharing and exchange efficiency. After WWW, information was universally available and efforts to the proliferation of Internet connectivity facilitated the creation of a vast digital ecosystem. This novel digital ecosystem enabled the rapid exchange of data/information, ideas, and innovations through several types of data for exchange such as Text, Image, Video, Audio, and other platform-specific formats. This led to the transformation of traditional systems either improving their effectiveness or efficiency or completely transforming them into new products, systems, processes, services etc. The widespread adoption of the Internet and the development of the WWW transformed communication, business and commerce, and information exchange for any purpose personal or professional. E-commerce platforms emerged utilising the capabilities of WWW such as Amazon in the late 90s which is now one of the most valuable companies. Businesses started to explore new digital channels for communicating with customers, marketing their products, and customer engagement and feedback (Fig. 1.6). Later on, the Mobile Revolution in the 2000s led to the proliferation of smartphones and mobile devices which completely changed how people interacted with technology and how it became a full-time companion of human beings (Helal et al. 1999). In this technological phase, businesses started to invest and adopt mobile apps and responsive web design in addition to websites to cater to the growing mobile audience and improve user experience. New technological concepts such as Cloud Computing and their implementation started with how information is stored and how services are delivered by highly centralising them using cloud computing. Cloud computing technologies provide scalable and cost-effective infrastructure for businesses to host applications, provide services, and store data moving away from decentralised management of web applications and data. This era saw a move away from traditional on-premises IT infrastructure for computing and storage towards cloud-based services, enabling greater flexibility and agility (Zhu 2010). The exponential growth of data generated by digital interactions led to the emergence of big data technologies and advanced analytics tools. Businesses began leveraging data-driven insights to make informed decisions and gain a competitive edge in the market. Another emerging technology IoT led to connected devices, sensors, and smart appliances enabling the collection of real-time data from physical and social environments (Din et al. 2018). IoT technologies found applications in various industries, from manufacturing and healthcare to transportation and agriculture. Emerging technologies have become increasingly accessible, enabling automation, predictive analytics, and personalised customer experiences. Throughout this evolution, digital transformation has fundamentally reshaped industries, business models, and societal interactions, driving innovation and economic growth.

1.4 Convergence of Digital Transformation and Artificial Intelligence

The convergence of digital transformation and artificial intelligence represents a pivotal moment in the technological landscape. Intelligent systems, powered by AI algorithms, have become integral to the fabric of digital transformation. Automation, predictive analytics, and data-driven decision-making are reshaping industries, from healthcare and finance to manufacturing and education (Jagatheesaperumal et al. 2021). The symbiotic relationship between digital transformation and AI is evident in the transformative potential they offer collectively. Digital transformation provides the infrastructure and data ecosystems necessary for AI to thrive, while AI enhances the capabilities of digital systems, unlocking new dimensions of efficiency, innovation, autonomous actions, and intelligence. Digital technologies provide the

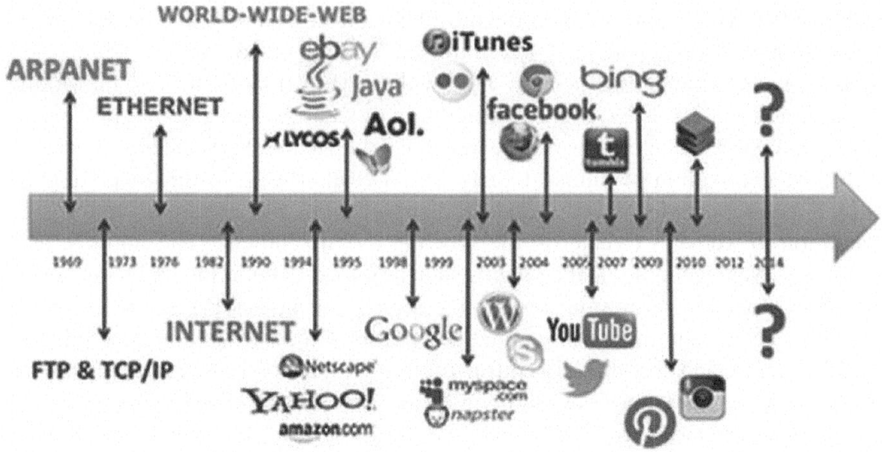

Fig. 1.6 Evolution of Internet and its products (http://digiwonderz.weebly.com/the-internet-for-business/the-evolution-of-the-internet)

infrastructure, data, and connectivity that fuel AI applications to help grow business by automating human decision-making.

AI augments the capabilities of machines/software/tools, enabling them to process vast datasets, derive insights, and make intelligent decisions at unimaginable speeds and scales. The idea of machines or devices demonstrating human intelligence is not new. It has always been in human curiosity and imagination to develop an autonomous machine/agent which can take care of all the work without human intervention. The computational age provided the tools and frameworks and required infrastructure to breathe life into these ambitions. Early AI research and development starting from 1950 focused on rule-based systems and expert systems, laying the groundwork for more sophisticated approaches. The turning point for AI came with machine learning, a paradigm that allowed systems to learn from data of experiences and improve their performance iteratively (Govender 2023). The rise of neural networks and the development of deep learning algorithms marked a watershed moment, enabling AI systems to tackle complex tasks with remarkable accuracy and efficiency. From image recognition to natural language processing, AI began to transcend its theoretical contribution, becoming an integral part of our technological landscape by being used in daily life applications and systems. AI is also being used in a variety of other industries. In finance, AI is being used to detect fraud, manage risk, and make investment decisions. In retail, it is being used to personalise the shopping experience, recommend products, and manage inventory. In the transportation sector, AI is being used to develop self-driving cars and improve traffic management. AI is also being used to improve energy efficiency, predict energy demand in residential and commercial buildings, and improve the efficiency of smart Grid (Pannu 2015). To improve citizen experience and safety in governance, AI is being used to improve public safety, detect crime, and provide citizen services centric welfare distribution services.

1.5 Digital Transformation and Artificial Intelligence and Societal Implications

Digital technologies driving Digital transformation and AI permeate society and their impact extends far beyond the realm of business and industry. The integration of digital technologies and AI has profound implications for individuals, communities, society, and governments. There is hardly any domain where digital technologies and AI are not penetrating and have not shown the potential to disrupt the existing ecosystem. Few technologists such as Professor Andrew N G have said that "AI will have the same transformative impact as electricity" (Lynch 2022). However, along with these opportunities come challenges that demand thoughtful consideration. Privacy concerns, ethical use of AI, job displacement, and societal inequalities have become focal points of discussions surrounding the societal implications of digital transformation and AI (Whittlestone et al. 2019).

1.5.1 Reshaping of Socio-economic Systems

The economic landscape is undergoing a metamorphosis due to digital transformation and AI revolution. Traditional industries and business models are facing disruption as automation and AI-driven technologies redefine customer expectations and requirements, value creation in production systems and processes, and marketing and advertising systems. Social media influencers impact the way we purchase products and services using digital marketing methods and tools. The nature of employment is also changing due to the emergence of the Gig economy and free-lancing successes as they empower capable individuals and allow freedom (Carlos Alvarez de la Vega et al. 2021). New technologies are forcing us to adopt new skills and reskilling as per the demand of the economy. Emerging educational technology platforms are coming to skill and upgrade the workforce in data science, artificial intelligence, cybersecurity, blockchain, IoT, etc. (Almufarreh and Arshad 2023). Every industry is now under the influence of digital transformation restructuring its ways of doing business and prioritising future goals of product portfolios and research and development priorities. This has led to restricting internal systems and team formation as per the societal and economic requirements resulting in layoffs even from large companies such as Amazon, Google, and Microsoft (Magazzo 2023). These developments are also reflecting the job losses and reduction in jobs in the market which forces the government to provide financial assistance to unemployed people in society. The concept of Universal basic income (UBI) has also come due to the threat of job losses as a result of automation and intelligent automation (Kelly 2023).

Digital transformation and AI are revolutionising big businesses and small busses as like and transforming financial markets through optimising trading strategies and risk management. Moreover, the rise of AI-powered platforms such as Uber and Airbnb has disrupted traditional business models, creating new forms of asset monetisation and the gig economy. These examples highlight how AI is not only enhancing freedom of choice of work and productivity but also fundamentally restructuring the socio-economic dynamics of the existing economy and social systems and their interdependence (Vlados et al. 2018). Such dynamic and uncertain changes in socio-economic systems and domains necessitate policy responses to ensure equitable distribution of benefits and address emerging challenges of wealth inequality and reduction of the middle class in a few countries.

The influence of digital transformation and AI extends beyond the economic realm, shaping cultural norms and social dynamics. AI is increasingly shaping cultural norms and social dynamics, impacting various aspects of human interaction and behavior (Walther 2021). Social media platforms employ AI algorithms to personalise content delivery, influencing users' preferences and perceptions, and manipulating their choices and decisions about social economic events and global perception (Krishna 2024). For instance, recommendation systems on platforms like YouTube and Netflix suggest content based on users' past interactions, expressed interests, and choices of past content which potentially reinforces existing beliefs and preferences of the user and prevents it from experiencing new and other dimensions outside echo chambers (Ko et al. 2022). Moreover, AI-powered chatbots and virtual assistants are changing communication patterns, with people interacting more frequently with automated systems rather than humans. Few tools are being used by users to treat their loneliness. Additionally, AI is influencing creative expression through tools like generative adversarial networks (GANs), enabling the creation of art, music, and literature with minimal human intervention (Gülaçti and Kahraman 2021). These examples illustrate how AI is not only reshaping cultural norms but also altering the dynamics of social interactions, posing both opportunities and challenges for individuals and societies to navigate.

1.5.2 Education and Digital Literacy and Knowledge Economy

As the pace of adoption of digital technologies and offerings accelerates, the importance of education, skilling, innovation, and digital literacy becomes paramount. Society must grapple with the challenge of preparing individuals for a future technological landscape where the ability to adapt and reskill them as learn, unlearn, and relearn are prerequisites for participation and serving in the knowledge and digital economy (Ahmad 2020). Bridging the digital divide and ensuring equitable access to educational resources become central tenets in crafting a just and equitable society that can harness the opportunities presented by digital transformation and AI. The emergence of the knowledge economy marks a significant shift in the way societies generate knowledge, wealth, progress, and sustain themselves. Unlike traditional economies reliant on tangible goods and services, the knowledge economy thrives on intangible assets such as creativity, information, innovation, and expertise and develops products and services which enhance the life and intellectual experiences of individuals (Hadad 2017). This transition has been fueled by rapid advancements in technology, globalisation, and changing market demands across the world. The emergence of the knowledge economy needs reformation of education and learning systems which presents both opportunities and challenges for policymakers, businesses, and society as a whole. Embracing digital transformation, investing in education and skills development, and fostering a culture of innovation are key strategies for harnessing the potential of the digital economy (Garritzmann et al. 2022). By leveraging information, innovation, and expertise, societies can unlock new sources of growth and prosperity in the twenty-first century.

1.5.3 Digital Governance and Smart Cities and Administration

Digital transformation adoption provided for digital public infrastructure (DPI) which has led to digital governance, smart administration, and e-governance systems (Eaves et al. 2024). The outcome of these in digital space has led to the smart city development which has successfully delivered tangible and intangible benefits to citizens, businesses, and other stakeholders. Digital governance smart cities and smart governance systems have improved their experiences and quality of interaction and access to governance products and services in society. For example, several types of certificates are developed and downloaded from digital platforms (Milakovich 2021). The government has reached the people rather than the previous situation in which citizens needed to come to governance institutions for such works. DPI created the foundation and adoption of AI and other emerging technologies such as blockchain have transformed record/document keeping and security for validation and verification purposes (Oliveira et al. 2020). These technologies integrated with AI and data analysis have improved the efficiency and effectiveness of digital governance and smart city initiatives on public service delivery. By streamlining administrative processes, enhancing transparency, and facilitating citizen participation, digital technologies products in governance and smart administration have the potential to improve the responsiveness and effectiveness of government services. The role of citizen engagement in shaping the design and implementation of smart city initiatives and other government programmes and policies is important. These technologies and social media platforms also help the government to gauge the public mood and feedback of citizens about the policies easily from several dimensions. Empowering citizens to co-create solutions, provide feedback, and participate in decision-making is essential for building inclusive and resilient cities (Leino and Puumala 2021). By identifying best practices, addressing key challenges, and promoting citizen engagement, policymakers and urban planners can harness the full potential of digital technologies to create more sustainable, equitable, and resilient cities and administrations for the future.

1.5.4 Manufacturing and Intelligent Factories

Manufacturing and the advent of intelligent factories represent a paradigm shift in industrial production, characterised by the integration of advanced technologies such as digital transformation, automation, robotics, artificial intelligence, the Internet of Things (IoT), and cyber-physical systems (Abikoye et al. 2021). There are huge advantages of adopting digital intelligent products and services in manufacturing processes, supply chains, and workforce dynamics. Intelligent factories leverage digital technologies to get feedback from stakeholders, analyse the state of inventory, optimise production resources and processes, and enhance efficiency. By deploying sensors and interconnected systems, these factories can collect real-time data on equipment performance, production metrics, and quality control, enabling predictive maintenance, proactive problem-solving, and continuous improvement (LaCasse et al. 2019). These technologies implement intelligent manufacturing systems and assess their impact on productivity, cost-effectiveness, and product quality. Due to real-time monitoring and decision-making, efficient use of inventory, product development, and other resources can be made. By enabling real-time monitoring and coordination across the entire value chain, these technologies have the potential to enhance supply chain resilience, agility, and responsiveness to changing market conditions and global affairs (Arif et al. 2023). By identifying best practices, addressing key challenges, and promoting workforce development, policymakers and industry stakeholders can harness the full potential of these technologies to create more competitive, sustainable, and inclusive manufacturing ecosystems.

1.5.5 International Relations and Security

Digital transformation and the integration of artificial intelligence (AI) are reshaping the landscape of international relations and security as well. Digital transformation and AI including machine learning and data analytics are influencing decision-making processes, strategic calculations, and power dynamics among states and non-state actors. From cyber warfare and information manipulation to surveillance and predictive analytics, these technologies have the potential to redefine the nature of conflict and cooperation in the twenty-first century (Iqbal et al. 2023). There are dimensions of implications of AI-driven digital transformation for traditional notions of sovereignty, security, and governance in the international system. These technologies are also contributing to digital diplomacy and cyber strategy in shaping statecraft and diplomatic relations in an interconnected world and protecting the interests of countries. As governments increasingly rely on digital platforms for communication, engagement, and influence, the boundaries between traditional diplomacy and digital diplomacy become blurred as information, misinformation, and international pressures are exerted through social media platforms and opinion formation on them (Cull 2019). Digital technologies also advance their strategic interests, project soft power, and respond to emerging threats in cyberspace. In addition to that, the implications of AI-driven automation and autonomy for military capabilities, deterrence strategies, and arms control regimes are also important contributions (Johnson 2019). Local issues and their reflection on tough trends on social media platforms have also provided valuable feedback for better international policies in multilateral institutions and bodies. From autonomous drones and unmanned vehicles to AI-enabled decision support systems, these technologies are revolutionising the conduct of warfare raising complex ethical and legal questions in International relations domains and requesting to reform the existing systems according to the digital technologies-driven world provided opportunities and challenges (Jones 2022).

1.5.6 Information Consumption, Fake News Deep Fake

At present, Digital transformation and AI technologies specifically generative AI have influenced the creation, distribution, sharing, and reception of information and leading to the complete transformation of information ecosystems (Mannuru et al. 2023). With the rise of social media platforms, recommendation algorithms, and personalised content recommendations, individuals are increasingly exposed to echo chambers and filter bubbles, which can amplify the spread of false or misleading information and manipulate their sane behaviour to exercise their choice in any manner (Fig. 1.7). Information highways now do not have an editing phase which is responsible for their accuracy and quality of content. They have entered into the post-truth era. Due to intelligent AI technologies and tools and generative AI, information in any form is created which can lead to high penetration of the phenomenon of fake news and deepfake leading to manipulation and outages in masses instantly and creating law and order situations (Karnouskos 2020). This forces us to examine properly and ethically the technological capabilities and socio-political implications of AI-generated content. AI has made it possible to create highly realistic and persuasive fake videos, audio recordings, and text, blurring the line between fact and fiction (Kaplan 2020). There is a need to be aware of cognitive and behavioural factors that influence individuals' susceptibility to misinformation and their ability to discern credible sources from deceptive content. By understanding the psychological mechanisms underlying information processing and belief formation, stakeholders need to develop interventions and educational strategies to enhance media literacy and

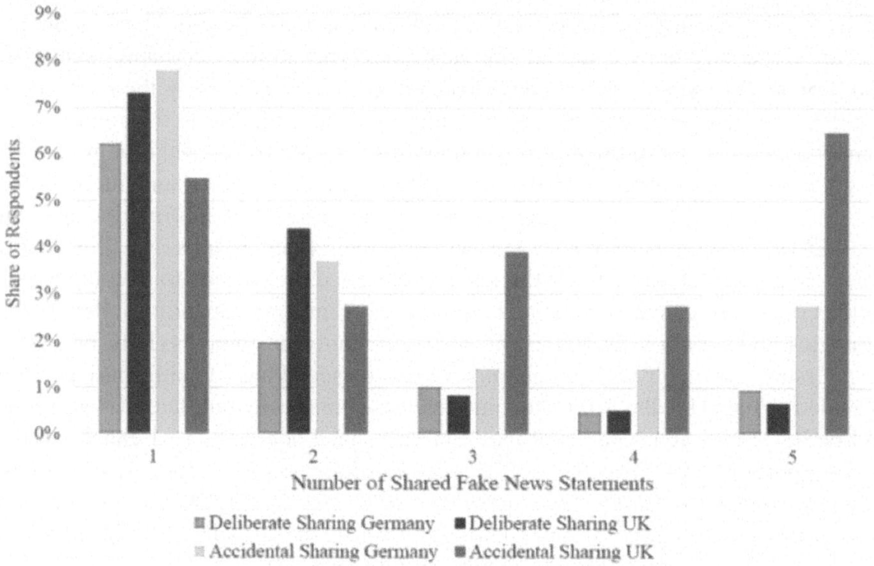

Notes. The diagram shows the share of respondents who wanted to share 1...5 fake news statements either deliberately or accidentally.

Fig. 1.7 Fake news and trends on sharing it (Arin et al. 2023). Ability of detecting and willingness to share fake news. *Scientific Reports*, *13*(1), 7298

critical thinking skills, empowering individuals to navigate the digital information landscape more effectively.

1.5.7 AI, Climate Change, and Climate Actions

Digital transformation, the Internet, and sensing methods have revolutionised the way we collect, analyse, and disseminate data. Present-day capabilities allow for more comprehensive and real-time monitoring of climate change indicators. This provides opportunities for scientists and other stakeholders to solve climate-related problems with data-driven experimental insights and monitor the trends and progress to set accountability on institutions (Kaack et al. 2022). AI, with its ability to process vast amounts of data and identify complex patterns, holds immense promise for enhancing climate modelling, forecasting extreme weather events, and optimising resource management strategies (Fig. 1.8). However, these technological advancements also present significant challenges (Kaack et al. 2022). One major concern is the environmental footprint of digital infrastructure and AI algorithms, which consume substantial amounts of energy and contribute to carbon emissions. Addressing this challenge requires developing energy-efficient computing systems and promoting renewable

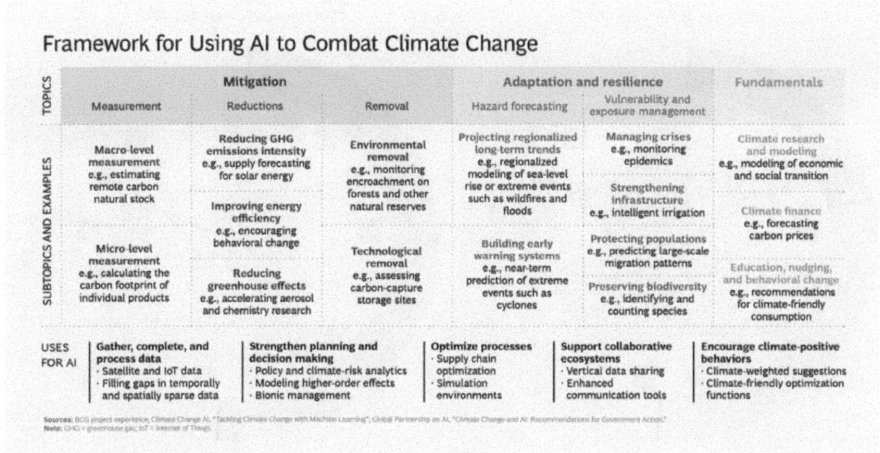

Fig. 1.8 Artificial intelligence and climate change mitigation (https://www.bcg.com/publications/2022/how-ai-can-help-climate-change)

energy sources to power digital technologies. Additionally, there are ethical considerations surrounding the use of AI in climate-related decision-making, such as ensuring transparency, accountability, and equity in algorithmic processes.

1.5.8 Sustainable Development of Society

The potential of Digital Transformation and AI can streamline processes, optimise resource allocation, and improve productivity across various sectors. Such capabilities and tools can be adopted to address societal challenges and achieve Sustainable Development Goals (SDGs). More specifically, AI can contribute to progress towards SDG 9 which is responsible for "Industry, Innovation, and Infrastructure" and SDG 8 which aims to address and provide "Decent Work and Economic Growth" (Vinuesa et al. 2020). Digital transformation enables better data collection, analysis, and interpretation of data, providing policymakers and organisations with valuable insights to inform evidence-based policies and strategies for achieving multiple SDGs (Vinuesa et al. 2020). AI can help in addressing the targets of SDG 2 in achieving "Zero Hunger." For example, One research study used digital data and machine learning with mobile phone data to predict poverty in African country which helped in designing programmes and policies specifically targeted at poor regions (Blumenstock et al. 2015). This can also help in monitoring the progress of targeted programmes in poor regions at a very low cost. AI has the potential to help in addressing issues related to Public health in SDG 3 (Good Health and Well-being) (Fernandez 2020). SDG 4 is centred around "Quality Education Innovation and Solutions" where AI can foster innovation by enabling the development of

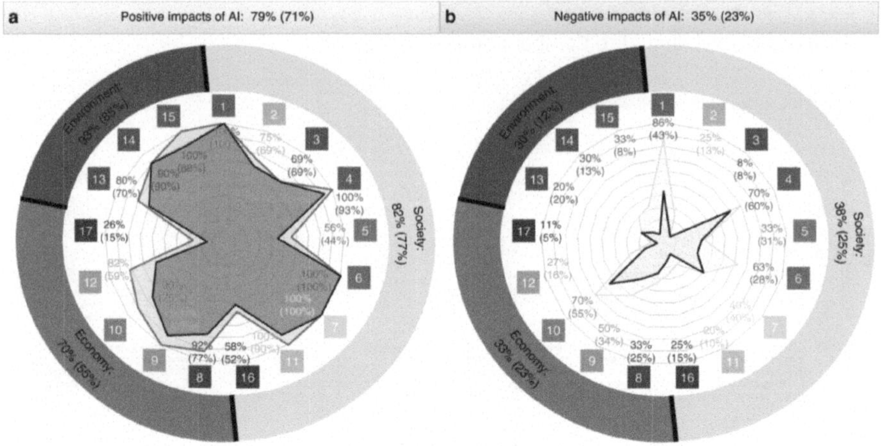

Fig. 1.9 Artificial intelligence and SDGs (Vinuesa et al. 2020)

new technologies, personalised learning products, and services for students (Pedro et al. 2019). AI and emerging innovation can support progress towards SDG 7 also aiming for "Affordable and Clean Energy" and SDG 11 for "Sustainable Cities and Communities" (Vinuesa et al. 2020). Similarly, AI can help in addressing "Climate change and climate action monitoring" and setting accountability for actions and their evaluation to stakeholders (Fig. 1.9).

1.5.9 Challenges and Ethical Considerations

The advent of Digital technologies, Digital transformation, and AI raises several socio-economic and ethical challenges. There are several issues related to Digital technologies and digital transformation such as the digital divide which is unequal access to digital technologies, digital products, and their benefits that exacerbate existing disparities, hindering community progress to become the mains stream and is against SDG 1 (No Poverty) and SDG 5 (Gender Equality), and SDG 10 (Reduced Inequalities) (DiMaggio et al. 2004). The most affected sections of society are marginalised communities, particularly those coming from disadvantageous groups, low-income regions, and the Global South. These regions may lack the DPI, physical infrastructure, skills, and human resources to benefit from digital transformation and AI (Carey and Mc Donnell 2021). Automation and AI-driven technologies may lead to job displacement, particularly in sectors vulnerable to automation, impacting progress towards SDG 8 (Decent Work and Economic Growth) and potentially exacerbating poverty and inequality (Yadav et al. 2024). There is the proliferation of digital technologies that raise concerns about data privacy, security breaches, and misuse of personal information, undermining trust and posing risks to individuals' rights and freedoms. This has been a big challenge after the Cambridge Analytica Scandal in the USA elections (Berghel 2018). As intelligent machines take on decision-making roles, questions of accountability, transparency, and bias demand proper scrutiny. Ethical frameworks become essential guides in navigating the ethical minefield of AI applications and intelligent algorithms, from autonomous vehicles making split-second decisions to algorithms influencing hiring processes and governance welfare distribution to the masses. The need for responsible AI development becomes a critical aspect of societal dialogue.

As we embark on this intellectual journey, the following chapters delve into specific facets of digital transformation, AI, and its impact on one of the domains or aspects of society. From the intricate technicalities of Data, Digital Technologies, and AI to the nuances of policymaking and social interventions, each chapter contributes to a comprehensive understanding of the digital and AI impact in that particular domain and the opportunities and challenges that define digital transformation and artificial intelligence. The road ahead is complex, marked by uncertainties and possibilities. Through rigorous analysis, thoughtful discourse, and a commitment to ethical innovation, we navigate the contours of a future where the fusion of digital transformation, artificial intelligence, and society creates a landscape of promise and potential. Together, we embark on a journey that transcends disciplinary boundaries, fostering a holistic perspective that is essential for navigating the transformative forces that shape our interconnected world and society we live in.

References

Abikoye OC, Bajeh AO, Awotunde JB, Ameen AO, Mojeed HA, Abdulraheem M, ... Salihu SA (2021) Application of internet of thing and cyber physical system in Industry 4.0 smart manufacturing. In: Emergence of cyber physical system and IoT in smart automation and robotics: computer engineering in automation. Springer International Publishing, Cham, pp 203–217

Ahmad T (2020) Scenario based approach to re-imagining future of higher education which prepares students for the future of work. Higher Educ, Skills Work-Based Learn 10(1):217–238

Alberts DS, Papp DS (eds) (1997) The information age: an anthology on its impacts and consequences. Center for Advanced Concepts and Technologies, p 0312

Almufarreh A, Arshad M (2023) Promising emerging technologies for teaching and learning: recent developments and future challenges. Sustainability 15(8):6917

Arif J, Samadhiya A, Kumar A (2023) Net zero supply chain performance and industry 4.0 technologies: past review and present introspective analysis for future research directions. Heliyon 9(11)

Arin KP, Mazrekaj D, Thum M (2023) Ability of detecting and willingness to share fake news. Sci Rep 13(1):7298

Auriga (2016) Digital transformation: history, present, and future trends. https://auriga.com/blog/digital-transformation-history-present-and-future-trends/. Accessed 01 April 2024

Belenguer L (2022) AI bias: exploring discriminatory algorithmic decision-making models and the application of possible machine-centric solutions adapted from the pharmaceutical industry. AI Ethics 2(4):771–787

Berghel H (2018) Malice domestic: the Cambridge analytica dystopia. Computer 51(5):84–89

Bhatia A, Bhabha J (2017) India's Aadhaar scheme and the promise of inclusive social protection. Oxf Dev Stud 45(1):64–79
Blumenstock J, Cadamuro G, On R (2015) Predicting poverty and wealth from mobile phone metadata. Science 350(6264):1073–1076
Breuer A (2016) The role of social media in mobilizing political protest. In: Young generation awakening: economics, society, and policy on the eve of the Arab spring, pp 110–131
Carey E, Mc Donnell I (2021) Overview: powering an inclusive digital future
Carlos Alvarez de la Vega J, Cecchinato ME, Rooksby J (2021, May) "Why lose control?" A study of freelancers' experiences with gig economy platforms. In: Proceedings of the 2021 CHI conference on human factors in computing systems, pp 1–14
Choudrie J, Tsatsou P, Kurnia S (eds) (2018) Social inclusion and usability of ICT-enabled services. Routledge, New York City
Cull NJ (2019) Public diplomacy: foundations for global engagement in the digital age. John Wiley & Sons.
Desk (2023) Digital payment via UPI spikes on person-to-merchant transaction growth: Report Read more at: https://economictimes.indiatimes.com/tech/technology/digital-payment-via-upi-spikes-on-person-to-merchant-transaction-growth-report/articleshow/103958457.cms?utm_source=contentofinterest&utm_medium=text&utm_campaign=cppst
DiMaggio P, Hargittai E, Celeste C, Shafer S (2004) From unequal access to differentiated use: a literature review and agenda for research on digital inequality. Soc Inequal 1:355–400
Din IU, Guizani M, Hassan S, Kim BS, Khan MK, Atiquzzaman M, Ahmed SH (2018) The Internet of Things: a review of enabled technologies and future challenges. IEEE Access 7:7606–7640
Eaves D, Mazzucato M, Vasconcellos B (2024) Digital public infrastructure and public value: what is 'public' about DPI. UCL Institute for Innovation and Public Purpose, Working Paper Series (IIPP WP 2024-05). UCL Institute for Innovation and Public Purpose, London. Accessed 28 March 2024
Faboye M (2024) Disruptive technology: how businesses are adapting to AI, Blockchain, and IoT. https://em360tech.com/tech-article/disruptive-technology-how-businesses-are-adapting-ai-blockchain-and-iot Accessed 01 April 2024
Fernandez RM (2020) SDG3 good health and well-being: integration and connection with other SDGs. In: Good health and well-being, pp 629–636
Fuloria S (2023) Unified payments interface: revolutionizing digital payments in India. In: Doing business in South Asia. Routledge, pp 92–98
Garritzmann JL, Häusermann S, Palier B (eds) (2022) The world politics of social investment: Volume I: welfare states in the knowledge economy. Oxford University Press
Gong C, Ribiere V (2021) Developing a unified definition of digital transformation. Technovation 102:102217
Govender K (2023) Age of agency: rise with AI. CRC Press
Gülaçti İE, Kahraman ME (2021) The impact of artificial intelligence on photography and painting in the post-truth era and the issues of creativity and authorship. Medeniyet Sanat Dergisi 7(2):243–270
Hadad S (2017) Knowledge economy: characteristics and dimensions. Manag Dyn Knowl Econ 5(2):203–225
Hanelt A, Bohnsack R, Marz D, Antunes Marante C (2021) A systematic review of the literature on digital transformation: insights and implications for strategy and organizational change. J Manag Stud 58(5):1159–1197
Helal AA, Haskell B, Carter JL, Brice R, Woelk D, Rusinkiewicz M (1999) Any time, anywhere computing: mobile computing concepts and technology, vol 522. Springer Science & Business Media
Iqbal S, Rizvi SWA, Haider MH, Raza S (2023) Artificial intelligence in security and defense: explore the integration of AI in military strategies, security policies, and its implications for global power dynamics. Int J Human Soc 3(4):341–353

Jagatheesaperumal SK, Rahouti M, Ahmad K, Al-Fuqaha A, Guizani M (2021) The duo of artificial intelligence and big data for industry 4.0: applications, techniques, challenges, and future research directions. IEEE Internet of Things J 9(15):12861–12885

Jain A (2021) Impact of digitalization and artificial intelligence as causes and enablers of organizational change. Nottingham University Business School, UK

Johnson J (2019) Artificial intelligence & future warfare: implications for international security. Def Secur Anal 35(2):147–169

Jones H (2022) When AI rules the world: China, the US, and the race to control a smart planet. Bombardier Books

Kaack LH, Donti PL, Strubell E, Kamiya G, Creutzig F, Rolnick D (2022) Aligning artificial intelligence with climate change mitigation. Nat Clim Chang 12(6):518–527

Kaplan A (2020) Artificial intelligence, social media, and fake news: Is this the end of democracy? In: Media & society, 149

Karnouskos S (2020) Artificial intelligence in digital media: the era of deepfakes. IEEE Trans Technol Soc 1(3):138–147

Kelly P (2023) AI is coming for our jobs! Could universal basic income be the solution? https://www.theguardian.com/global-development/2023/nov/16/ai-is-coming-for-our-jobs-could-universal-basic-income-be-the-solution?CMP=share_btn_url

Ko H, Lee S, Park Y, Choi A (2022) A survey of recommendation systems: recommendation models, techniques, and application fields. Electronics 11(1):141

Krishna VV (2024) AI and contemporary challenges: the good, bad and the scary. J Open Innov: Technol, Market, Complex 10(1):100178

Kumar Sharma E (2018) AI is the new electricity, says Coursera's Andrew Ng. https://www.businesstoday.in/opinion/interviews/story/ai-is-the-new-electricity-says-courseras-andrew-ng-248210-2018-03-05. Accessed 01 April 2024

LaCasse PM, Otieno W, Maturana FP (2019) A survey of feature set reduction approaches for predictive analytics models in the connected manufacturing enterprise. Appl Sci 9(5):843

Legner C, Eymann T, Hess T, Matt C, Böhmann T, Drews P, ... Ahlemann F (2017) Digitalization: opportunity and challenge for the business and information systems engineering community. Bus Inf Syst Eng 59:301–308

Leiner BM, Cerf VG, Clark DD, Kahn RE, Kleinrock L, Lynch DC, ... Wolff SS (1997) The past and future history of the Internet. Commun ACM 40(2):102–108

Leino H, Puumala E (2021) What can co-creation do for the citizens? Applying co-creation for the promotion of participation in cities. Environ Plann C: Polit Space 39(4):781–799

Lynch S (2022) Andrew Ng: why AI Is the new electricity, 11 March 2017. https://www.gsb.stanford.edu/insights/andrew-ng-why-ai-new-electricity. Accessed 22 April 2024)

Macarthy A (2021) 500 social media marketing tips: essential advice, hints and strategy for business: facebook, twitter, pinterest, Google+, YouTube, instagram, LinkedIn, and mor

Magazzo S (2023) Latest mass Layoffs: detailed list & reporting of notable company cutbacks. https://mondo.com/insights/mass-layoffs-in-2022-whats-next-for-employees/. Accesed 01 April 2024

Mannuru NR, Shahriar S, Teel ZA, Wang T, Lund BD, Tijani S, ... Vaidya P (2023) Artificial intelligence in developing countries: the impact of generative artificial intelligence (AI) technologies for development. Inf Dev, 02666669231200628

Mergel I, Edelmann N, Haug N (2019) Defining digital transformation: results from expert interviews. Gov Inf Q 36(4):101385

Milakovich ME (2021) Digital governance: applying advanced technologies to improve public service. Routledge

Min S, So KKF, Jeong M (2021) Consumer adoption of the Uber mobile application: insights from diffusion of innovation theory and technology acceptance model. In: Future of tourism marketing. Routledge, pp 2–15

Oliveira TA, Oliver M, Ramalhinho H (2020) Challenges for connecting citizens and smart cities: ICT, e-governance and blockchain. Sustainability 12(7):2926

O'Regan G, O'Regan (2008) A brief history of computing. Springer, London, pp I–XIX
Palvia P, Baqir N, Nemati H (2018) ICT for socio-economic development: a citizens' perspective. Inf Manag 55(2):160–176
Pannu A (2015) Artificial intelligence and its application in different areas. Artif Intell 4(10):79–84
Pedro F, Subosa M, Rivas A, Valverde P (2019) Artificial intelligence in education: challenges and opportunities for sustainable development
Sarker IH (2021) Machine learning: algorithms, real-world applications and research directions. SN Comput Sci 2(3):160
Siebel TM (2019) Digital transformation: survive and thrive in an era of mass extinction. RosettaBooks
Suchman L, Weber J (2016) Human-machine autonomies. In: Autonomous weapons systems: law, ethics, policy, pp 75–102
Thalanany S (2015) Mobile evolution: insights on connectivity and service. CRC Press
Tien JM (2017) Internet of Things, real-time decision-making, and artificial intelligence. Ann Data Sci 4:149–178
Tyagi AK, Nair MM (2020) Internet of Everything (IoE) and Internet of Things (IoTs): threat analyses, possible opportunities for future. J Inf Assur Secur 15(5)
Verma N, Kumaran GMM (2021) Digital transformation in government—A case study of India. In: Citizen empowerment through digital transformation in government. Chapman and Hall/CRC, pp 1–22
Vinuesa R, Azizpour H, Leite I, Balaam M, Dignum V, Domisch S, ... Fuso Nerini F (2020) The role of artificial intelligence in achieving the sustainable development goals. Nat Commun 11(1):1–10
Vlados C, Deniozos N, Chatzinikolaou D, Demertzis M (2018) Towards an evolutionary understanding of the current global socio-economic crisis and restructuring: from a conjunctural to a structural and evolutionary perspective. Res World Econ 9(1):15–33
Walther CC (2021) Technology, social change and human behavior: influence for impact. Springer Nature
West DM (2004) E-government and the transformation of service delivery and citizen attitudes. Public Adm Rev 64(1):15–27
Whittlestone J, Nyrup R, Alexandrova A, Dihal K, Cave S (2019) Ethical and societal implications of algorithms, data, and artificial intelligence: a roadmap for research. Nuffield Foundation, London
Whyte C (2020) Deepfake news: AI-enabled disinformation as a multi-level public policy challenge. J Cyber Policy 5(2):199–217
Yadav P, Tudela LAM, Marco-Lajara B (2024) The role of AI in assessing and achieving the sustainable development goals (SDGs). In: Issues of sustainability in AI and new-age thematic investing. IGI Global, pp 1–17
Zhu J (2010) Cloud computing technologies and applications. In: Handbook of cloud computing, pp 21–45

Chapter 2
Historical Aspects of Technological Revolutions and Society Transformation

Abstract This chapter delves into the historical aspects of several technological revolutions and their transforming impact on society. It surveys significant technological advancements in human history, from the hunting-gathering society to the agricultural society to the digital revolution-driven Information Age. It explores the technological revolutions driving socio-economic, cultural, political, and environmental transformations. The last revolution, the Industrial Revolution, for instance, brought about the mechanisation of the production of goods and services, urbanisation, and the modern factory system, drastically altering the economic and social dimensions of societies and social interactions. The present technological revolution, the digital and information age, characterised by the advent of computers, the Internet, and digital technologies, ushered in a new era of connectivity, information access, and communication and has had a huge impact on several sectors of economies and social life from multiple dimensions.

Keywords Technological revolutions · Industrial revolution · Information age · Historical aspects · Society impact · Changes in socio-economic systems

2.1 Introduction to Technological Revolutions

Human history is very long but taking technology as the yardstick for the measurement, it can be majorly divided based on how new technologies have transformed society's journey. The historical narrative of humanity is entangled with a series of technological revolutions. Technological Revolutions have been pivotal in shaping human civilisation since ancient times, propelling societies to move forward through new tools, inventions, and innovation (Ede 2019). In this journey, each technological revolution has left an unforgettable mark on the socio-economic, cultural, political, and environmental fabric of societies across the world. From the invention of the wheel to the dawn of the Internet age, these revolutions have redefined the way we live, work, and interact with the world around us (Perez 2004). One of the earliest technological revolutions occurred with the advent of agriculture around 10,000

S. Kumar et al., *Digital Transformation, Artificial Intelligence and Society*, Frontiers of Artificial Intelligence, Ethics and Multidisciplinary Applications,
https://doi.org/10.1007/978-981-97-5656-8_2

BCE, marking the transition from nomadic hunter-gatherer lifestyles of survival to settled agricultural ways of living in local communities (National Geographic 2020). This led to the transformation of human living and several institutions emerged as for the necessity. The Industrial Revolution, which began in the late eighteenth century, sparked a series of significant transformations in many dimensions specifically in manufacturing, transportation, and communication (Stearns 2020). Steam engines, mechanised production, and the development of railroads revolutionised industry and transportation, leading to unprecedented economic growth and urbanisation in Europe and its colonies (Landes 2003). After that, The Information Age, ushered in by the rise of computers and digital technology in the late twentieth century, represents another significant technological revolution. The invention of the microprocessor in the 1970s paved the way for the democratisation of computation through the personal computer revolution, enabling individuals to access vast amounts of information and communicate globally through the Internet and influencing the masses instantly (da Motta e Albuquerque 2023). Today, smartphones, social media platforms, and cloud computing continue to reshape the way we communicate, work, and access information, with more than 4.66 billion people worldwide using the Internet as of 2021 (Sangmeister and Villhauer 2022). Technological revolutions have been instrumental in driving human progress throughout history, from the agricultural revolution to the digital age and beyond. These transformative shifts have not only improved our quality of life but also posed new challenges and opportunities for societies to adapt and thrive in an ever-changing world (Fig. 2.1).

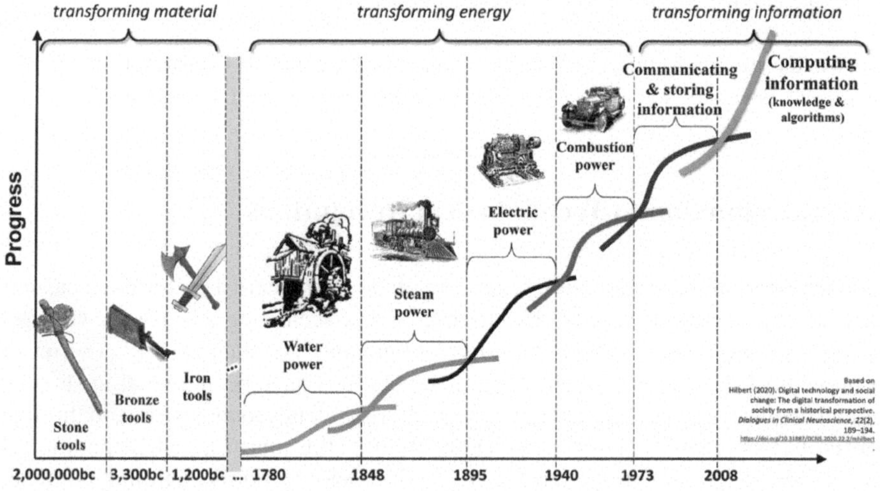

Fig. 2.1 Technological revolutions and transformation of tools and energy systems (Perez 2003)

2.2 From Hunter-Gatherers to Agricultural Societies

Approximately 10,000 years ago, humanity underwent a tremendous shift as communities across the globe began to embrace agriculture as a way of life (McNeill 2009). This transition is often referred to as the Neolithic Revolution. It represented a fundamental departure from millennia of nomadic existence for survival and sustenance. Through the cultivation of crops and the domestication of animals, humans unlocked the potential for surplus food production, leading to the establishment of permanent settlements, less thinking about the future food requirements, the rise of complex societies, and the dawn of civilisation. Central to the Neolithic Revolution was the domestication of plants and animals, a process that transformed human society and ecosystems alike. In regions such as the Fertile Crescent, the birthplace of agriculture, ancient peoples selectively bred wild plants such as wheat, barley, and lentils, gradually transforming them into domesticated crops optimised for human consumption (Abbo et al. 2022). Similarly, animals like cattle, sheep, and pigs were domesticated for food, labour, and other resources, leading to significant changes in human-animal relationships and ecological dynamics. The shift to agriculture brought about a wave of technological innovations that revolutionised food production and daily life. Agricultural communities developed tools such as ploughs, sickles, and grinding stones to cultivate crops and process food. Irrigation systems, including canals and ditches, were constructed to control water flow and maximise agricultural productivity. Pottery emerged as a crucial technology for storing and transporting surplus food, while the invention of the wheel facilitated trade and transportation networks (Brown 1989). The adoption of agriculture led to profound changes in settlement patterns, as nomadic hunter-gatherer bands gave way to permanent villages and towns. Archaeological sites such as Çatalhöyük in Anatolia and Jericho in the Levant offer glimpses into the early stages of sedentary life, with evidence of densely populated settlements, complex social structures, and rudimentary forms of governance (Bennison-Chapman 2014).

Agricultural societies witnessed the emergence of complex social hierarchies and specialised labour roles. The surplus food generated by agriculture allowed for the development of non-farming professions such as artisans, traders, and religious leaders (Bernstein 2010). Social stratification became more pronounced, with elites wielding political and economic power, while commoners toiled in the fields. This division of labour laid the groundwork for the development of urban economies and the exchange of goods and services.

The transition to agriculture was accompanied by profound cultural and religious developments, as humans grappled with the complexities of settled life and the rhythms of the agricultural calendar. Cultures around the world developed myths, rituals, and religious beliefs tied to the cycles of planting, harvesting, and fertility (Kirk 1973). Monumental architecture, including temples, pyramids, and megalithic structures, served as focal points for communal worship and political authority, reflecting the growing complexity of human societies.

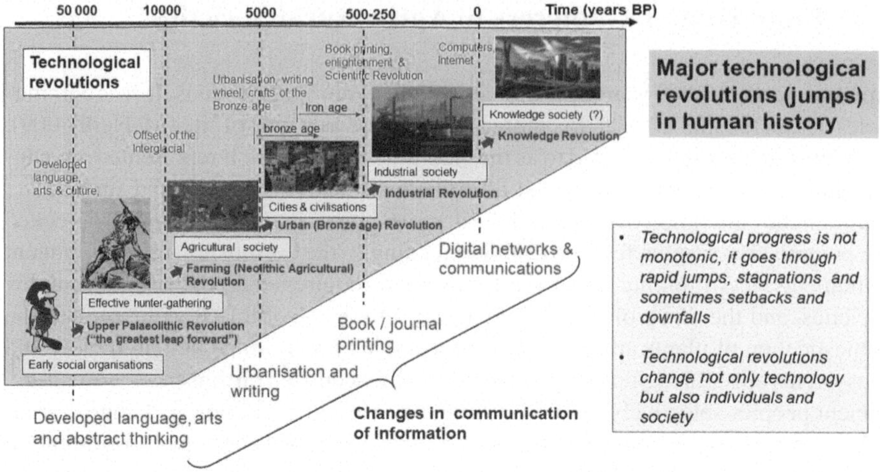

Fig. 2.2 Major technological revolutions and their impact and contributions to humanity (https://images.app.goo.gl/TsCM514qnisqptPE8)

While the Neolithic Revolution brought about unprecedented social and technological advancements, it also had profound environmental impacts that continue to resonate today. The clearing of land for agriculture led to deforestation, soil erosion, and loss of biodiversity, altering ecosystems and contributing to long-term environmental degradation. Additionally, the reliance on monoculture crops and intensive farming practices depleted soil nutrients and increased vulnerability to pests and diseases. As societies grappled with the consequences of their agricultural innovations, they began to develop strategies for sustainable land management and resource conservation (Fig. 2.2).

2.3 Industrial Revolution: Mechanisation, Urbanisation, and Societal Transformation

The Industrial Revolution marks a significant chapter in human history. It encompasses the mechanisation of production processes and the advent of factories leading to surplus production and the consequent search for a market for finished goods (Marsh 2012). Urbanisation became a hallmark, with populations migrating to industrial centres, leading to the development of the modern factory system. The First Industrial Revolution occurred in England at the end of the eighteenth century (1780–1830), and it was characterised by two important inventions: the steam engine and the locomotive. These technologies significantly increased industrial production, transport, and distribution of goods, transforming society from rural to urban

(Mohajan 2019). This led to the emergence of town and city-associated administration systems. The Second Industrial Revolution, known as the "age of steel and electricity," emerged in the metallurgical and chemical sectors, with steel becoming a basic material and the chemical and automobile industries taking great importance (Skilton and Hovsepian 2018). Countries like Germany, France, Russia, Italy, and the United States also industrialised during this period. Key inventions of this period include the Bessemer process for transforming iron into steel, the dynamo for replacing steam with electricity, and the internal combustion engine for large-scale use of oil, creating conditions for the invention of automobiles and aeroplanes (Ayres 1990). The automobile industry took great importance during this period, with the Fordist technique and work system being the paradigm of technical regulation and work known across the industrial world. The characteristic technology of this period was steel, metallurgy, electricity, electromechanics, petroleum, internal explosion engines, and petrochemicals. Electricity and oil were the main forms of energy. The Third Industrial Revolution, which occurred in the 1970s, was inspired by Toyotism, developed by engineers at Toyota, the Japanese automobile industry (Steinberg 2022). This method abolished the role of specialised professional workers and made them multifunctional workers. The characteristic technology of this period was microelectronics, information technology, the CNC machine (Computer Numerical Control), the robot, and computerised telematics. Toyotism began in 1962 and aimed to produce only what was necessary and in the shortest time (Price 1994). It was just in time, producing only what was ordered with minimal stock, resulting in faster, better, and lower inventory and production costs (Fig. 2.3). This led to a multipurpose, flexible, team-integrated, less hierarchical work system that allowed for creative action by workers. Industry 4.0, or Industry 4.0, is characterised by the integration of cyber-physical production systems, where intelligent sensors inform machines about their processing (Santos et al. 2018). Processes must be governed in a decentralised modular system, with smart production systems communicating wirelessly or through an Internet "cloud" (Internet of Things or IoT). The machine-to-machine and devices-to-device concept represents the interconnection between production cells, allowing autonomous decision-making regarding production, cost, contingency, and safety through artificial intelligence models complemented by IoT.

2.4 Information Revolution

The Information Revolution, a defining era of the late twentieth and early twenty-first centuries, has reshaped the fabric of human society again similar to previous technological revolutions through the rapid advancement of digital technologies and the ubiquitous connectivity afforded by the Internet and associated technological advancements in information and communication technology (Robins and Webster 2020). The roots of the Information Revolution can be traced back to the mid-twentieth century when seminal developments in computing laid the foundation for the digital age. The inventions and innovations in electronics specifically the

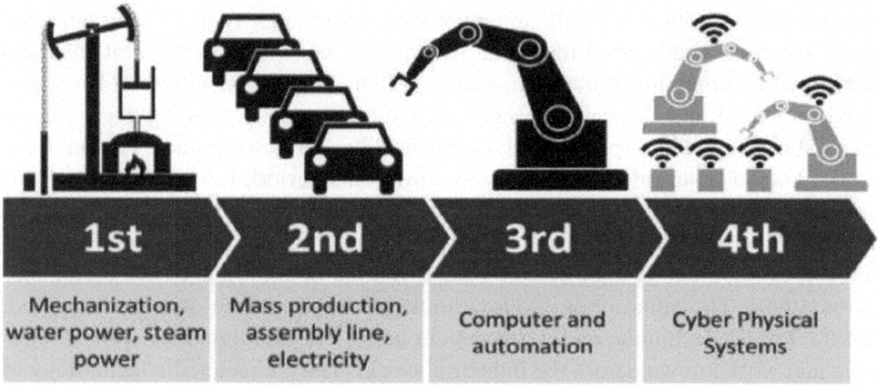

Fig. 2.3 Several industrial revolutions (Prasongko and Adianto 2019)

invention of the transistor in 1947 paved the way for the miniaturisation of electronic components, leading to the development of integrated circuits (IC) and microprocessors (Dummer 2013). The creation of ARPANET, the precursor to the Internet, in 1969 marked a major milestone in the development of computer networking (Hauben 1997). Such developments enable researchers to share important resources and communicate across vast distances with significant efficiency. The advent of personal computers in the 1970s and 1980s democratised computation brought computing power into the hands of individuals and catalysed the democratisation of the information ecosystem by empowering people to create, share, and process information and knowledge.

At the heart of the Information Revolution lies a constellation of interconnected components that together form the backbone of the digital ecosystem. The Internet, a global network of networks, serves as the primary medium for transmitting and accessing information. Through a combination of wired and wireless connections, users can communicate, collaborate, and consume content from virtually anywhere in the world. WWW, invented by Tim Berners-Lee in 1989, provides a user-friendly interface for navigating the vast expanse of digital content, linking documents and resources through hyperlinks (Berners-Lee 1996).

The Information Revolution has given rise to a plethora of tools and technologies that empower individuals and organisations to harness the power of data and information. Data analytics tools, such as machine learning algorithms and data visualisation software, enable organisations to extract insights from vast amounts of data and make data-driven decisions. Cloud computing platforms, such as Amazon Web Services and Microsoft Azure, provide scalable and flexible infrastructure for hosting applications and storing data, reducing the cost and complexity of IT operations and infrastructure. Mobile technologies, including smartphones and tablets, have transformed the way we access information and conduct business, enabling mobile commerce, location-based services, and on-the-go productivity (Fig. 2.4).

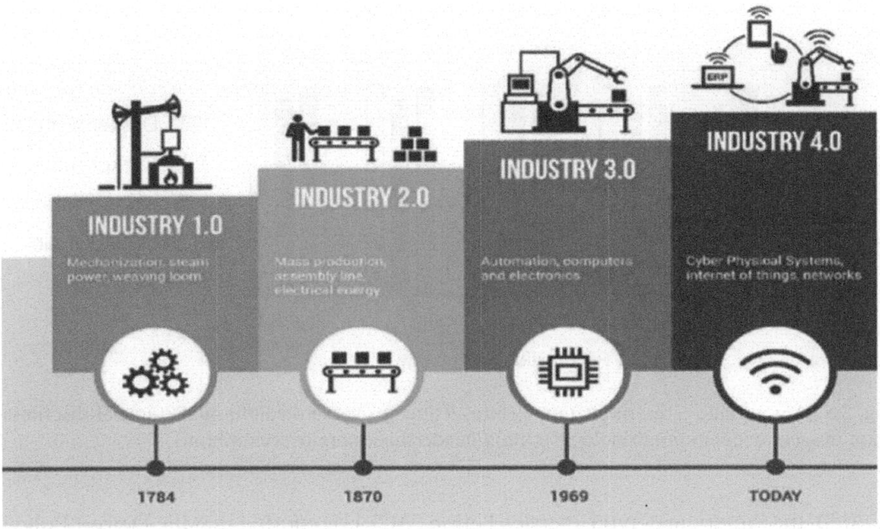

Fig. 2.4 Macro perspective and industrialisation revolution. https://medium.com/@lawrenceamartin/the-5th-industrial-revolution-244f10ee4cc1

The proliferation of personal computers, smartphones, and other Internet-enabled devices has further democratised access to information, empowering individuals to communicate, collaborate, and create in ways previously unimaginable (Wheeler 2011). Industries across the board, from media and entertainment to retail and finance, have been disrupted by digital technologies, forcing businesses to adapt to the digital information ecosystem or risk obsolescence. The rise of e-commerce giants like Amazon and Alibaba has revolutionised the way we shop while streaming platforms like Netflix and Spotify have revolutionised the way we consume media to entertain (Chalaby and Plunkett 2021). Digital currencies such as Bitcoin have challenged traditional notions of money and finance, while advances in artificial intelligence and machine learning have unlocked new possibilities for automation and data analysis, prediction, and decision-making (Singh 2023).

In the workplace, digital technologies have automated routine tasks, augmented human capabilities, and transformed business models, giving rise to the gig economy and remote work arrangements (Kraus et al. 2023). In education, online learning platforms and digital textbooks have expanded access to education and personalised learning experiences (Haleem et al. 2022). In healthcare, telemedicine and wearable devices have revolutionised patient care and remote monitoring, improving outcomes and reducing costs (Kalasin and Surareungchai 2023). In entertainment, streaming services and digital distribution platforms have disrupted traditional media industries and empowered content creators to reach global audiences with unprecedented ease (Evangelista et al. 2014).

Let us take specific examples, Facial recognition technology used by law enforcement agencies without proper regulations can lead to privacy violations. For instance,

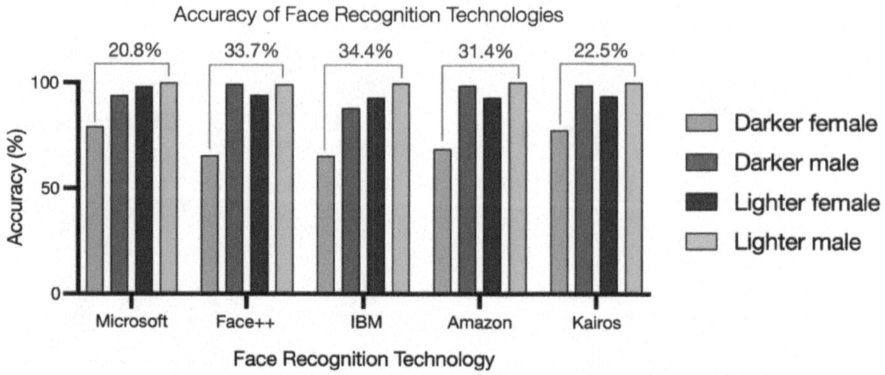

Fig. 2.5 Algorithmic discrimination (https://sitn.hms.harvard.edu/flash/2020/racial-discrimination-in-face-recognition-technology/) (http://gendershades.org/overview.html)

in 2020, the American Civil Liberties Union (ACLU) reported that the Detroit Police Department's facial recognition software was flawed, misidentifying individuals up to 96% of the time, and disproportionately affecting people of colour (Gee 2020). AI-powered hiring platforms may inadvertently perpetuate gender or racial biases if they are trained on biased data. For instance, Amazon scrapped an AI recruitment tool in 2018 because it was biased against female candidates (Albaroudi et al. 2024). Predictive policing algorithms, if trained on historical data that reflects biased policing practices, can perpetuate racial disparities in law enforcement (Drage and Mackereth 2022). For example, in Broward County, Florida, a predictive policing algorithm was found to be twice as likely to falsely flag black defendants as future criminals compared to white defendants (Flores et al. 2016). A ProPublica investigation revealed that COMPAS, a widely used algorithm for predicting recidivism, was biased against African American defendants, incorrectly labelling them as high risk at nearly twice the rate of white defendants (Dressel and Farid 2018) (Fig. 2.5).

Deepfake technology can be used to create highly realistic fake videos or audio recordings that can be used to spread misinformation or manipulate public opinion (Masood et al. 2023). For instance, in 2020, a deepfake video depicting political figures engaging in inappropriate behaviour went viral, causing public outrage. A report by Deeptrace Labs in 2019 estimated that the number of deepfake videos online had doubled within nine months, with 96% of them being pornographic, raising concerns about the potential for widespread misuse of the technology for malicious purposes (Schick 2020). The proliferation of fake news and misinformation erodes trust in traditional media and institutions, undermining democratic norms and public discourse (Stark et al. 2020).

2.5 Socio-economic Impacts of Digital and Information Age

Transitioning to the present, the narrative unfolds to the Digital and Information Age. Characterised by the proliferation of computers, the Internet, and globalisation, this era marks a paradigm shift in connectivity, information access, and communication. The Digital and Information Age has reshaped the labour market, leading to both opportunities and challenges. Automation and artificial intelligence have automated routine tasks, resulting in job displacement in some sectors. According to a report by the World Economic Forum, around 85 million jobs may be displaced by 2025 due to automation, particularly in sectors such as manufacturing and transportation (Russo 2020). However, this same report also projects the creation of 97 million new jobs in emerging fields like data analytics, artificial intelligence, robotics, ethics of machines, digital marketing, content creation renewable energy, etc. Additionally, the gig economy has emerged as a prominent feature of the modern workforce, offering flexibility and autonomy to workers but also raising concerns about job security and labour rights (De Stefano 2015).

The Digital and Information Age has revolutionised education, expanding access to learning opportunities and transforming pedagogical approaches. Online learning platforms like Coursera, Udemy, and Khan Academy offer a wide range of courses and resources, enabling individuals to acquire new skills and knowledge from anywhere in the world (Bakhshi and Amees 2022). Massive Open Online Courses (MOOCs) have democratised access to education, with millions of learners enrolled in courses on diverse subjects. Digital technologies have also transformed traditional classrooms, facilitating personalised learning experiences through adaptive learning software and interactive multimedia resources. However, the digital divide remains a significant barrier to equitable access to education, particularly in underserved communities and developing countries.

The Information Age has revolutionised healthcare delivery, enabling remote consultations, telemedicine, and digital health monitoring. Telemedicine platforms like Teladoc Health and Doctor on Demand provide virtual consultations with healthcare professionals, offering convenience and accessibility to patients, especially those in rural or underserved areas (Eisenberg et al. 2018). Wearable devices like fitness trackers and smartwatches monitor vital signs and track health metrics, empowering individuals to take a proactive approach to their health and well-being (Tariq 2024). Artificial intelligence and machine learning algorithms analyse vast amounts of medical data to identify patterns and make diagnostic predictions, improving patient outcomes and reducing healthcare costs. However, concerns about data privacy and security remain paramount in the digital healthcare landscape, as the sharing and analysis of sensitive health information raise ethical and regulatory challenges (Ellahham et al. 2020).

Information Age has transformed the way we buy, sell, and consume goods and services, giving rise to the e-commerce revolution. Online retail giants like Amazon, Alibaba, and eBay have disrupted traditional brick-and-mortar retail models, offering a vast selection of products at competitive prices and unparalleled convenience.

According to Statista, global e-commerce sales reached $4.28 trillion in 2020 and are projected to exceed $6.38 trillion by 2024 (Chevalier 2024). The COVID-19 pandemic further accelerated the shift to online shopping, with lockdowns and social distancing measures driving consumers to embrace digital channels for their shopping needs. However, the rise of e-commerce has also raised concerns about the concentration of market power among tech giants, as well as issues related to counterfeit goods, data privacy, and consumer protection.

Despite the transformative potential of the Digital and Information Age, significant disparities persist in access to digital technologies and information. The digital divide, both within and between countries, reflects unequal access to broadband Internet, digital devices, and digital literacy skills. According to the International Telecommunication Union (ITU), around 3.7 billion people worldwide remain unconnected to the Internet, with the majority residing in developing countries (Raina 2017). Inadequate infrastructure, high costs, and lack of digital literacy contribute to this digital divide, exacerbating existing socio-economic inequalities. Bridging the digital divide requires concerted efforts from governments, private sector actors, and civil society organisations to expand access to affordable broadband infrastructure, provide digital skills training, and promote inclusive digital policies (Lythreatis et al. 2022).

Information Age has unleashed unprecedented opportunities for innovation, economic growth, and social progress. However, it also poses significant challenges related to job displacement, digital inclusion, privacy, and equity. Addressing these challenges requires a multifaceted approach that prioritises investment in digital infrastructure, education, and workforce development while safeguarding fundamental rights and values in the digital realm. By harnessing the power of technology for the greater good and ensuring that its benefits are equitably distributed, we can leverage the transformative potential of the Digital and Information Age to build a more inclusive and sustainable future for all.

References

Abbo S, Gopher A, Bar-Gal GK (2022) The origins of agriculture in the ancient near east. Cambridge University Press

Albaroudi E, Mansouri T, Alameer A (2024) A comprehensive review of AI techniques for addressing algorithmic bias in job hiring. AI 5(1):383–404

Amanda Russo WEF (2020) Recession and automation changes our future of work, but there are jobs coming, Report Says, Published 20 Oct 2020 2020 Share Amanda Russo, Public Engagement, World Economic Forum. https://www.weforum.org/press/2020/10/recession-and-automation-changes-our-future-of-work-but-there-are-jobs-coming-report-says-52c5162fce/. Accessed 22 April 2024

Ayres RU (1990) Technological transformations and long waves. Part I. Technol Forecast Soc Change 37(1):1–37

Bakhshi SI, Amees M (2022) Legal education through MOOCs: a study of select international online platforms. Indian J Educ Technol 4(2):169–185

Bennison-Chapman LE (2014) The role and function of "Tokens" and sealing practices in the neolithic of the near east: The question of early recording systems, symbolic storage, precursors to writing, gaming, or monitoring devices in the world's first villages. The University of Liverpool (United Kingdom)
Berners-Lee T (1996) WWW: past, present, and future. Computer 29(10):6
Bernstein H (2010) Class dynamics of agrarian change, vol 1. Kumarian Press
Brown JA (1989) 10 The beginnings of pottery as an economic process
Chalaby JK, Plunkett S (2021) Standing on the shoulders of tech giants: media delivery, streaming television and the rise of global suppliers. New Media Soc 23(11):3206–3228
Chevalier S (2024) Global retail e-commerce sales 2014–2027. https://www.statista.com/statistics/379046/worldwide-retail-e-commerce-sales/. Accessed 22 April 2024
da Motta e Albuquerque E (2023) The microprocessor and the world wide web–two technological revolutions and a second reversal?–1971, 1991. In: Technological revolutions and the periphery: understanding global development through regional lenses. Springer International Publishing, Cham, pp 159–189
De Stefano V (2015) The rise of the just-in-time workforce: on-demand work, crowdwork, and labor protection in the gig-economy. Comp Lab l. Pol'y J 37:471
Drage E, Mackereth K (2022) Does AI derbies recruitment? Race, gender, and AI's "eradication of difference." Philos Technol 35(4):89
Dressel J, Farid H (2018) The accuracy, fairness, and limits of predicting recidivism. Sci Adv 4(1):eaao5580
Dummer GWA (2013) Electronic inventions and discoveries: electronics from its earliest beginnings to the present day. Elsevier
Ede A (2019) Technology and society: a world history. Cambridge University Press
Eisenberg E, Louk R, Mohammad S, Vaughan D (2018) Telemedicine: the next generation of healthcare. Muma Case Rew 3(6):1–21
Ellahham S, Ellahham N, Simsekler MCE (2020) Application of artificial intelligence in the health care safety context: opportunities and challenges. Am J Med Qual 35(4):341–348
Evangelista R, Guerrieri P, Meliciani V (2014) The economic impact of digital technologies in Europe. Econ Innov New Technol 23(8):802–824
Flores AW, Bechtel K, Lowenkamp CT (2016) False positives, false negatives, and false analyses: a rejoinder to machine bias: There's software used across the country to predict future criminals. and it's biased against blacks. Fed. Probation 80, 38
Gee H (2020) Surveillance state: fourth amendment law, big data policing, and facial recognition technology
Haleem A, Javaid M, Qadri MA, Suman R (2022) Understanding the role of digital technologies in education: a review. Sustain Oper Comput 3:275–285
Hauben R (1997) The birth and development of the ARPANET. In: Hauben M, Hauben R (eds) Netizens: on the history and impact of usenet and the internet. John Wiley and Sons
Kalasin S, Surareungchai W (2023) Challenges of emerging wearable sensors for remote monitoring toward telemedicine healthcare. Anal Chem 95(3):1773–1784
Kirk GS (1973) Myth: its meaning and functions in ancient and other cultures. University of California Press
Kraus N, Kraus K, Manzhur O, Ishchenko I, Radzikhovska Y (2023) Digital transformation of business processes of enterprises on the way to becoming industry 5.0 in the gig economy. WSEAS Trans Bus Econ 93(20):1008–1029
Landes DS (2003) The unbound PROMETHeus: technological change and industrial development in Western Europe from 1750 to the present. Cambridge University Press
Lythreatis S, Singh SK, El-Kassar AN (2022) The digital divide: a review and future research agenda. Technol Forecast Soc Change 175:121359
Marsh P (2012) The new industrial revolution: consumers, globalization and the end of mass production. Yale University Press

Masood M, Nawaz M, Malik KM, Javed A, Irtaza A, Malik H (2023) Deepfakes generation and detection: state-of-the-art, open challenges, countermeasures, and way forward. Appl Intell 53(4):3974–4026
McNeill WH (2009) The rise of the West: a history of the human community. University of Chicago Press
Mohajan H (2019) The first industrial revolution: creation of a new global human era
National Geographic (2020) The development of agriculture. https://education.nationalgeographic.org/resource/development-agriculture/. Accessed 02 April 2024
Perez C (2003) Technological revolutions and financial capital. Edward Elgar Publishing
Perez C (2004) Technological revolutions, paradigm shifts and socio-institutional change. In: Globalization, economic development and inequality: an alternative perspective, pp 217–242
Prasongko A, Adianto T (2019) The role of the agile leadership model as a competitive advantage for the future leader in the era of globalization and industrial revolution 4.0. Jurnal Pertahanan: Media Informasi tentang Kajian dan Strategi Pertahanan yang Mengedepankan Identity, Nasionalism dan Integrity 5(3):126–133
Price J (1994) Lean production at Suzuki and Toyota: a historical perspective. Stud Polit Econ 45(1):66–99
Raina R (2017) Connectivity and information and communications technology. In: A sustainable future for small states: pacific 2050, 289
Robins K, Webster F (2020) The long history of the information revolution: the long history of the information revolution. In: The information society reader. Routledge, pp 62–80
Sangmeister H, Villhauer B (2022) Digitalization and global responsibility. In: Handbook industry 4.0: law, technology, society. Springer Berlin Heidelberg, Berlin, Heidelberg, pp 1161–1170. https://datareportal.com/reports/digital-2020-july-global-statshot
Santos BP, Charrua-Santos F, Lima TM (2018, July) Industry 4.0: an overview. In: Proceedings of the world congress on engineering, vol 2. IAEN, London, UK, pp 4–6
Schick N (2020) Deep fakes and the infocalypse: what you urgently need to know. Hachette UK
Singh S (2023) An analysis of artificial intelligence and its role in the cryptocurrency. Samvakti J Res Inf Technol 4(1)
Skilton M, Hovsepian F (2018) The 4th industrial revolution. Springer Nature
Stark B, Stegmann D, Magin M, Jürgens P (2020) Are algorithms a threat to democracy? The rise of intermediaries: a challenge for public discourse. Algorithm Watch 26
Stearns PN (2020) The industrial revolution in world history. Routledge
Steinberg M (2022) From automobile capitalism to platform capitalism: toyotism as a prehistory of digital platforms. Organ Stud 43(7):1069–1090
Tariq MU (2024) Advanced wearable medical devices and their role in transformative remote health monitoring. In: Transformative approaches to patient literacy and healthcare innovation, pp 308–326. IGI Global
Wheeler DL (2011) Does the Internet empower? A look at the internet and international development. In: The handbook of internet studies, pp 188–211

Chapter 3
Digitalisation, Artificial Intelligence, IoT, and Industry 4.0 and Digital Society

Abstract This chapter introduces the foundation of digital transformation taking place due to Digital technologies, Artificial Intelligence, Machine Learning, the Internet of Things (IoT), and Industry 4.0. This chapter discusses developments that led to digital transformation from a definition point of view. It also provides real-life examples to demonstrate their impact and explore the synergies between digitalisation, AI, and Industry 4.0 and their implications for society and businesses. This chapter explores the concept of digital transformation and its impact on the emergence of a digital society. It examines the fundamental shifts brought about by digital technologies in various aspects of life, including communication, economy, governance, and culture. The chapter also explores the concept of a digital society, where digital technologies have become deeply embedded in everyday life, transforming how people communicate, work, learn, and participate in civic activities. It discusses the opportunities and challenges arising from the digital society.

Keywords Digitalisation · Digital transformation · Artificial intelligence · IoT and industry 4.0 · Digital society · Impact and assessment

3.1 Introduction to Digitisation, Digitalisation, and Digital Transformation

The present canvas of society is undergoing a profound transformation due to the rapid technological advancements and adoption in various systems of society. This technological adoption is making changes in almost all aspects of our lives and facilitating our lives by providing comfort and convenience. Digital transformation integration into the fabric of organisations and societies goes beyond theoretical discussions and mere adoption. It signifies a fundamental shift in how societal entities operate, deliver value, and interact with several stakeholders such as citizens, community, public and private institutions, and governments (OECD 2017). We have

S. Kumar et al., *Digital Transformation, Artificial Intelligence and Society*, Frontiers of Artificial Intelligence, Ethics and Multidisciplinary Applications,
https://doi.org/10.1007/978-981-97-5656-8_3

gone through a lot as a society and economy in the process of digitisation and digitalisation. At present, we are in digital transformation and it facilitates the seamless flow of data and information, transcending traditional boundaries.

Driving digital transformation foundation, digital technologies, AI, machine learning, big data analytics (BDA), and IoT catalyse a revolution in each domain such as communication, manufacturing, healthcare, education, finance, and entertainment (Heidari et al. 2022). Communication becomes instantaneous and large-scale, manufacturing processes evolve with smart technologies and intelligent decision-making and data collection from sensors, healthcare embraces digital solutions for the prediction of disease, precision medicine, robotic surgery, etc., and financial landscapes undergo a digital revolution (George and George 2024).

We have been using the terms digitisation, digitalisation, and digital transformation casually and interchangeably but they are fundamentally different and convey different meanings which need to be understood. We need to understand them from a definitional point of view and understand the fundamental shift they have been bringing into society and why it is happening. Each concept carries distinct meanings and implications for organisations, industries, and societies. We need to understand these concepts by providing insights into their definitions, key differences, and real-world examples.

3.1.1 Digitisation: Defining the Digital Frontier

We have been using data for ages. We create data, use and store it for processing, and extract information/knowledge from it. Till the beginning of the twentieth century, we used information in the form of analogue representation or stored it in physical forms such as papers, registers, copies, etc. Real-world information about things that can be represented as values and from a continuous space is termed an analogue. For example, quantities such as mass, length, time, temperature, current, voltage, and colour are stored as analogue information. Opposite to this is another representation called digital format and processing methods (Hilbert and López 2011). Digitisation is the process of changing information/data from analogue to digital form. It is also known as the digital enablement of information. More specifically, Digitisation takes an analogue process and changes it to a digital form without any different-in-kind changes in its nature and value (Bloomberg 2018). Digitisation refers to the process of converting analogue information into digital format, enabling storage, processing, manipulation, and transmission very efficiently and easily. This digitisation of data, documents, and processes facilitates seamless access, updation, sharing, and analysis resulting in efficiency and innovation across all domains where digitisation is integrated and adopted in systems. For example, the digitisation of paper-based documents into electronic formats streamlines document management processes, the creation of copies, and the performing of several important operations on such stored documents individually and collectively. It reduces storage costs and enhances the information accessibility and processing abilities of organisations. Digitisation converts analogue data, such as text, images, and audio, into digital form through scanning, encoding, or other available and emerging digitisation techniques (Bloomberg 2018). In addition to the conversion, digitisation also facilitates process automation that leverages digital tools and software to automate repetitive tasks, streamline workflows, and improve operational efficiency. Moreover, it enables information access in digital format anytime, anywhere across the world through several types of platforms.

3.1.2 *Digitalisation: Transforming Business Operations*

Digitalisation extends beyond the conversion of analogue data to digital data format. Digitalisation encompasses the integration of digital technologies/their products into business models, operations, and customer experiences. It involves leveraging digital tools/software and strategies to optimise processes, enhance customer experience and engagement, and drive competitive advantage in the digital economy (Bloomberg 2018). For instance, digitalisation in retail encompasses online sales channels, digital marketing campaigns, and personalised customer experiences tailored to individual preferences by the particular business organisation through system automation (Vrana and Singh 2021). Digitalisation provides access and efficiency through automation software and transforms individual business operations. Moreover, while digitisation aims to convert and record data, digitalisation focuses on developing processes and changing workflows to improve existing manual systems. For example, digitised customer data from different sources to automatically generate insights from their purchasing behavior (Bloomberg 2018). It harnesses the power of data analytics tools and techniques to derive actionable insights from digital data, inform decision-making, and drive business growth. For example, business owners use customer purchase and product data to identify purchasing patterns, optimise product assortments, and personalise marketing campaigns. Digitalisation fosters a culture of innovation, experimentation, and continuous improvement within organisations (Fig. 3.1).

3.1.3 *Digital Transformation: Orchestrating Transformation of Business Models and Strategy*

Digital transformation represents a holistic and strategic approach to leveraging digital technologies to fundamentally transform business models, operations, and organisational culture leading to completely new entities and substantially modified versions of previous entities to provide more value to end users. It goes beyond

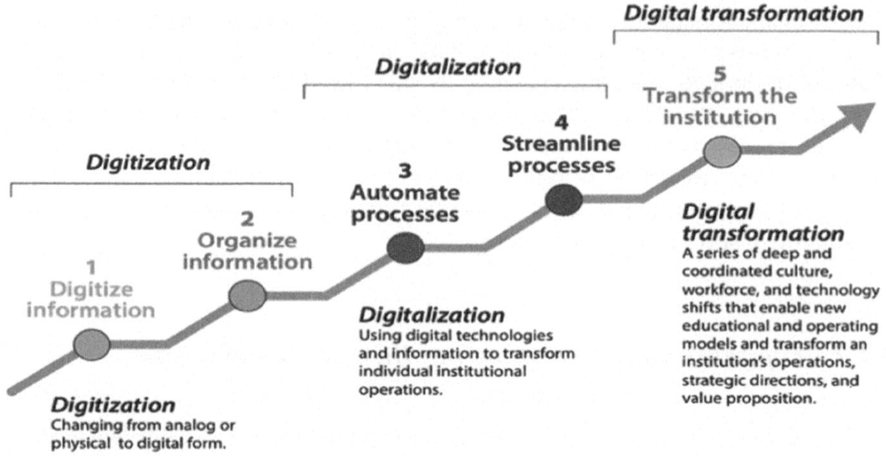

Fig. 3.1 Digitisation, digitalisation, and digital transformation (Reinitz, B. "Consider the Three Ds When Talking about Digital Transformation," https://er.educause.edu/blogs/2020/6/consider-the-three-ds-when-talking-about-digital-transformation)

incremental improvements and encompasses radical shifts in processes and capabilities. Digital transformation is not merely about adopting new technologies but rather about reimagining business models, creating new value propositions, and driving sustainable growth in the digital era for customers and citizens in the case of governance systems. This is driven by the foundation of previous developments of digitisation and digitalization (Bloomberg 2018). Digital transformation is a revolutionary extension of digitisation and digitalisation. Digital transformation enables companies to create innovative products and services, revenue streams, partnerships, and ecosystem collaborations that disrupt existing systems and industry norms and redefine competitive landscapes. It also cultivates a digital-first mindset and fosters a culture of innovation, collaboration, and continuous learning within and outside organisations and among organisations (Bloomberg 2018). For example, Digital transformation in payment systems, online e-commerce, etc. places customer needs, preferences, convenience experience, and feedback at the centre. By adopting a customer-centric approach, organisations can design products, services, and experiences that deliver tangible value and differentiate them from competitors in the digital marketplace. For example, Amazon's transformation from an online bookstore to a global e-commerce juggernaut exemplifies digital transformation. It integrated several stakeholders and developed products based on offerings of digital technologies (Dodge 1999). By leveraging software development, data analytics, machine learning, and cloud computing, Amazon has disrupted traditional retail models, pioneered same-day delivery services, and diversified into new business verticals, such as cloud computing through (Amazon Web Services) and streaming and entertainment media (Amazon Prime Video) (Kahn 2021). Similarly, in the entertainment domain, Netflix transformed the way we access entertainment by forcing a transition from a DVD rental service to a leading streaming platform representing a classic example of digital transformation (Vieželytė 2022). By investing in original content production, personalised recommendation algorithms, and global expansion strategies, Netflix has revolutionised the entertainment industry, challenging traditional broadcast and cable television models. Similarly, Tesla's vision to accelerate the transition to sustainable energy through electric vehicles (EVs) and renewable energy technologies embodies digital transformation (Romeu Lezama 2016). By integrating AI-driven autonomous driving features, over-the-air software updates, and energy storage solutions, Tesla has redefined the automotive industry, driving innovation and sustainability in transportation for a better future. All three concepts of digitisation, digitisation, and digital transformation are depicted in (Fig. 3.1).

3.2 Introduction to Artificial Intelligence

AI encompasses everything responsibly and involves the creation of systems, machines, software, and devices which are capable of behaving, working, or making decisions such as human beings do (Samoili et al. 2020). More specifically AI systems/tools/softwares can do the learning, reasoning, and problem-solving, often mimicking human cognitive functions. AI has emerged as one of the most transformative technologies of the twenty-first century which is revolutionising industry after industry, reshaping economies, and redefining the human–machine interface and technology and society interface (West and Allen 2018). AI refers to the development of machines/systems capable of performing tasks that typically require human intelligence, such as understanding natural language, recognising patterns, solving complex problems, and learning from experience and doing those tasks with the help of machines/devices/tools/softwares/agents (McCarthy 2007). Formally, the goal of AI is to create intelligent agents that can perceive their environment, reason about it, and take appropriate actions to achieve specific goals.

3.2.1 Fundamental Components of Artificial Intelligence

There are several dimensions of defining components of AI. Here the components that are internal to the intelligence and type of data and processes of intelligence from that data together.

- Machine Learning is a subfield of AI focused on developing intelligent algorithms that enable computers to learn from data and previous experiences, identify patterns, and make predictions without explicit programming (Pramod et al. 2021). It is further subdivided into Supervised learning, unsupervised learning, and reinforcement learning. Recent advancements in machine learning, particularly in deep learning, have led to significant breakthroughs in areas such as image recognition, natural language processing, and autonomous decision-making (Dargan et al. 2020). Deep learning is a subset of machine learning, a branch of artificial intelligence (AI) that focuses on algorithms inspired by the structure and function of the brain's neural networks. Deep learning algorithms attempt to model high-level abstractions in data by using multiple processing layers composed of complex structures called neural networks (Indrakumari et al. 2021). These networks can learn representations of data with multiple levels of abstraction, leading to better performance on tasks such as classification, regression, and pattern recognition (Pramod et al. 2021) (Fig. 3.2). For example, Prediction of Crime, Face recognition systems, Recommendation systems for entertainment content on Netflix, etc. are prime examples of machine learning and its real-world applications (Shanthamallu and Spanias 2022).

- Natural Language Processing (NLP) is a branch of AI that deals with the interaction between computers and human language (Joshi 1991). NLP algorithms enable computers to understand, interpret, and generate human language, facilitating tasks such as language translation, sentiment analysis, and chatbot interactions (Chowdhary and Chowdhary 2020). Recent developments in NLP, such as transformer models like BERT and GPT, have achieved remarkable performance in tasks such as language understanding and text generation. For example, the latest ChatGPT, Bard, etc. are actual products which now users are using for their daily tasks such as writing letters of recommendation, solving assignments,

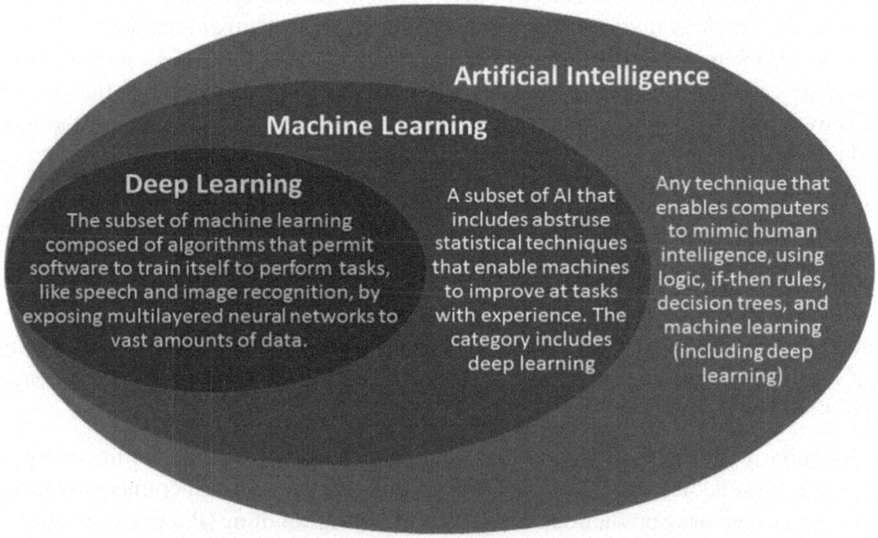

Fig. 3.2 Artificial intelligence, machine learning, and deep learning (https://www.geospatialworld.net/blogs/difference-between-ai%EF%BB%BF-machine-learning-and-deep-learning/)

generating ideas, asking questions, and getting answers as per their background (Min et al. 2023).

- Computer Vision is a field of AI concerned with enabling computers to interpret and understand visual information such as images/videos/audio from the real world. Computer vision algorithms allow machines to analyse images and videos, recognise objects, and extract meaningful insights and knowledge from images and videos (Szeliski 2022). Recent advancements in computer vision, driven by deep learning techniques, have led to breakthroughs in applications such as facial recognition, autonomous vehicles, and medical image analysis (Paneru and Jeelani 2021).
- Robotics combines AI with mechanical engineering to create intelligent machines capable of performing physical tasks in various environments (Murphy 2019). Robotics applications range from industrial robots used in manufacturing to autonomous drones, self-driving cars, and humanoid robots. Recent developments in robotics focus on enhancing autonomy, dexterity, and adaptability in robotic systems, enabling them to operate in complex and dynamic environments. (Govers 2018). There is an example of Boston Dynamics. Boston Dynamics is a pioneering robotics company renowned for its groundbreaking creations that blur the lines between science fiction and reality. Founded in 1992 by Marc Raibert, the company has revolutionised the field of robotics with its innovative designs and cutting-edge technology. Their robots, including Spot, Atlas, and Handle, exhibit unprecedented agility, balance, and adaptability. One of their most famous creations, Spot, is a versatile quadruped robot capable of navigating various terrains and performing tasks like inspection and data collection autonomously. Atlas, a humanoid robot, showcases remarkable mobility, demonstrating capabilities such as walking, running, and even performing gymnastic manoeuvers (Fig. 3.3). Boston Dynamics' work extends beyond mere functionality, often capturing the public's imagination with viral videos showcasing their robots' abilities, from dancing to parkour. These demonstrations not only highlight the technical prowess of their creations but also spark discussions about the future of robotics and automation in society (Guizzo 2019).

3.2.2 Real-World Applications of Artificial Intelligence

In the digital age, from healthcare to finance, manufacturing to retail, AI applications are permeating every facet of modern life, offering unprecedented opportunities for efficiency, productivity, and advancement in the growth of individuals and businesses (Sheikh 2020).

AI is revolutionising healthcare by empowering clinicians and researchers with powerful tools for diagnosis, treatment, and patient care (Alowais et al. 2023). Medical imaging analysis, a prime example, has witnessed remarkable advancements. AI algorithms can detect abnormalities in radiology scans with accuracy comparable to or even surpassing human experts. According to a study published, AI

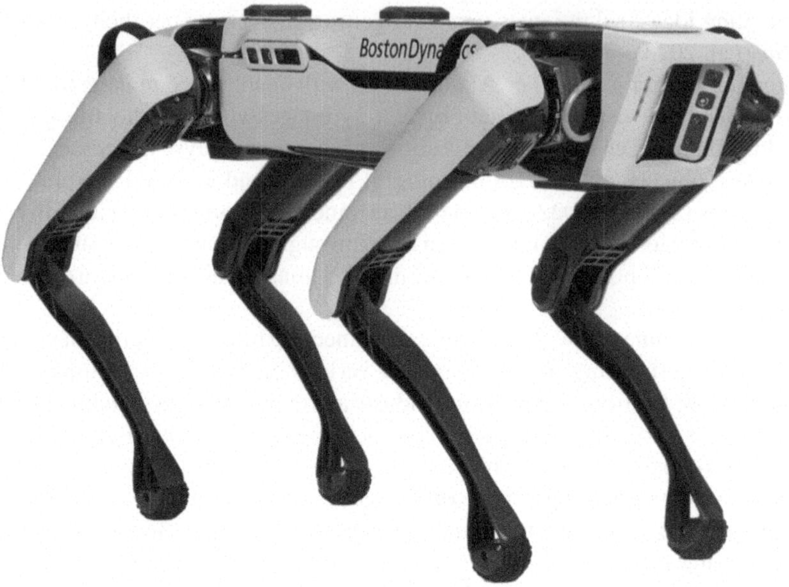

Fig. 3.3 Boston dynamics spot robot (https://bostondynamics.com/news/boston-dynamics-expands-global-sales-of-spot-robot/)

outperformed radiologists in diagnosing breast cancer from mammograms, reducing false positives by 5.7% and false negatives by 9.4% (McKinney et al. 2020). Moreover, AI-driven predictive analytics are enhancing patient outcomes by forecasting diseases and identifying at-risk populations.

In the financial sector, AI is transforming operations across various domains, from risk management to customer service. Algorithmic trading, enabled by AI-powered predictive analytics, has surged in popularity, accounting for over 80% of stock market trading volume in the United States (McGowan 2010). High-frequency trading algorithms leverage AI to execute trades at lightning speed, capitalising on market inefficiencies and generating significant profits for financial institutions (Zhou and Kalev 2019). Fraud detection is another critical application of AI in finance, safeguarding against fraudulent activities such as identity theft and credit card fraud. According to a report by Juniper Research, AI-based fraud detection systems are projected to save businesses over $40 billion annually by 2023, reducing false positives and enhancing security measures (Mill et al. 2023).

AI is reshaping the retail landscape by revolutionising customer experiences. Recommendation systems, powered by machine learning algorithms, drive personalised shopping experiences by analysing customer preferences and behaviour. Amazon, a trailblazer in this domain, attributes a major portion of its revenue to recommendation algorithms, significantly boosting sales and customer satisfaction (Weinstein 2012). Moreover, AI-driven supply chain optimisation is streamlining inventory management and logistics operations, reducing costs and minimising stock outs. Walmart, for instance, implemented an AI-powered inventory management system that reduced excess inventory by less than 15% while improving product availability by more than 90% (Mohan 2021).

AI's impact on manufacturing is profound, ushering in the era of Industry 4.0 with its transformative capabilities (Fig. 3.4). Predictive maintenance, facilitated by AI-driven analytics and IoT sensors, enables proactive equipment maintenance, minimising downtime and optimising asset utilisation. According to a study by McKinsey, predictive maintenance can reduce maintenance costs by up to 40% and unplanned downtime by 50%. AI-powered quality control systems enhance product quality and yield rates by detecting defects with unparalleled accuracy (Manyika et al. 2015). Tesla's utilisation of computer vision and deep learning algorithms for quality inspection in its manufacturing process has resulted in a more than 80 per cent reduction in defects, ensuring superior product reliability and customer satisfaction (Grigorescu et al. 2020).

The automotive industry is undergoing a paradigm shift with the advent of AI-powered autonomous vehicles and advanced driver assistance systems (ADAS). According to a report by Allied Market Research, the global autonomous vehicle market is projected to reach $556.67 billion by 2026, driven by the proliferation of AI technologies such as computer vision, sensor fusion, and deep learning (Allied Market Research 2019). Tesla, a frontrunner in autonomous driving technology, leverages AI algorithms trained on vast amounts of real-world data to enable features such as Autopilot and Full Self-Driving (FSD). These systems continuously learn and adapt to diverse driving conditions, paving the way for safer and more efficient transportation solutions (Shah 2023).

AI-powered chatbots and virtual assistants are revolutionising customer service by providing personalised, round-the-clock support across various channels. According

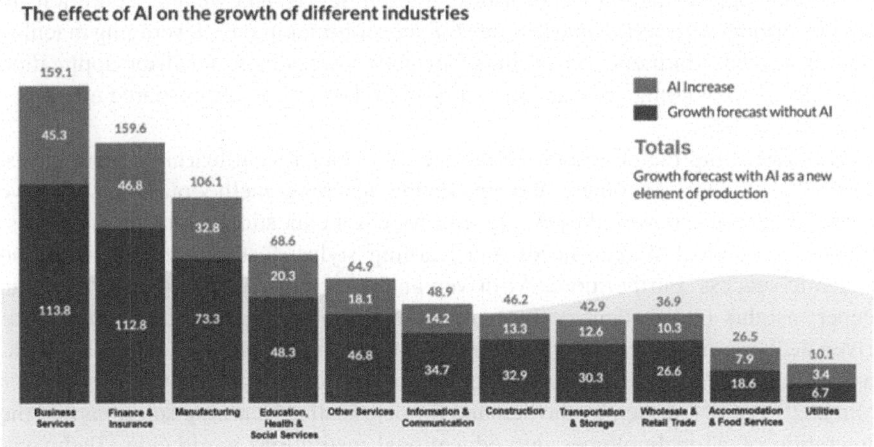

Fig. 3.4 Effect of AI on growth of different industries (https://www.plantautomation-technology.com/articles/the-future-of-artificial-intelligence-in-manufacturing-industries)

to a study by Grand View Research, the global chatbot market is expected to reach $1.25 billion by 2025, driven by the demand for automated customer interactions and operational efficiency (Ground View Research 2023). Companies such as Google, Amazon, and Apple have integrated AI-powered virtual assistants such as Google Assistant, Alexa, and Siri into their products and services, enhancing user experiences and enabling seamless voice interactions (Roslan and Ahmad 2023). These virtual assistants leverage natural language processing (NLP) and machine learning algorithms to understand and respond to user queries with human-like accuracy and efficiency.

In an increasingly interconnected world, cybersecurity is paramount, and AI is playing a pivotal role in fortifying digital defences against evolving threats. AI-powered threat detection systems analyse vast network traffic and security logs to identify anomalous behaviour indicative of cyberattacks. According to a report by MarketsandMarkets, the global AI in cybersecurity market is projected to reach $38.2 billion by 2026, driven by the escalating cybersecurity threats and the need for proactive defence mechanisms (Mehra 2024).

IBM's Watson for Cyber Security, for instance, leverages AI algorithms to analyse structured and unstructured data from diverse sources, enabling early detection and rapid response to cyber threats. This proactive approach enhances threat visibility and resilience, safeguarding organisations against potential breaches and data compromises (Vähäkainu and Lehto 2022).

AI is revolutionising agriculture by enabling precision farming techniques that optimise resource usage, improve crop yields, and mitigate environmental impacts. According to a report by Research and Markets, the global AI in agriculture market is expected to reach $4.6 billion by 2026, driven by the adoption of AI-driven solutions for crop monitoring, yield prediction, and pest detection (Reportlinker 2023). Precision agriculture systems, equipped with AI algorithms and IoT sensors, collect and analyse data on soil moisture, nutrient levels, and weather conditions to provide farmers with actionable insights for decision-making. By leveraging machine learning models, farmers can optimise irrigation schedules, fertiliser application rates, and crop planting patterns, resulting in higher yields and resource efficiency (Islam et al. 2023).

AI is reshaping the education landscape by personalising learning experiences, improving student outcomes, and enhancing teaching methodologies. Adaptive learning platforms, powered by AI algorithms, tailor educational content and assessments to individual student needs and learning styles, fostering engagement and academic success. Furthermore, AI-driven analytics tools enable educators to gain deeper insights into student performance and learning progress, facilitating data-driven decision-making and targeted interventions. According to a report by Technavio, the global AI in education market is expected to grow at a CAGR of over 33% from 2020 to 2024, driven by the demand for personalised learning solutions and the integration of AI technologies into educational institutions worldwide (Technavio 2023).

AI is driving the transformation of urban infrastructure and governance, ushering in the era of smart cities characterised by connectivity, sustainability, and efficiency.

According to a report by MarketsandMarkets, the global smart cities market is projected to reach $820.7 billion by 2025, driven by the adoption of AI-driven solutions for transportation, energy management, public safety, and environmental monitoring (Markets and Markets 2024). Digital technologies and AI-powered traffic management systems optimise traffic flow and reduce congestion by analysing real-time data from sensors, cameras, and GPS devices. Singapore's Smart Mobility 2030 vision, for instance, leverages AI algorithms to predict traffic patterns and optimise traffic signal timings, resulting in smoother traffic flow and reduced travel times (Keong and Grace 2015).

3.3 Internet of Things (IoT)

At its core, Digital Technologies encompass the expansive realm of innovations that convert analogue information into digital formats. This includes the digitisation of data, processes, and communication channels, laying the groundwork for subsequent integrations. The Internet has provided a way for the connection of humans through devices and web applications to facilitate the sharing of information and expression. However, billions of devices and machines can also be connected and made to share information on demand or in real time. The Internet of Things (IoT) involves connecting everyday devices to the Internet, enabling them to send and receive data and do the processing of information for desired purposes (Borgia 2014). This interconnected web of devices forms the backbone of personal lives and Industry 4.0 and provides huge potential for further transformation of society. IoT has emerged as a transformative force in the digital era, revolutionising how devices, objects, and systems communicate, interact, and operate (Fig. 3.5).

3.3.1 Foundational and Component of IoT

The IoT refers to the network of interconnected devices, sensors, and actuators that communicate and exchange data over the Internet, without requiring human intervention. The IoT ecosystem encompasses various devices, ranging from smartphones and wearables to household appliances, industrial machinery, and equipment in smart city infrastructure. By embedding sensors and connectivity features into physical objects, IoT enables seamless monitoring, control, and automation of processes, unlocking new levels of efficiency, productivity, and convenience (Gubbi et al. 2013).

Sensors are fundamental components of IoT devices, capable of detecting and measuring physical parameters, such as temperature, humidity, motion, and light. On the other hand, actuators enable IoT devices to perform physical actions or control external systems based on input from sensors. For example, a smart thermostat equipped with temperature and humidity sensors can adjust heating and cooling settings to maintain optimal indoor comfort levels for human beings. IoT devices

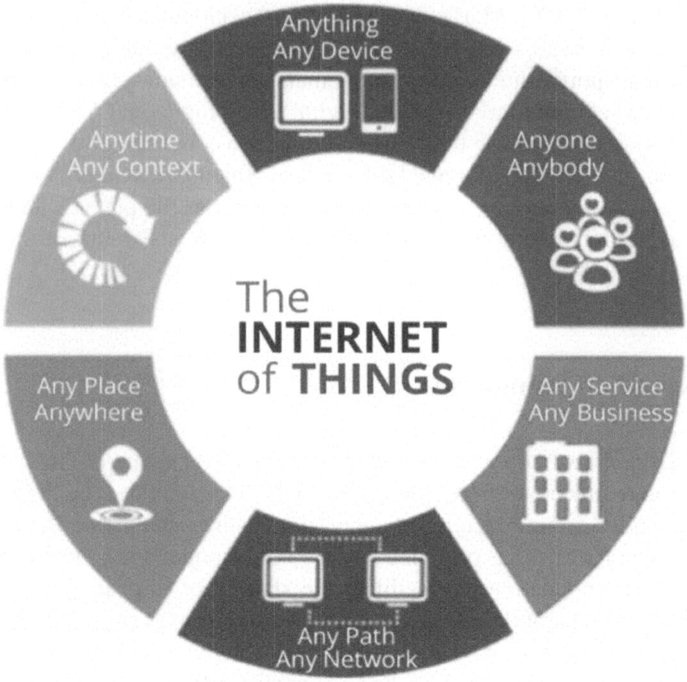

Fig. 3.5 Concept of IoT (https://medium.com/@kunalmohta/what-is-meant-by-the-term-internet-of-things-iot-287cfc233865)

rely on various communication protocols and technologies to transmit data over the Internet or local networks. Common connectivity options include Wi-Fi, Bluetooth, Zigbee, LoRaWAN, and cellular networks (e.g., 4G LTE, 5G) (Gubbi et al. 2013). These connectivity technologies facilitate seamless data exchange and enable remote monitoring and control of IoT devices from anywhere in the world. IoT generates vast amounts of data that require storage, processing, and analysis to derive actionable insights and support decision-making. Cloud computing platforms, such as Amazon Web Services (AWS) and Microsoft Azure, provide scalable infrastructure and analytics tools for managing IoT data and deploying AI and machine learning models. Edge computing complements cloud computing by processing data locally on IoT devices or gateways, reducing latency and bandwidth usage for real-time applications (Firouzi et al. 2020).

3.3.2 Real-World Applications of IoT

IoT enables homeowners to automate and remotely control various aspects of their homes, including lighting, heating, security, and entertainment systems. For example, smart thermostats like Nest Learning Thermostat learn users' preferences and adjust temperature settings automatically, while smart security cameras send alerts and footage to users' smartphones in case of suspicious activity. In the industrial sector, IoT technologies are revolutionising manufacturing, logistics, and supply chain management processes (Attia 2019). Industrial IoT (IIoT) solutions enable predictive maintenance, asset tracking, and real-time monitoring of equipment and production lines. For instance, sensors embedded in manufacturing equipment can detect signs of wear or malfunction, triggering maintenance alerts and preventing costly downtime. IoT plays a crucial role in building smart and sustainable cities by optimising resource management, enhancing public services, and improving the quality of life for residents. Smart city initiatives leverage IoT sensors and data analytics to monitor traffic flow, reduce energy consumption, manage waste, and enhance public safety. Examples include smart traffic lights that adjust signal timings based on real-time traffic conditions and smart waste bins that optimise waste collection routes (Khanna and Kaur 2020). The Internet of Things (IoT) represents a paradigm shift in connectivity and automation, connecting billions of devices and enabling data-driven insights and actions across industries and domains. With its foundational principles, key components, and real-world applications, IoT is poised to continue reshaping the way we live, work, and interact with the world around us. As IoT adoption continues to accelerate, organisations and societies must navigate challenges related to data privacy, security, and interoperability to harness the full potential of this transformative technology (Khanna and Kaur 2020) (Fig. 3.6).

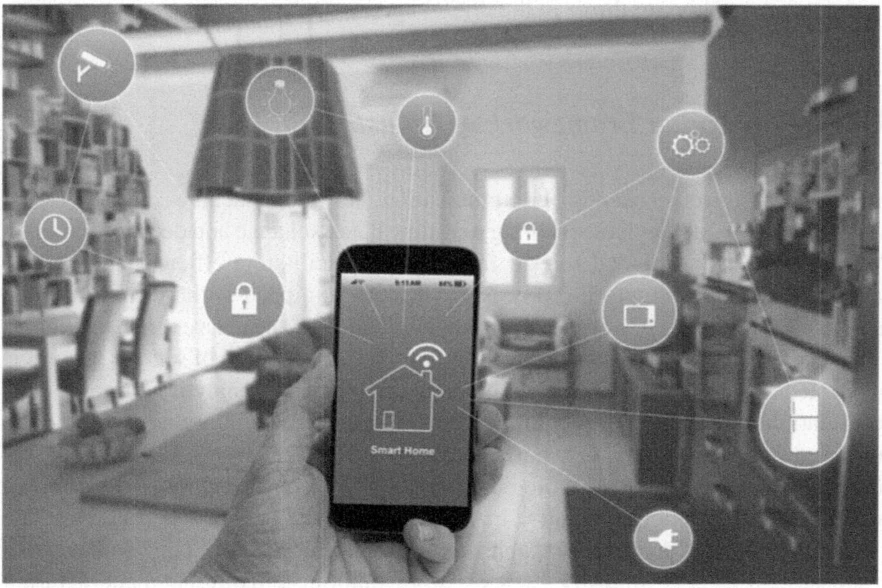

Fig. 3.6 Smart home concept using IoT (https://letstalkscience.ca/educational-resources/backgrounders/what-internet-things)

3.4 Introduction to Industry 4.0

Industry 4.0, also known as the Fourth Industrial Revolution, represents a paradigm shift in manufacturing and production processes driven by advanced digital technologies. Industry 4.0 represents a transformative shift in manufacturing processes, driven by advancements in digital technologies (Lasi et al. 2014). This paradigm encompasses the integration of cyber-physical systems, the Internet of Things (IoT), cloud computing, and artificial intelligence (AI) to create smart factories and revolutionise traditional production methods. The global market for Industry 4.0 technologies is projected to reach $310 billion by 2026, with a compound annual growth rate (CAGR) of 14.4% (Longati et al. 2023). Manufacturers embracing Industry 4.0 report an average increase in productivity by 25% and a reduction in maintenance costs by 30% (Ghobakhloo 2018). According to a survey by McKinsey, nearly 70% of companies have accelerated their digital transformation initiatives due to the COVID-19 pandemic, further driving the adoption of Industry 4.0 technologies (https://www.mckinsey.com/~/media/mckinsey/business%20functions/mckinsey%20digital/our%20insights/how%20six%20companies%20are%20using%20technology%20and%20data%20to%20transform%20themselves/the-next-normal-the-recovery-will-be-digital.pdf). Germany leads the adoption of Industry 4.0, with over 70% of its manufacturing companies implementing smart factory solutions (Veile et al. 2020). Industry 4.0 represents a paradigm shift in manufacturing, empowering companies to drive efficiency, innovation, and competitiveness in a rapidly evolving global landscape. Embracing this revolution is not just a choice but a necessity for organisations seeking to thrive in the digital age.

3.4.1 Conceptual Framework of Industry 4.0

Industry 4.0 fosters seamless communication between machines, systems, and humans through IoT devices, enabling real-time data exchange and decision-making. Automation plays a pivotal role in Industry 4.0, facilitating efficient and precise manufacturing and monitoring processes. Robots, equipped with AI and machine learning capabilities, perform tasks with minimal human intervention, leading to enhanced efficiency, productivity, and quality. The proliferation of sensors and interconnected devices generates vast amounts of data. Big data analytics harnesses this information to optimise production processes, predict maintenance needs, and drive informed decision-making (Kumar and Agrawal 2022). Industry 4.0 encompasses the convergence of digital technologies, such as the Internet of Things (IoT), artificial intelligence (AI), robotics, additive manufacturing, and big data analytics, to create smart, interconnected systems capable of autonomous decision-making and adaptive responses. At its core, Industry 4.0 seeks to revolutionise traditional manufacturing paradigms by enabling the seamless integration of cyber-physical systems (CPS) across the entire value chain, from design and production to logistics and service delivery (Fig. 3.7).

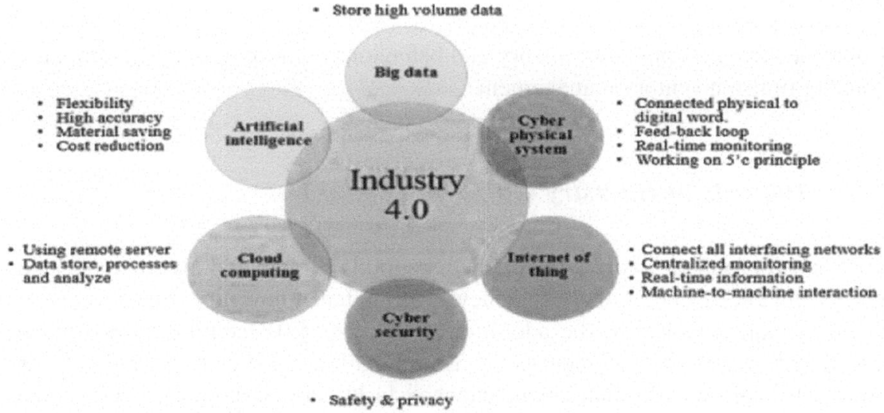

Fig. 3.7 A conceptual framework for the implementation of Industry 4.0. Kumar and Agrawal (2022). A conceptual framework for the implementation of Industry 4.0 in legal informatics. *Sustainable Computing: Informatics and Systems*, *33*, 100650

3.4.2 Technological Enablers of Industry 4.0

- Internet of Things (IoT): The proliferation of IoT devices embedded with sensors and actuators facilitates real-time monitoring and control of physical assets and processes. For example, in smart factories, IoT-enabled sensors collect data on machine performance, energy consumption, and product quality, enabling predictive maintenance and process optimisation.
- Artificial Intelligence (AI): AI algorithms power cognitive capabilities, including machine learning, natural language processing, and computer vision, enabling machines to analyse vast datasets, learn from experience, and make intelligent decisions autonomously. In manufacturing, AI-driven predictive analytics optimise production schedules, detect defects, and enhance quality control.
- Robotics and Automation: Advanced robotics technologies, including collaborative robots (cobots) and autonomous mobile robots (AMRs), automate repetitive tasks, enhance worker safety, and improve operational efficiency. For instance, in automotive assembly lines, robots work alongside human workers to perform complex tasks with precision and speed.
- Additive Manufacturing (3D Printing): Additive manufacturing techniques, such as selective laser sintering (SLS) and fused deposition modelling (FDM), enable on-demand production of customised parts and prototypes with reduced material waste and lead times. Additive manufacturing revolutionises supply chain management by enabling distributed manufacturing and decentralised production networks (Ngo et al. 2018).
- Big Data Analytics: The proliferation of big data analytics platforms facilitates real-time data processing, pattern recognition, and predictive modelling, unlocking insights for operational optimisation, demand forecasting, and

customer personalisation. For example, in retail, big data analytics algorithms analyse customer purchase history and behaviour to tailor marketing campaigns and optimise inventory management.

3.4.3 *Impacts of Industry 4.0*

Industry 4.0 promises to drive significant economic growth and productivity gains through enhanced operational efficiency, accelerated innovation cycles, and new revenue streams. However, the adoption of Industry 4.0 technologies also raises concerns about job displacement, such as automation. AI-driven technologies are assumed to replace traditional labour-intensive tasks (Fig. 3.8). Industry 4.0 enables reshoring initiatives by reducing labour costs, minimising supply chain risks, and enabling agile production processes (Rosin et al. 2020). As a result, many companies are bringing manufacturing operations back to domestic or regional markets, leveraging advanced technologies to compete in global markets effectively. Industry 4.0 offers opportunities to promote sustainable development by optimising resource utilisation, reducing environmental footprint, and enabling circular economy practices (Oláhet al. 2020). For instance, in smart cities, IoT-enabled sensors monitor energy consumption, optimise transportation routes, and reduce carbon emissions, contributing to environmental conservation and climate resilience (Oláhet al. 2020). The adoption of Industry 4.0 technologies necessitates upskilling and reskilling the workforce to meet the demands of a rapidly evolving labour market with new skills. Governments, educational institutions, and industry stakeholders must collaborate to develop training programmes and curricula aligned with emerging digital skills, such as data analytics, cybersecurity, and robotics programming. Industry 4.0 represents a transformative force reshaping industries, economies, and societies worldwide (Mourtzis, et al. 2022). By harnessing the power of advanced digital technologies, Industry 4.0 promises to drive unprecedented levels of innovation, efficiency, and sustainability across the manufacturing landscape. However, realising the full potential of Industry 4.0 requires concerted efforts to address challenges related to workforce readiness, ethical considerations, and equitable access to technology, ensuring that the benefits of the Fourth Industrial Revolution are shared inclusively and sustainably (Moraes and Lepikson 2017).

3.5 The Digital Society: A Paradigm Shift in Everyday Life

Present society due to digital transformation is transforming into the digital version of society. It is a society in which technology is an invariable part of human life and community. In a digital society, it permeates digital technologies in every facet of

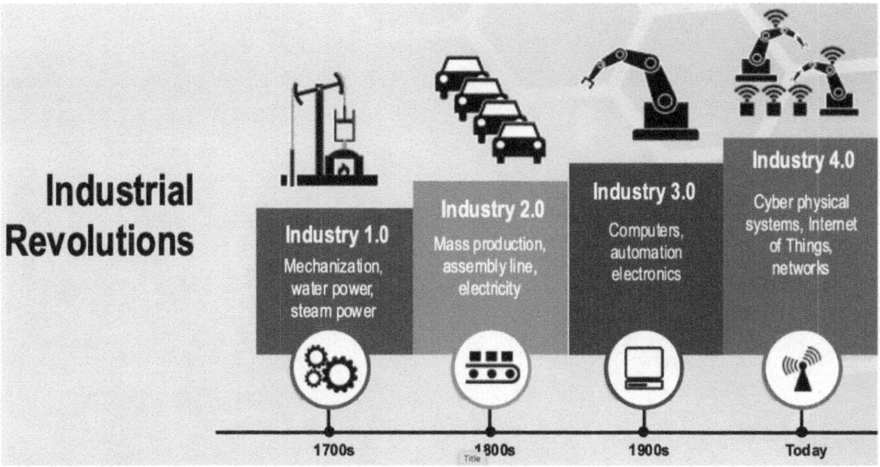

Fig. 3.8 Several phases of industrial revolutions. https://www.nist.gov/blogs/manufacturing-innovation-blog/cybersecurity-and-industry-40-what-you-need-know

daily existence starting from personal to professional domains such as communication to work, education and learning, and civic activities, impacting societal structures, culture, and individual behaviours (Dufva and Dufva 2019). The digital society, characterised by the pervasive influence of digital technologies on various aspects of human life, has transformed the way we communicate, work, learn, and interact. From social media platforms connecting people across the globe to AI revolutionising industries, the digital society has ushered in an era of unprecedented connectivity, information sharing, information generation, and research and innovation (Fig. 3.9).

In the digital society, communication has become instantaneous and ubiquitous. Social media platforms like Facebook, Twitter, and Instagram boast billions of users worldwide. As of 2022, there were approximately 4.33 billion active social media users globally, with the number expected to reach 4.41 billion by 2025. This immense connectivity has transformed how people share information, engage with each other, and even participate in socio-political movements. For instance, the Arab Spring uprisings in 2010–2012 saw the extensive use of social media platforms for organising protests and disseminating information, highlighting the transformative power of digital communication on the political landscape and global affairs (Brownlee et al. 2015).

The digital society has reshaped economies, creating new opportunities while disrupting traditional industries' business models and customer engagement methods. E-commerce has witnessed explosive growth, with platforms like Amazon, Alibaba, and eBay dominating the online retail space. In 2021, global e-commerce sales amounted to $4.9 trillion, representing a significant increase from previous years (Allali and Allali 2020). Moreover, the rise of the gig economy, fueled by platforms such as Uber, Airbnb, Freelance, and Upwork, has transformed labour markets, offering flexibility but also raising concerns about job security and worker

Fig. 3.9 Digital society (https://www.japan.go.jp/kizuna/2020/aiming_for_a_digital_society.html)

rights (Tan et al. 2021). For example, Uber, founded in 2009, has revolutionised the transportation industry, with millions of drivers globally using the platform to earn income (Isaac and Davis 2014). The digital society has democratised access to education and knowledge. Online learning platforms like Coursera, Udemy, and Khan Academy offer a plethora of courses across various subjects, enabling individuals to acquire new skills from the comfort of their homes and access to world's best content and knowledge. As of 2021, Coursera alone had over 82 million registered users and offered more than 5,000 courses from over 200 universities. Additionally, Massive Open Online Courses (MOOCs) have gained popularity, with prestigious institutions like Harvard and MIT offering free or low-cost courses to learners worldwide, fostering lifelong learning and skill development (Xiong et al. 2021).

Digital technologies have revolutionised healthcare delivery, making it more accessible and efficient. Telemedicine platforms allow patients to consult healthcare professionals remotely, overcoming geographical barriers and improving access to medical services, especially in underserved areas. During the COVID-19 pandemic, telemedicine witnessed a surge in adoption as people sought alternative ways to receive healthcare while minimising the risk of exposure to the virus. For instance, Teladoc Health, one of the largest telemedicine providers, reported a significant increase in virtual visits during the pandemic, highlighting the growing importance of digital health solutions (Bokolo 2021). Despite its numerous benefits, the digital society also raises concerns about privacy and security. Data breaches and cyberattacks pose significant threats to individuals, businesses, and governments. According to a report by Risk-Based Security, there were over 36 billion records exposed in data breaches in the first half of 2021 alone, highlighting the scale of the cybersecurity challenge (CrowdStrike 2024). Moreover, issues such as online surveillance, data mining, and algorithmic bias raise questions about the ethical implications of digital technologies and the need for robust regulatory frameworks to protect individuals' rights and interests.

The digital era has ushered in unprecedented connectivity and immense power of generating information, but it has also exposed societies to a myriad of cybersecurity threats where many loopholes are not examined by stakeholders in cyberspace and information technology products and services. From data breaches and ransomware attacks to identity theft and state-sponsored espionage and malign campaigns, the landscape of cyber threats and national security due to emerging technologies is constantly evolving. For instance, the notorious WannaCry ransomware attack in 2017 affected over 200,000 computers across 150 countries, highlighting the vulnerability of interconnected systems (Grammatikakis and Kolokotronis 2021; Sophos Labs 2024). Moreover, the rise of Internet of Things (IoT) devices has expanded the attack surface, amplifying concerns about the security of critical infrastructure and personal privacy.

In the digital age, personal data has become a highly valuable commodity, fueling the growth of the data economy. However, this data-driven paradigm has raised significant privacy concerns, as individuals grapple with the trade-off between convenience and surveillance. The Cambridge Analytica scandal, where the personal data of millions of Facebook users was harvested without consent for political profiling, exemplifies the ethical dilemmas inherent in the collection and exploitation of personal data (Veer 2019). Additionally, the proliferation of facial recognition technology and biometric surveillance systems has intensified debates surrounding the right to privacy in public spaces.

In the digital society, every person having access to mobile and portable computing devices is an information generator. The proliferation of social media platforms and online news outlets has democratised the creation, processing, manipulation, and dissemination of information, but it has also facilitated the spread of misinformation and disinformation at an unprecedented scale instantly (Levak 2020). Whether it's fake news, conspiracy theories, or propaganda, false information can manipulate public opinion, undermine trust in institutions, and incite social unrest which can create a loss of socio-economic nature and social fabric. The COVID-19 infodemic, characterised by the rampant spread of misinformation about the virus, its origins, and potential treatments, has underscored the urgent need for media literacy and fact-checking initiatives to combat the spread of falsehoods (Johnson 2022).

AI and Algorithmic decision-making processes underpin various facets of modern digital life, starting from hiring systems and credit scoring softwares to predictive policing and crime and healthcare diagnostics and precision medicine. However, algorithms are not immune to wrong and biased decisions, reflecting and perpetuating societal prejudices embedded in training data and design choices at large scale and threatening the social equilibrium (Fig. 3.10).

For instance, research has revealed racial and gender biases in facial recognition algorithms, leading to erroneous and discriminatory outcomes for minority groups such as black and unrepresentative groups (Lee 2018). Addressing algorithmic bias requires interdisciplinary collaboration, algorithm transparency, and the development

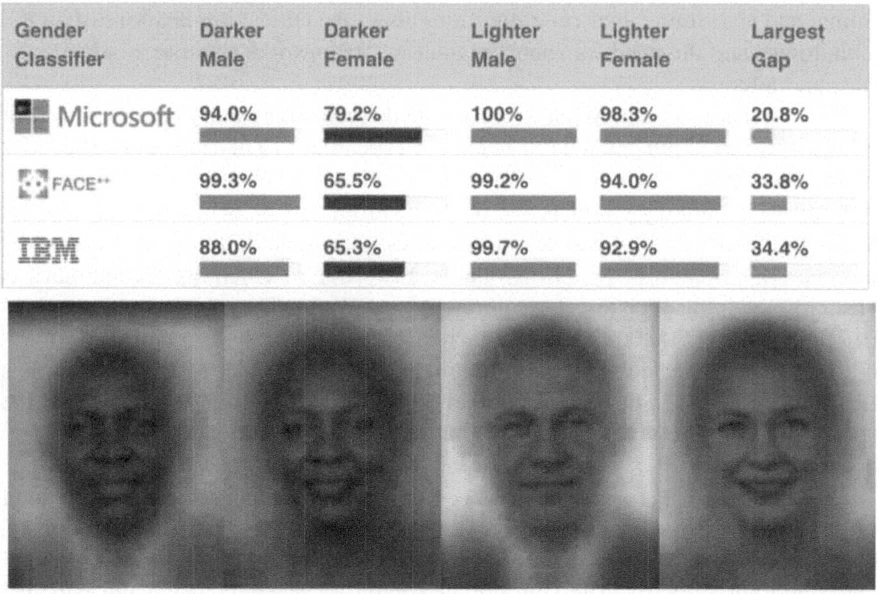

Gender Classifier	Darker Male	Darker Female	Lighter Male	Lighter Female	Largest Gap
Microsoft	94.0%	79.2%	100%	98.3%	20.8%
FACE++	99.3%	65.5%	99.2%	94.0%	33.8%
IBM	88.0%	65.3%	99.7%	92.9%	34.4%

Fig. 3.10 Examples of AI and its biased decision-making (https://physicsworld.com/a/fighting-algorithmic-bias-in-artificial-intelligence/)

of fairness-aware AI techniques to mitigate discrimination and promote algorithmic accountability and justice.

References

Allali F, Allali Z (2020).The impact of the COVID-19 pandemic on the development of e-commerce in word. World, 01

Allied Market Research (2019) Global autonomous vehicle market is expected to reach $556.67 billion by 2026. https://www.globenewswire.com/news-release/2019/07/03/1877861/0/en/Global-Autonomous-Vehicle-Market-is-Expected-to-Reach-556-67-Billion-by-2026.html

Alowais SA, Alghamdi SS, Alsuhebany N, Alqahtani T, Alshaya AI, Almohareb SN, ... Albekairy AM (2023) Revolutionizing healthcare: the role of artificial intelligence in clinical practice. BMC Med Educ 23(1):689

Artificial Intelligence (AI) market in the education sector by end-user, learning method and geography-forecast and analysis 2023–2027 Published: Oct 2023 Pages: 165 SKU: IRTNTR70660. https://www.technavio.com/report/artificial-intelligence-market-in-the-education-sector-industry-analysis

Attia TM (2019) Challenges and opportunities in the future applications of IoT technology

Bloomberg J (2018) Digitization, digitalization, and digital transformation: confuse them at your Peril. https://www.forbes.com/sites/jasonbloomberg/2018/04/29/digitization-digitalization-and-digital-transformation-confuse-them-at-your-peril/?sh=647a441b2f2c. Accessed 03 April 2024

Bokolo AJ (2021) Application of telemedicine and eHealth technology for clinical services in response to the COVID-19 pandemic. Heal Technol 11(2):359–366

Borgia E (2014) The Internet of Things vision: key features, applications and open issues. Comput Commun 54:1–31

Brownlee J, Masoud TE, Reynolds A (2015) The Arab Spring: pathways of repression and reform. Oxford University Press

Chowdhary K, Chowdhary KR (2020) Natural language processing. In: Fundamentals of artificial intelligence, pp 603–649

CrowdStrike (2024) Global threat report uncover the adversaries hiding in plain sight. https://go.crowdstrike.com/rs/281-OBQ-266/images/GlobalThreatReport2024.pdf

Dargan S, Kumar M, Ayyagari MR, Kumar G (2020) A survey of deep learning and its applications: a new paradigm to machine learning. Archiv Comput Methods Eng 27:1071–1092

Dodge M (1999) Finding the source of the Amazon. com: examining the truth behind the hype of 'earth's biggest bookstore'. In: E* Space 5 conference, Cape Town, July, pp 10–15

Dufva T, Dufva M (2019) Grasping the future of the digital society. Futures 107:17–28

Firouzi F, Farahani B, Weinberger M, DePace G, Aliee FS (2020) IoT fundamentals: Definitions, architectures, challenges, and promises. In: Intelligent Internet of Things: from device to fog and cloud, pp 3–50

George AS, George AH (2024) Riding the wave: an exploration of emerging technologies reshaping modern industry. Partners Univers Int Innov J 2(1):15–38

Ghobakhloo M (2018) The future of manufacturing industry: a strategic roadmap toward industry 4.0. J Manuf Technol Manag 29(6):910–936

Govers FX (2018) Artificial intelligence for robotics: build intelligent robots that perform human tasks using AI techniques. Packt Publishing Ltd

Grammatikakis KP, Kolokotronis N (2021) System threats. In: Cyber-security threats, actors, and dynamic mitigation. CRC Press, pp 81–122

Grigorescu S, Trasnea B, Cocias T, Macesanu G (2020) A survey of deep learning techniques for autonomous driving. J Field Robot 37(3):362–386

Ground View Research (2023) Chatbot market worth $27,297.2 million by 2030 | CAGR: 23.3%. https://www.grandviewresearch.com/press-release/global-chatbot-market. Accessed 04 April 2024

Gubbi J, Buyya R, Marusic S, Palaniswami M (2013) Internet of Things (IoT): a vision, architectural elements, and future directions. Futur Gener Comput Syst 29(7):1645–1660

Guizzo E (2019) By leaps and bounds: an exclusive look at how boston dynamics is redefining robot agility. IEEE Spectr 56(12):34–39

Heidari A, Navimipour NJ, Unal M (2022) Applications of ML/DL in the management of smart cities and societies based on new trends in information technologies: a systematic literature review. Sustain Cities Soc 85:104089

Hilbert M, López P (2011) The world's technological capacity to store, communicate, and compute information. Science 332(6025):60–65

Indrakumari R, Poongodi T, Singh K (2021). Introduction to deep learning. In: Advanced deep learning for engineers and scientists: a practical approach, pp 1–22

Isaac E, Davis UC (2014) Disruptive innovation: risk-shifting and precarity in the age of Uber. Berkeley Roundtable on the International Economy, University of California, Berkeley, p 7

Islam MR, Oliullah K, Kabir MM, Alom M, Mridha MF (2023) Machine learning enabled IoT system for soil nutrient monitoring and crop recommendation. J Agric Food Res 14:100880

Johnson SS (2022) Knowing well, being well: well-being born of understanding: the urgent need for coordinated and comprehensive efforts to combat misinformation. Am J Health Promot 36(3):559–581

Joshi AK (1991) Natural language processing. Science 253(5025):1242–1249

Kahn BE (2021) The shopping revolution, updated and expanded edition: how retailers succeed in an era of endless disruption accelerated by COVID-19. University of Pennsylvania Press

Keong CK, Grace ONG (2015) Smart mobility 2030–ITS strategic plan for Singapore. Land Transport Authority of Singapore

Khanna A, Kaur S (2020) Internet of things (IoT), applications and challenges: a comprehensive review. Wirel Pers Commun 114:1687–1762

Kumar R, Agrawal N (2024) Shaping the future of industry: understanding the dynamics of industrial digital twins. Comput Ind Eng 191:110172

Lasi H, Fettke P, Kemper HG, Feld T, Hoffmann M (2014) Industry 4.0. Bus Inf Syst Eng 6:239–242

Lee NT (2018) Detecting racial bias in algorithms and machine learning. J Inf Commun Ethics Soc 16(3):252–260

Levak T (2020) Disinformation in the new media system—Characteristics, forms, reasons for its dissemination and potential means of tackling the issue. Medijska istraživanja: znanstveno-stručni časopis za novinarstvo i medije 26(2):29–58

Longati AA, Elias AM, Furlan FF, Miranda EA, Giordano RDC (2023) Techno-economic-environmental analysis of the production of biosurfactants in the context of biorefineries. In: Biosurfactants and sustainability: from biorefineries production to versatile applications, pp 281–300

Manyika J, Chui M, Bisson P, Woetzel J, Dobbs R, Bughin J, Aharon D (2015) Unlocking the potential of the Internet of Things. McKinsey Global Institute, 1

Markets and Markets (2024) Smart cities global forecast 2028. https://www.marketsandmarkets.com/Market-Reports/smart-cities-market-542.html, Accessed 04 April 2024

McCarthy J (2007) What is artificial intelligence? https://cse.unl.edu/~choueiry/S09-476-876/Documents/whatisai.pdf. Accessed 04 April 2024

McGowan MJ (2010) The rise of computerized high-frequency trading: use and controversy. Duke Law Technol Rev 9:1

McKinney SM, Sieniek M, Godbole V, Godwin J, Antropova N, Ashrafian H, ... Shetty S (2020) International evaluation of an AI system for breast cancer screening. Nature 577(7788):89–94

Mehra A (2024) Artificial intelligence in cybersecurity industry worth $60.6 billion by 2028. https://www.marketsandmarkets.com/Market-Reports/artificial-intelligence-ai-cyber-security-market-220634996.html. Accessed 04 April 2024

Mill ER, Garn W, Ryman-Tubb NF, Turner C (2023) Opportunities in real time fraud detection: an explainable artificial intelligence (XAI) research agenda. Int J Adv Comput Sci Appl 14(5):1172–1186

Min B, Ross H, Sulem E, Veyseh APB, Nguyen TH, Sainz O, ... Roth D (2023) Recent advances in natural language processing via large pre-trained language models: a survey. ACM Comput Surv 56(2):1–40

Mohan S (2021) Artificial intelligence in retail. In: Demystifying AI for the enterprise. Productivity Press, pp 193–222

Moraes EC, Lepikson HA (2017) Industry 4.0 and its impacts on society. In: Proceedings of the international conference on industrial engineering and operations management, vol 2017, pp 729–735

Mourtzis D, Angelopoulos J, Panopoulos N (2022) A literature review of the challenges and opportunities of the transition from industry 4.0 to society 5.0. Energies 15(17):6276

Murphy RR (2019) Introduction to AI robotics. MIT Press

Ngo TD, Kashani A, Imbalzano G, Nguyen KT, Hui D (2018) Additive manufacturing (3D printing): a review of materials, methods, applications and challenges. Compos B Eng 143:172–196

OECD (2017, July) Going digital: making the transformation work for growth and well-being. In: Meeting of the OECD council at ministerial level

Oláh J, Aburumman N, Popp J, Khan MA, Haddad H, Kitukutha N (2020) Impact of Industry 4.0 on environmental sustainability. Sustainability 12(11):4674

Paneru S, Jeelani I (2021) Computer vision applications in construction: current state, opportunities & challenges. Autom Constr 132:103940

Pramod A, Naicker HS, Tyagi AK (2021) Machine learning and deep learning: open issues and future research directions for the next 10 years. In: Computational analysis and deep learning for medical care: principles, methods, and applications, pp 463–490

Reportlinker (2023) The global artificial intelligence in agriculture market size is expected to reach $4.9 billion by 2028, rising at a market growth of 24.1% CAGR during the forecast period. https://www.globenewswire.com/news-release/2023/04/20/2651247/0/en/The-Global-Artificial-Intelligence-in-Agriculture-Market-size-is-expected-to-reach-4-9-billion-by-2028-rising-at-a-market-growth-of-24-1-CAGR-during-the-forecast-period.html. Accessed 04 April 2024

Romeu Lezama JJ (2016) Architectural innovation in the automotive industry: Tesla and the renaissance of the battery electric vehicle. Doctoral dissertation, Massachusetts Institute of Technology

Rosin F, Forget P, Lamouri S, Pellerin R (2020) Impacts of industry 4.0 technologies on Lean principles. Int J Prod Res 58(6):1644–1661

Roslan FABM, Ahmad NB (2023) The rise of AI-powered voice assistants: analyzing their transformative impact on modern customer service paradigms and consumer expectations. Q J Emerg Technol Innov 8(3):33–64

Samoili S, Cobo ML, Gómez E, De Prato G, Martínez-Plumed F, Delipetrev B (2020) AI Watch. Defining Artificial Intelligence. Towards an operational definition and taxonomy of artificial intelligence

Shah A (2023) How Tesla uses and improves its AI for autonomous driving, Accessed 03 April 2024. https://www.enterpriseai.news/2023/03/08/how-tesla-uses-and-improves-its-ai-for-autonomous-driving/

Shanthamallu US, Spanias A (2022) Machine and deep learning applications. Machine and deep learning algorithms and applications. Springer International Publishing, Cham, pp 59–72

Sheikh S (ed).(2020) Understanding the role of artificial intelligence and its future social impact. IGI Global

Sophos Labs (2024) WannaCry: the ransomware that didn't arrive on a phishing hook. May 17, 2017. nakedsecurity.sophos.com/2017/05/17/wannacry-the-ran-somware-worm-that-didnt-arrive-on-a-phishing-hook/. Accessed 04 April 2024

Szeliski R (2022) Computer vision: algorithms and applications. Springer Nature

Tan ZM, Aggarwal N, Cowls J, Morley J, Taddeo M, Floridi L (2021) The ethical debate about the gig economy: a review and critical analysis. Technol Soc 65:101594

Vähäkainu P, Lehto M (2022) Use of artificial intelligence in a cybersecurity environment. Artificial intelligence and cybersecurity: theory and applications. Springer International Publishing, Cham, pp 3–27

Veer R (2019) Connecting the world: privacy violations and the harm principle in the facebook-Cambridge Analytica scandal

Veile JW, Kiel D, Müller JM, Voigt KI (2020) Lessons learned from Industry 4.0 implementation in the German manufacturing industry. J Manuf Technol Manag 31(5):977–997

Viežėlytė K (2022) Media transformation in the age of Netflix: user interface and user experience trends of svod platforms. Doctoral dissertation, Kauno technologijos universitetas

Vrana J, Singh R (2021) Digitization, digitalization, and digital transformation. In: Handbook of nondestructive evaluation 4.0, pp 1–17

Weinstein A (2012) Superior customer value: strategies for winning and retaining customers. CRC Press

West DM, Allen JR (2018, April 24) How artificial intelligence is transforming the world. https://www.brookings.edu/articles/how-artificial-intelligence-is-transforming-the-world/. Accessed 04 April 2024

Xiong Y, Ling Q, Li X (2021) Ubiquitous e-Teaching and e-Learning: China's massive adoption of online education and launching MOOCs internationally during the COVID-19 outbreak. Wirel Commun Mob Comput 2021:1–14

Zhou H, Kalev PS (2019) Algorithmic and high-frequency trading in Asia-Pacific, now and the future. Pac Basin Financ J 53:186–207

Chapter 4
Digital Transformation and Knowledge Economy

Abstract This chapter delves into the concept of the digital technologies-driven knowledge economy and its transformative impact on industries, economies, and societies. It explores how the rapid advancement of digital technologies and the availability of vast amounts of data have reshaped the way businesses operate, create value, and interact with customers. This chapter examines the key drivers of the digital economy and knowledge economy, such as the internet, mobile devices, cloud computing, and data analytics and digital platforms. It discusses the opportunities and challenges that arise from this digital transformation, including increased efficiency, innovation, and global connectivity, as well as concerns. It discusses the importance of education, research institutions, and lifelong learning in fostering a thriving knowledge economy. It discusses the need for investments in digital infrastructure, fostering digital skills and literacy, promoting research and development, and creating supportive regulatory frameworks.

Keywords Digital transformation · Knowledge economy · Education · Digital economy · Digital skills · Literacy

4.1 Introduction to Digital Transformation and Knowledge Economy

The digital transformation has brought about a paradigm shift in the way societies, economies, and industries function. With the advent of digital technologies, the world has witnessed a transition to what is commonly referred to as the knowledge economy. This shift is characterised by the growing importance of knowledge and information as key drivers of economic growth and societal progress (Powell and Snellman 2004). The rise of the knowledge economy can be attributed to various factors. Technological advancements, particularly in areas such as computing, telecommunications, and data analytics, have enabled the rapid generation, dissemination, and utilisation of knowledge on a global scale. As a result, knowledge has become a valuable

S. Kumar et al., *Digital Transformation, Artificial Intelligence and Society*, Frontiers of Artificial Intelligence, Ethics and Multidisciplinary Applications,
https://doi.org/10.1007/978-981-97-5656-8_4

commodity, driving innovation, productivity, and competitiveness in today's interconnected world. Scholars and researchers have extensively studied the concept of the knowledge economy and its implications. For instance, the seminal work of Drucker emphasised the centrality of knowledge and innovation in driving economic prosperity. Drucker argued that in the knowledge economy, the primary source of wealth is no longer tangible assets such as land and labour but rather intangible assets such as intellectual capital, creativity, and expertise (Drucker 1993). Furthermore, Tapscott et al. (2008) highlighted the transformative impact of digital technologies on business models and organisational structures. They argued that digital technologies have enabled companies to transcend traditional boundaries and embrace new forms of collaboration, communication, and value creation. This, in turn, has led to the emergence of agile, knowledge-intensive organisations that are better equipped to thrive in today's fast-paced, interconnected world (Fig. 4.1).

The knowledge economy has become a cornerstone of global economic development, with statistics reflecting its growing significance. In 2020, the World Bank reported that knowledge-based industries contributed over 70% to the GDP of high-income countries(). Notably, the United States allocated approximately 3.14% of its GDP towards research and development (R&D), underscoring its commitment to innovation (Budget 2021). The digital economy surged to a value of $11.5 trillion globally, projected to reach $23 trillion by 2025, as reported by leading market analysts (Srivastava 2023). Moreover, Intellectual property-intensive industries played a substantial role, accounting for over 30% of GDP and more than

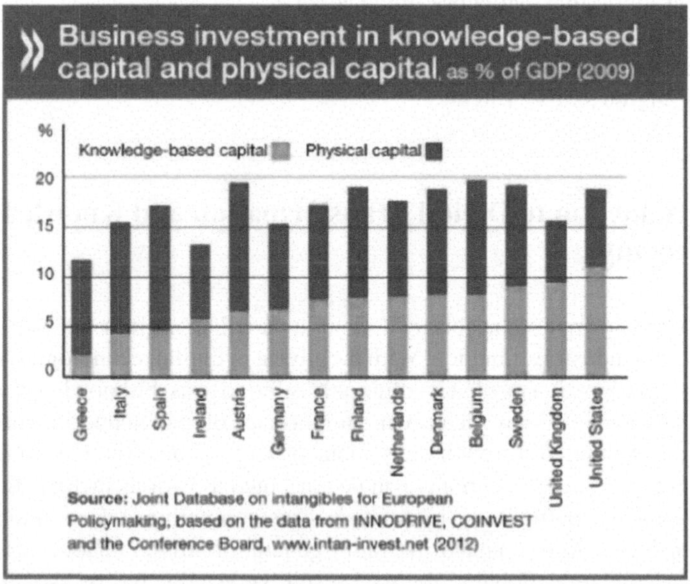

Fig. 4.1 Share of physical and knowledge capital in GDP (https://www.oecd.org/innovation/knowledge-is-growth.htm)

50% of exports in the United States. Emerging economies like China and India also demonstrated a remarkable shift towards knowledge-driven growth, significantly increasing R&D investments (Anand et al. 2021). Despite these strides, challenges persist, including the digital divide, skills gap, and regulatory frameworks, highlighting the need for concerted efforts to harness the full potential of the knowledge economy for sustained global prosperity.

4.2 Key Drivers of Digital Economy

The digital economy, propelled by a convergence of technological advancements, stands as a testament to the transformative power of innovation. Each component of this digital ecosystem plays a crucial role in shaping the landscape of modern business and society. Let's delve deeper into the key drivers that fuel this digital revolution (Fig. 4.2).

4.2.1 The Internet

The internet serves as the foundation upon which the digital economy is built. It is the primary conduit through which information flows, transactions occur, and connections are made. With its vast reach and accessibility, the Internet has dismantled traditional barriers to communication and commerce, enabling businesses to engage with customers across the globe. From online retail giants like Amazon to

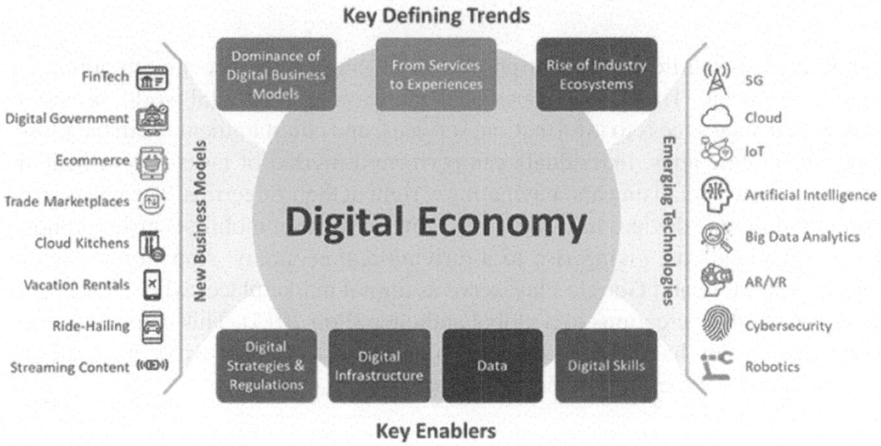

Fig. 4.2 Digital economy and key enablers (https://e.huawei.com/kz/blogs/industries/insights/2021/accelerating-digital-economy)

social media platforms like Facebook, the internet has spawned a myriad of digital enterprises that have reshaped industries and consumer behaviour. Moreover, the internet has catalysed the democratisation of information, empowering individuals with unprecedented access to knowledge and resources (Williams 2021). Educational platforms like Khan Academy and Coursera offer free, high-quality courses to learners worldwide, democratizing access to education and levelling the playing field for aspiring professionals.

The benefits of the internet are vast and far-reaching, evidenced by numerous compelling facts and figures. As of 2021, approximately 4.66 billion people around the globe were active internet users, representing over 59% of the world's population (Datareportal 2021). This widespread connectivity has transformed communication, commerce, education, and countless other aspects of modern life. E-commerce, for instance, has experienced exponential growth, with global online retail sales surpassing $4.2 trillion in 2020 alone (UNCTAD 2021). The internet has facilitated unprecedented access to information and resources, with over 1.83 billion websites available to users worldwide (Open Access Government 2023). Moreover, the internet has revolutionised education, enabling remote learning and providing access to a wealth of educational materials and courses. Socially, it has fostered global connectivity and collaboration, with over 4.2 billion active social media users engaging and interacting across various platforms (Datareportal 2021). The internet has played a crucial role in driving innovation and economic growth, with digital technologies contributing an estimated $2.3 trillion to the global economy in 2020 (Cepal 2021). These facts and figures underscore the profound impact of the internet on society, economy, and human progress.

4.2.2 Mobile Devices and Applications

Mobile devices, particularly smartphones and tablets, have become ubiquitous in today's digital age. They serve as personal gateways to the digital world, providing users with instant access to information, services, and entertainment. With the proliferation of mobile apps, individuals can perform a myriad of tasks—from banking and shopping to socialising and navigating—right at their fingertips. The widespread adoption of mobile devices has spurred the development of mobile-centric technologies and applications, giving rise to a thriving app economy. App stores, such as Apple's App Store and Google Play, serve as digital marketplaces where developers can distribute their creations to a global audience (Pon 2015). This democratisation of app distribution has lowered barriers to entry for aspiring developers, fostering innovation and competition in the mobile ecosystem.

4.2.3 Cloud Computing

Cloud computing refers to the delivery of computing services—including servers, storage, databases, networking, software, analytics, and intelligence—over the internet ("the cloud") to offer faster innovation, flexible resources, and economies of scale (Islam et al. 2023). Essentially, cloud computing enables users to access and utilise computing resources and services on-demand, without the need for direct management or ownership of physical infrastructure. This model allows organisations and individuals to leverage computing power, storage, and applications without having to invest heavily in hardware, maintain infrastructure, or worry about scalability issues. By providing a scalable and elastic environment, cloud computing empowers businesses to efficiently deploy applications, store and manage data, and deliver services to users worldwide, thereby revolutionizing the way computing resources are utilized and accessed in the digital age.

Cloud computing has revolutionized the way businesses manage their IT infrastructure and deliver services to customers. By leveraging cloud-based resources, organisations can scale their operations dynamically, without the need for costly investments in physical hardware. This flexibility and scalability empower businesses to innovate rapidly and respond to changing market demands with agility. Furthermore, cloud computing democratises access to computing power, enabling startups and small businesses to compete on a level playing field with industry giants. Cloud-based services, such as Amazon Web Services (AWS) and Microsoft Azure, offer a wide range of tools and resources that empower businesses to build, deploy, and scale applications with ease (Attaran and Woods 2019).

4.2.4 Data Analytics

In today's data-driven economy, the ability to extract actionable insights from vast amounts of data is paramount to success. Data analytics, fueled by advancements in machine learning and artificial intelligence, enables businesses to unlock hidden patterns, trends, and correlations within their data. By leveraging sophisticated algorithms and predictive models, organisations can make informed decisions, optimise processes, and drive innovation. Data analytics has permeated every facet of modern business from personalised recommendations on e-commerce websites to predictive maintenance in manufacturing (Ogbuke et al. 2022). Organisations that harness the power of data analytics gain a competitive edge by understanding customer preferences, identifying market trends, and anticipating future demand.

4.2.5 Digital Platforms

Digital platforms serve as the cornerstone of the digital economy, facilitating interactions between businesses and customers in an increasingly connected world. Social media networks like Facebook and Twitter enable individuals to connect with friends, share content, and discover new products and services (Syn and Oh 2015). E-commerce marketplaces like Amazon and Alibaba provide a seamless shopping experience, offering a vast array of products and personalised recommendations to shoppers worldwide. Moreover, digital platforms have given rise to new business models and revenue streams, such as the sharing economy and the gig economy. Platforms like Uber and Airbnb connect service providers with consumers in need of transportation and accommodation, creating new opportunities for income generation and entrepreneurship (Barbu et al. 2018). The digital economy is propelled by a constellation of technological innovations that have revolutionized the way businesses operate and interact with customers. From the internet and mobile devices to cloud computing, data analytics, and digital platforms, each component plays a crucial role in shaping the digital landscape of today and tomorrow. As technology continues to evolve, businesses must embrace digital transformation to stay competitive and thrive in the digital economy of the future.

4.3 Digital Transformation and Knowledge Economy

The impact of digital transformation reverberates across businesses, economies, and societies, reshaping their structures, operations, and interactions. This seismic shift is evident in various dimensions, each carrying significant implications and challenges that accompany the rapid advancement of digital technologies and their contribution to knowledge economy.

4.3.1 Transformation of Business Operations

Digital technologies have ushered in a new era of efficiency and productivity for businesses and organisations small or large. By streamlining processes, automating tasks, and optimising workflows, businesses can achieve unprecedented levels of operational excellence. From supply chain management to customer relationship management, digital transformation empowers companies to enhance their agility, responsiveness, and cost-effectiveness. For instance, the adoption of enterprise resource planning (ERP) systems integrates disparate business functions into a unified platform, enabling real-time data sharing and decision-making (Zheng et al. 2000). Similarly, the implementation of robotic process automation (RPA) automates repetitive tasks, freeing up human capital for more strategic endeavours (Aguirre and Rodriguez

2017). These technological advancements not only boost efficiency but also drive innovation and competitive advantage in an increasingly digital marketplace.

4.3.2 Revolutionising Customer Engagement

Digital transformation has revolutionized the way businesses interact with customers, transcending geographical barriers and temporal constraints. Through digital channels such as websites, mobile apps, and social media platforms, companies can engage with a global audience in real-time, delivering personalised experiences and tailored solutions. For instance, data-driven marketing strategies leverage customer insights to deliver targeted messages and offers, enhancing customer satisfaction and loyalty. Moreover, the integration of artificial intelligence and chatbots enables round-the-clock customer support, resolving queries and issues promptly and efficiently (Kumar et al. 2013). By embracing digital transformation, businesses can forge deeper connections with their customers, driving brand loyalty and advocacy in an increasingly competitive landscape.

4.3.3 Fueling Innovation and Entrepreneurship

Digital transformation catalyses innovation and entrepreneurship, unlocking new avenues for value creation and disruption. Startups and small businesses, in particular, leverage digital technologies to challenge incumbents, disrupt traditional industries, and pioneer new business models. For instance, the rise of the sharing economy, exemplified by companies like Uber and Airbnb, transforms underutilised assets into revenue-generating opportunities, fostering economic empowerment and flexibility (Knight 2021). Similarly, the proliferation of fintech startups revolutionises the financial services industry, offering innovative solutions for payments, lending, and wealth management. However, digital transformation also presents challenges and risks that businesses must navigate to thrive in the digital age. One such challenge is cybersecurity, as the interconnectedness of digital systems exposes organisations to cyber threats such as data breaches, ransomware attacks, and phishing scams (Verma and Shri 2022). Furthermore, the growing concerns over privacy rights and data protection underscore the need for robust cybersecurity measures and regulatory compliance (Fig. 4.3).

4.3.4 Economic Implications and Societal Impact

The economic implications of digital transformation are profound, reshaping industries, labour markets, and economic structures. Research by the World Economic

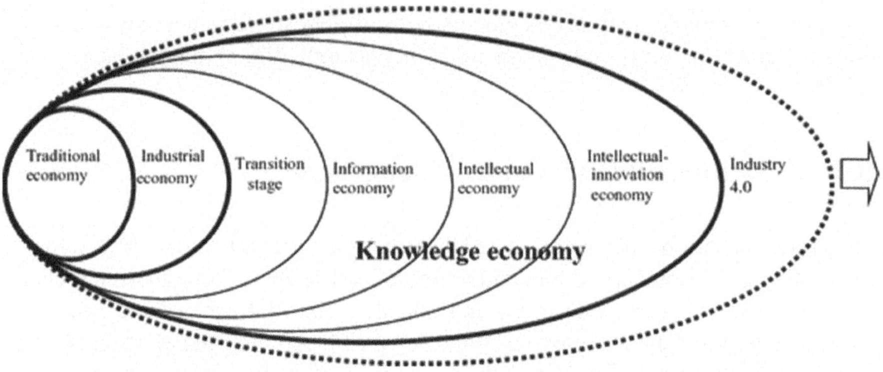

Fig. 4.3 Several types of knowledge economy (Kolesnichenko et al. 2019)

Forum (2018) highlights the potential of digital technologies to create jobs, boost productivity, and drive inclusive growth, particularly in developing economies (World Economic Forum 2018). However, the uneven distribution of digital benefits and the widening digital divide raise concerns about social equity and inclusion. Moreover, digital transformation has far-reaching implications for societal dynamics, influencing how people live, work, and interact. The rise of remote work and digital nomadism, accelerated by the COVID-19 pandemic, challenges traditional notions of employment and workplace dynamics (Wang et al. 2020). Similarly, the digitization of education and healthcare expands access to learning resources and medical services, bridging geographical barriers and empowering individuals to lead healthier, more fulfilling lives. In conclusion, the impact of digital transformation extends beyond business operations to encompass broader economic and societal dimensions. While it presents unprecedented opportunities for innovation, efficiency, and growth, it also poses significant challenges that require careful consideration and proactive management (Savastano et al. 2019). By embracing digital transformation thoughtfully and strategically, businesses, economies, and societies can harness their full potential to create a more prosperous and inclusive future for all.

4.4 Opportunities and Challenges in Knowledge Economy

Digital transformation has emerged as a double-edged sword, offering a plethora of opportunities while concurrently presenting significant challenges for businesses, economies, and societies worldwide. At the heart of this transformation lies the promise of enhanced efficiency, innovation, and global connectivity, propelled by the seamless integration of digital technologies into various facets of modern life. The advent of digital technologies has unlocked a wealth of opportunities for businesses to thrive and innovate in an increasingly competitive landscape. By harnessing the power of data analytics and digital platforms, companies gain invaluable insights

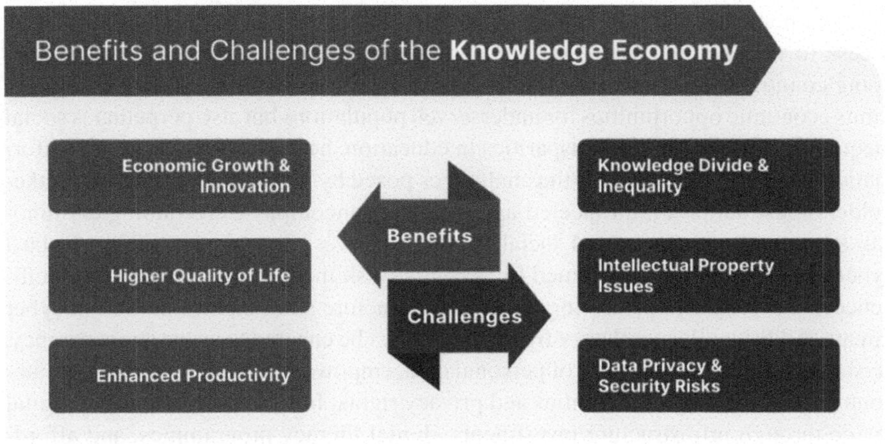

Fig. 4.4 Opportunities and challenges in knowledge economy (https://www.financestrategists.com/financial-advisor/knowledge-economy/)

into consumer behaviour, market trends, and competitive dynamics. Armed with this knowledge, businesses can tailor their products, services, and marketing strategies to meet evolving consumer demands, driving innovation and sustaining competitiveness in dynamic market environments. Moreover, digital transformation has catalysed the emergence of new business models, such as the sharing economy and the gig economy, which offer novel opportunities for income generation and employment. Platforms like Uber, Airbnb, and Upwork empower individuals to monetize their skills and assets, democratizing access to economic opportunities and fostering economic empowerment and social mobility (Parker et al. 2016) (Fig. 4.4).

However, the promises of digital transformation are accompanied by formidable challenges that demand vigilant attention and proactive mitigation strategies. Foremost among these challenges is cybersecurity, as the increasing reliance on digital technologies exposes businesses and societies to a myriad of cyber threats, including data breaches, ransomware attacks, and identity theft. The growing interconnectedness of digital systems and the proliferation of internet-connected devices further compound the challenge, expanding the attack surface for cybercriminals and necessitating robust cybersecurity measures to safeguard against sophisticated cyber threats. Privacy concerns also loom large in the digital age, as the widespread collection and utilisation of personal data by companies raise profound questions about individual privacy rights and data protection (Solove 2000). Heightened consumer awareness of data privacy issues, fueled by high-profile data breaches and privacy scandals, underscores the importance of transparency, accountability, and ethical data practices in digital business models. The rise of surveillance capitalism and the commodification of personal data by tech giants further amplify concerns about data privacy and consumer trust in digital platforms and institutions. Furthermore, the digital divide exacerbates existing social inequalities, as marginalised populations are left behind in an increasingly digital world. According to the International

Telecommunication Union (ITU), over half of the world's population still lacks access to the internet, with the digital divide disproportionately affecting developing countries and rural communities (Awotwi 2015). This digital divide not only limits economic opportunities for underserved populations but also perpetuates social inequalities and exacerbates disparities in education, healthcare, and access to information. To effectively address the challenges posed by digital transformation, stakeholders must adopt a multifaceted approach that encompasses technological innovation, regulatory reform, and social equity initiatives (Soto-Acosta 2024). Robust cybersecurity measures, informed by proactive risk management and threat intelligence, are essential to protecting digital infrastructure and sensitive data from cyber threats. Additionally, regulatory frameworks must be enacted to ensure transparency, accountability, and ethical use of personal data, empowering individuals with greater control over their digital identities and privacy rights. Initiatives to bridge the digital divide through infrastructure investments, digital literacy programmes, and affordable internet access are crucial to promoting equitable access to the benefits of the digital economy and fostering economic empowerment and social inclusion. Research by organisations like KPMG (2019) and scholars such as Acemoglu and Restrepo underscores the importance of addressing these challenges to ensure inclusive growth and sustainable development in the digital age (Acemoglu and Restrepo 2019). By confronting cybersecurity threats, protecting privacy rights, and bridging the digital divide, stakeholders can harness the transformative potential of digital technologies to create a more equitable, prosperous, and resilient future for all.

4.5 Education and Research and Knowledge Economy

In the contemporary global landscape, the significance of education and research cannot be overstated. In the transition towards a knowledge-based economy, these pillars serve as the bedrock for progress, prosperity, and societal advancement. Through a multifaceted lens, they contribute to the development of individuals, communities, and nations alike, fostering innovation, economic growth, and overall well-being (Peters 2008). Education stands as the cornerstone of human capital development. It equips individuals with the skills, knowledge, and competencies necessary to navigate an increasingly complex and interconnected world. In the digital age, where technological advancements redefine industries and job markets, continuous learning becomes imperative. Quality education not only enhances employability but also fosters critical thinking, creativity, and adaptability—attributes essential for success in the twenty-first-century workforce. Furthermore, education catalyses social mobility and equitable growth. By providing access to education for all segments of society, regardless of socioeconomic background, governments and institutions pave the way for inclusive development. This inclusivity not only reduces disparities but also unleashes the untapped potential of marginalized communities, thereby driving overall progress. Research, on the other hand, fuels the engine of innovation and drives progress across various sectors (Peters 2008). From scientific breakthroughs to technological advancements, research endeavours contribute to the creation of new knowledge, products, and solutions. Research institutions serve as hubs of discovery, bringing together bright minds to tackle complex challenges and push the boundaries of human understanding. The symbiotic relationship between education and research amplifies their impact manifold. Educational institutions that prioritise research integration provide students with opportunities to engage in hands-on learning experiences, fostering a culture of inquiry and exploration. This synergy not only enriches the educational experience but also nurtures a pipeline of talent equipped to address real-world problems through evidence-based approaches. Moreover, research findings often find practical applications, driving innovation and competitiveness in the marketplace. Collaborations between academia, industry, and government facilitate the translation of research insights into tangible outcomes, whether in the form of new technologies, processes, or policies. This innovation ecosystem not only stimulates economic growth but also addresses pressing societal challenges, ranging from healthcare to environmental sustainability. Empirical evidence underscores the transformative power of education and research. Few Studies, underscore the positive correlation between investments in education, research, and economic development (Hanushek 2019). They emphasise the need for sustained commitment to these domains to nurture human capital, foster innovation, and drive productivity gains—a prerequisite for long-term prosperity in the knowledge economy. Education and research stand as twin pillars of progress in the knowledge economy. Their importance transcends borders and disciplines, shaping the trajectory of nations and shaping the future of humanity. By prioritising investments in education and research, societies can unlock their full potential, driving innovation, prosperity, and societal well-being for generations to come.

4.6 Investments and Supportive Frameworks and Knowledge Economy

To fully realise the potential of the digital transformation and knowledge economy, it is essential to make investments in digital infrastructure, foster digital skills and literacy, promote research and development, and create supportive regulatory frameworks (Panel 2002). Investments in digital infrastructure, such as broadband networks and data centres, are critical for ensuring universal access to digital technologies and enabling businesses to harness the full power of the Internet and cloud computing. By expanding access to high-speed internet and investing in digital connectivity in underserved areas, governments can bridge the digital divide and unlock economic opportunities for all citizens. Similarly, investments in digital skills training and education programmes are essential for equipping individuals with the skills they need to thrive in the digital economy. By providing training in areas such as coding, data analytics, and digital marketing, governments and organisations can help bridge the digital divide and ensure that everyone has the opportunity to participate in the digital economy (Chetty et al. 2018). Moreover, efforts to promote digital literacy and digital citizenship are crucial for empowering individuals to navigate the digital landscape safely and responsibly. Promoting research and development is also crucial for driving innovation and economic growth in the knowledge economy. By investing in research institutions, funding research projects, and incentivizing collaboration between academia, industry, and government, countries can stimulate the creation of new knowledge, technologies, and solutions that address pressing societal challenges and fuel economic progress.

Moreover, creating supportive regulatory frameworks is essential for fostering innovation, protecting consumers, and ensuring a level playing field in the digital economy. Regulations related to data privacy, cybersecurity, intellectual property rights, and competition are essential for building trust in digital technologies, promoting fair competition, and safeguarding the rights and interests of all stakeholders (González and Jouanjean 2017). Furthermore, regulatory frameworks should be flexible and adaptive to keep pace with rapid technological advancements and evolving business models in the digital age. The digital transformation and knowledge economy present immense opportunities for economic growth, innovation, and societal progress. However, realising these opportunities requires concerted efforts from governments, businesses, academia, and civil society to invest in digital infrastructure, foster digital skills and literacy, promote research and development, and create supportive regulatory frameworks. By working together to harness the power of digital technologies and knowledge creation, we can build a more inclusive, prosperous, and sustainable future for all.

References

Acemoglu D, Restrepo P (2019) Automation and new tasks: how technology displaces and reinstates labor. J Econ Perspect 33(2):3–30. https://doi.org/10.1257/jep.33.2.3

Aguirre S, Rodriguez A (2017) Automation of a business process using robotic process automation (RPA): a case study. In: Applied computer sciences in engineering: 4th workshop on engineering applications, WEA 2017, Cartagena, Colombia, September 27–29, Proceedings 4. Springer International Publishing, pp 65–71

Anand J, McDermott G, Mudambi R, Narula R (2021) Innovation in and from emerging economies: new insights and lessons for international business research. J Int Bus Stud 52:545–559

Attaran M, Woods J (2019) Cloud computing technology: improving small business performance using the Internet. J Small Bus Entrep 31(6):495–519

Awotwi JE (2015) Challenging the digital divide in a developing country: Ghana case study. Digital Divides 47

Barbu CM, Bratu RŞ, Sîrbu EM (2018) Business models of the sharing economy. Revista de Management Comparat International 19(2):154–166

Budget (2021) Federally funded R&D declines as a share of GDP and total R&D. https://ncses.nsf.gov/pubs/nsf23339

Cepal NU (2021) Digital technologies for a new future

Chetty K, Aneja U, Mishra V, Gcora N, Josie J (2018) Bridging the digital divide in the G20: skills for the new age. Economics 12(1):20180024

Datareportal (2021) Digital 2021: global overview report, The full digital 2021 global report. https://datareportal.com/reports/digital-2021-global-overview-report#:~:text=Internet%3A%204.66%20billion%20people%20around,now%20stands%20at%2059.5%20percent. Accessed 04 April 2024

Drucker P (1993) Post capitalist society. Butter worth Heinemann, New York

González JL, Jouanjean MA (2017) Digital trade: developing a framework for analysis

Hanushek EA (2019) Testing, accountability, and the American economy. Ann Am Acad Pol Soc Sci 683(1):110–128

Islam R, Patamsetti V, Gadhi A, Gondu RM, Bandaru CM, Kesani SC, Abiona O (2023) The future of cloud computing: benefits and challenges. Int J Commun Netw Syst Sci 16(4):53–65

Knight AM (2021) The implications of the sharing economy for public relations theory and practice: a thematic analysis of Airbnb, Uber and TaskRabbit. Doctoral dissertation, Virginia Tech

Kolesnichenko EA, Radyukova YY, Pakhomov NN (2019) The role and importance of knowledge economy as a platform for formation of industry 4.0. In: Industry 4.0: industrial revolution of the 21st century, pp 73–82

KPMG (2019) Future of cyber security in the digital era. https://home.kpmg/xx/en/home/insights/2019/04/the-future-of-cybersecurity-in-the-digital-era.html

Kumar V, Chattaraman V, Neghina C, Skiera B, Aksoy L, Buoye A, Henseler J (2013) Data-driven services marketing in a connected world. J Serv Manag 24(3):330–352

Ogbuke NJ, Yusuf YY, Dharma K, Mercangoz BA (2022) Big data supply chain analytics: ethical, privacy and security challenges posed to business, industries and society. Prod Plann Control 33(2–3):123–137

Open Access Government (2023) Internet skyrockets to 1.88 billion websites and still growing. https://www.openaccessgovernment.org/internet-skyrockets-to-1-88-billion-websites-and-still-growing/168133/, Accessed 04 April 2024

Panel IL (2002) Digital transformation: a framework for ICT literacy. Educ Test Serv 1(2):1–53

Parker GG, Van Alstyne MW, Choudary SP (2016) Platform revolution: how networked markets are transforming the economy and how to make them work for you. WW Norton & Company

Peters MA (2008) Education and the knowledge economy. In: Knowledge policy. Edward Elgar Publishing, pp 27–44

Pon B (2015) Locating digital production: how platforms shape participa-tion in the global app economy. In: AAG 2015 workshop on geographies of production in digital economies of low-income countries.

Powell WW, Snellman K (2004) The knowledge economy. Annu Rev Sociol 30:199–220

Savastano M, Amendola C, Bellini F, D'Ascenzo F (2019) Contextual impacts on industrial processes brought by the digital transformation of manufacturing: a systematic review. Sustainability 11(3):891

Solove DJ (2000) Privacy and power: computer databases and metaphors for information privacy. Stanford Law Rev 53:1393

Soto-Acosta P (2024) Navigating uncertainty: post-pandemic issues on digital transformation. Inf Syst Manag 41(1):20–26

Srivastava DK (2023) How digital transformation will help India accelerate its growth in the coming years. https://www.ey.com/en_in/tax/economy-watch/how-digital-transformation-will-help-india-accelerate-its-growth-in-the-coming-years#:~:text=Joint%20collaborative%20research%20by%20Huawei,of%20global%20GDP)%20by%202025. Accessed 04 April 2024

Syn SY, Oh S (2015) Why do social network site users share information on Facebook and Twitter? J Inf Sci 41(5):553–569

Tapscott D, Williams AD, Herman D (2008) Government 2.0: transforming government and governance for the twenty-first century. New Paradigm, 1(15)

UNCTAD U (2021) Global e-commerce jumps to $26.7 trillion, COVID-19 boosts online sales. UNCTAD. Accessed 15 Feb 2022

Verma A, Shri C (2022) Cyber security: a review of cyber crimes, security challenges and measures to control. Vision. 09722629221074760.

Wang B, Schlagwein D, Cecez-Kecmanovic D, Cahalane MC (2020) Beyond the factory paradigm: digital nomadism and the digital future (s) of knowledge work post-COVID-19. J Assoc Inf Syst 21(6):10

Williams LD (2021) Concepts of digital economy and Industry 4.0 in intelligent and information systems. Int J Intell Netw 2:122–129

World Economic Forum (2018) The future of jobs report 2018. https://www.weforum.org/reports/the-future-of-jobs-report-2018.

Zheng S, Yen DC, Tarn JM (2000) The new spectrum of the cross-enterprise solution: the integration of supply chain management and enterprise resources planning systems. J Comput Inf Syst 41(1):84–93

Chapter 5
Artificial Intelligence-Driven Governance Systems: Smart Cities and Smart Governance

Abstract This chapter explores the integration of artificial intelligence (AI) driven systems in the context of smart cities and smart governance. It examines how AI technologies are revolutionising urban environments and transforming the way governments provide services, manage resources, and engage with citizens. Smart cities leverage AI-driven systems to enhance the efficiency, sustainability, and livability of urban areas. It explores how AI algorithms analyse vast amounts of data from sensors, devices, and citizens to enable real-time decision-making, optimise resource allocation, and improve overall city operations. Moreover, the chapter delves into the concept of smart governance, where AI technologies are employed to enhance the delivery of public services and increase citizen participation. It examines how AI-powered chatbots, virtual assistants, and data analytics tools enable governments to streamline administrative processes, provide personalised services, and make data-driven policy decisions. By leveraging AI technologies thoughtfully and collaboratively, governments can enhance the quality of life for citizens, improve resource management, and create sustainable and efficient urban ecosystems.

Keywords Artificial intelligence · Digital transformation · Smart cities · Smart governance

5.1 Introduction to Smart Cities

Smart cities are urban areas that utilise advanced technology and data-driven solutions to address various challenges and improve the quality of life for residents. These cities leverage interconnected infrastructure, ICT products and services, Software, AI, ML and Internet of Things (IoT) devices, and data analytics to optimise resource usage, enhance sustainability, and promote efficiency across various sectors such as transportation, energy, healthcare, and public services (Silva et al. 2018). Key characteristics of smart cities include the integration of ICT into urban systems, citizen engagement through digital platforms, data-driven decision-making, and the pursuit of sustainable development goals. Urbanisation poses numerous challenges,

S. Kumar et al., *Digital Transformation, Artificial Intelligence and Society*, Frontiers of Artificial Intelligence, Ethics and Multidisciplinary Applications,
https://doi.org/10.1007/978-981-97-5656-8_5

Fig. 5.1 Concept of smart city (https://aliga.sk/en/what-the-heck-is-a-smart-city/)

including issues of congestion, low-quality air and pollution, inequitable resource distribution, inefficiency in resource distribution, and rising social inequalities (Silva et al. 2018). Smart cities offer innovative solutions to these challenges by leveraging technology to optimise resource allocation, improve infrastructure efficiency, and enhance public service delivery. By adopting smart city initiatives, urban areas can achieve sustainable growth, reduce environmental impact, and enhance the overall quality of life for residents (Silva et al. 2018). The concept of smart cities has evolved in response to technological advancements and changing urban landscapes. Early initiatives focused on leveraging ICT to improve infrastructure physical and digital, improve resources management and public service delivery. However, modern smart cities integrate a wide range of technologies, including IoT, artificial intelligence, big data analytics, and blockchain, to create interconnected and data-driven urban ecosystems. These technologies enable cities to become more responsive, adaptable, and resilient in the face of evolving challenges (Fig. 5.1).

5.2 Role of Digital Transformation and Artificial Intelligence in Smart Cities

Artificial intelligence (AI) refers to the simulation of human intelligence in machines, enabling them to perform tasks that typically require human cognition, such as learning, problem-solving, and decision-making. In the context of smart cities, AI plays a crucial role in analysing vast amounts of data generated by smart city digital platforms and digital infrastructure, IoT devices, sensors, and other sources to derive actionable insights and optimise urban operations. AI algorithms enable predictive analytics, anomaly detection, and real-time decision-making, facilitating more efficient resource allocation and infrastructure management (Al Marzouqi et al. 2021).

Several AI-driven systems are deployed in smart cities to address specific challenges and enhance urban services. For example, AI-powered traffic management systems use real-time data from sensors and cameras to optimise traffic flow, reduce congestion, and minimise travel times. Machine learning algorithms are employed in predictive maintenance applications to identify potential infrastructure failures before they occur, thereby reducing downtime and maintenance costs (Mahmoud et al. 2021) (Fig. 5.2).

Additionally, AI-driven energy management systems optimise power distribution, maximise energy efficiency, and promote renewable energy integration within smart grids. Integrating AI technologies offers numerous benefits for smart cities, including increased efficiency, sustainability, and innovation. By leveraging AI algorithms for data analysis and decision-making, cities can optimise resource usage, improve service delivery, and enhance overall urban livability. AI-driven predictive analytics enable proactive problem-solving and risk mitigation, leading to cost savings and improved infrastructure resilience (Jagatheesaperumal et al. 2021).

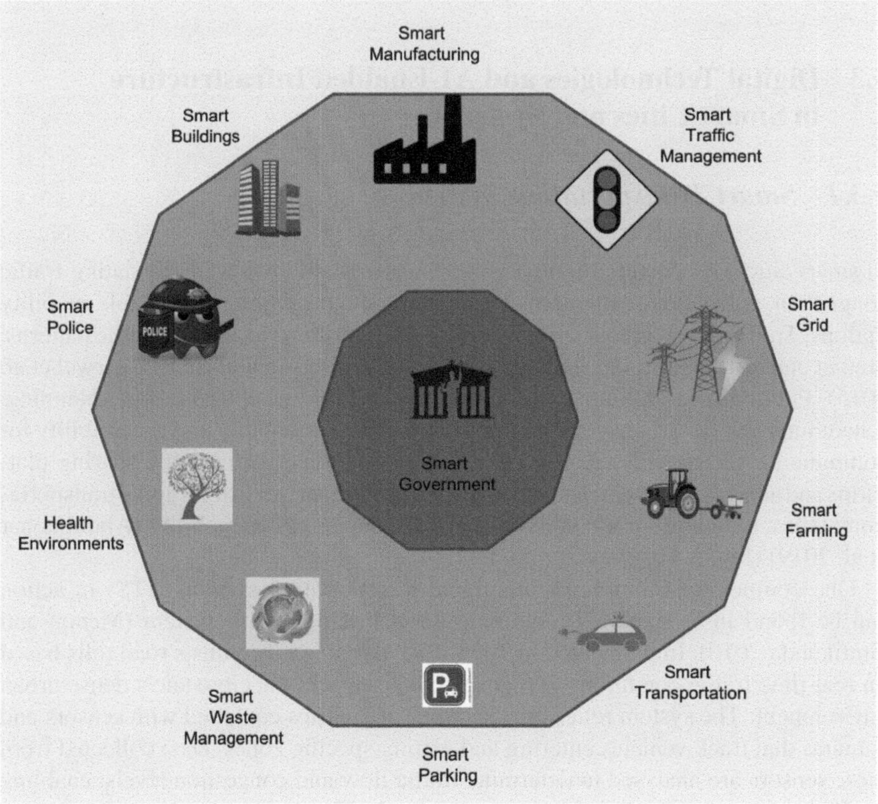

Fig. 5.2 Artificial intelligence and smart cities (https://www.oreilly.com/library/view/hands-on-artificial-intelligence/9781788836067/a302e0d8-20c0-4b5d-b75a-1d02c3aa046a.xhtml)

Digital transformation and artificial intelligence (AI) are catalysing a paradigm shift in the development of smart cities, revolutionising urban landscapes worldwide. For instance, predictive analytics algorithms enable precise forecasting in energy distribution, leading to up to a 30% reduction in energy consumption (Le et al. 2024). In transportation, AI-powered traffic management systems have reduced congestion by up to 25%, significantly improving mobility and air quality (Sanghavi 2024). Moreover, AI enhances public services and governance in smart cities. Chatbots and virtual assistants handle citizen queries efficiently, with over 80% accuracy, while AI-driven administrative platforms streamline processes, resulting in up to 40% reduction in bureaucratic overhead (Nirala et al. 2022). Empirical evidence from pioneering smart cities underscores the tangible benefits of AI integration. The synergy between digital transformation and AI offers unprecedented opportunities for smart cities to thrive. However, ethical considerations and data privacy concerns necessitate careful navigation. With strategic deployment and robust governance frameworks, smart cities can harness the full potential of AI to build sustainable, resilient urban environments for future generations.

5.3 Digital Technologies and AI-Enabled Infrastructure in Smart Cities and Systems

5.3.1 Smart Transportation Systems

In smart cities, AI-powered transportation systems are crucial in alleviating traffic congestion, enhancing public transit efficiency, and promoting sustainable mobility options. Traffic management systems utilise AI algorithms to analyse traffic patterns, predict congestion hotspots, and optimise signal timings in real-time (Agarwal et al. 2015). Public transit optimization systems leverage AI to optimise route planning, scheduling, and fleet management, improving service reliability and accessibility for commuters. Additionally, AI-driven mobility solutions, such as ride-sharing platforms and autonomous vehicles, offer innovative alternatives to traditional transportation modes, reducing carbon emissions and enhancing urban mobility (Abduljabbar et al. 2019) (Fig. 5.3).

One compelling example of intelligent transportation systems (ITS) in action can be found in Singapore's Electronic Road Pricing (ERP) system (Menon and Guttikunda 2010). Implemented in 1998, ERP dynamically adjusts road tolls based on real-time traffic conditions to manage congestion in the city-state's dense urban environment. The system relies on a network of gantries equipped with sensors and cameras that track vehicles entering and exiting specific zones. Data collected from these sensors are analysed to determine traffic flow and congestion levels, enabling the ERP system to calculate toll rates accordingly. The results have been impressive: according to the Land Transport Authority (LTA) of Singapore, ERP has helped to reduce peak-hour traffic speeds by up to 20%, while also cutting overall traffic

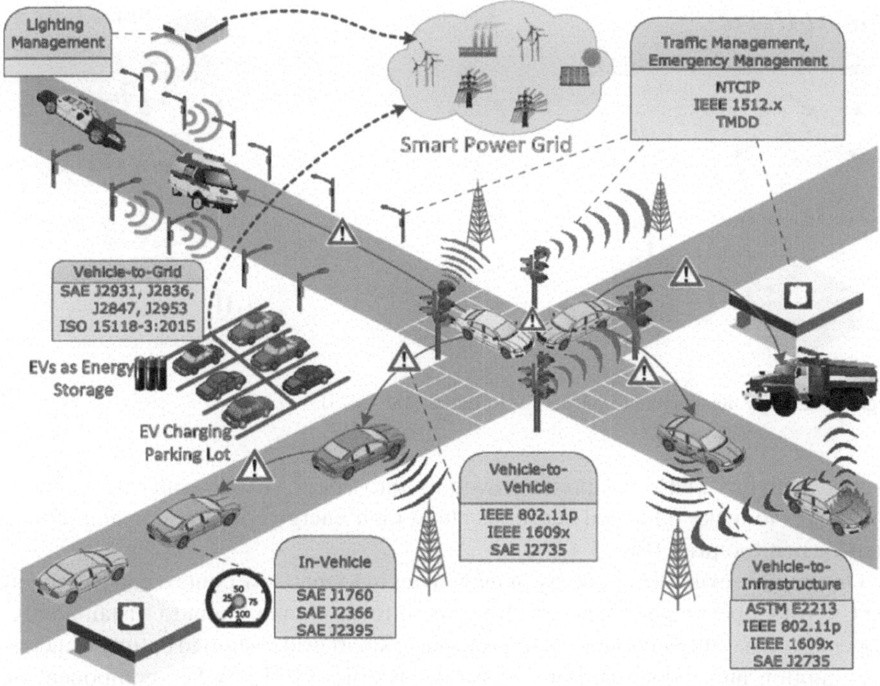

Fig. 5.3 Intelligent transportation systems (A Preliminary Work on Predicting Travel Times and Optimal Routes Using Istanbul's Real Traffic Data - Scientific Figure on ResearchGate. Available from: https://www.researchgate.net/figure/Intelligent-Transportation-System-and-Smart-City-are-closely-coupled_fig1_312040252 [accessed 23 Apr, 2024])

volumes by approximately 10% (Sagayaraj et al. 2024). Additionally, the LTA reports that ERP has contributed to a significant decrease in travel times, with commuters experiencing an average time savings of 15–20% during peak periods. These tangible outcomes underscore the effectiveness of intelligent transportation solutions like ERP in addressing traffic challenges in urban settings, leading to improved efficiency and quality of life for residents (Agarwal and Koo 2016).

5.3.2 Energy Management and Systems

AI-enabled energy management systems play a vital role in optimising energy production, distribution, and consumption within smart cities. Smart grids utilise AI algorithms to analyse energy demand patterns, optimise power generation, and balance supply and demand in real-time. AI-driven demand response systems enable dynamic pricing schemes and load management strategies, incentivizing energy conservation and peak shaving (Antonopoulos et al. 2020). Furthermore, AI-powered

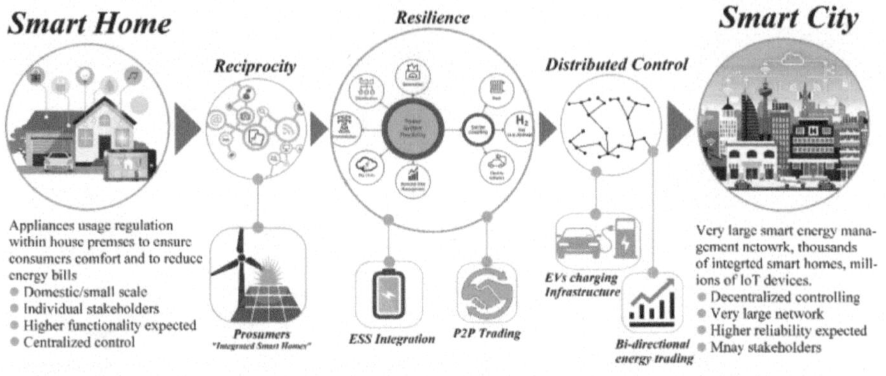

Fig. 5.4 Energy management systems (ur Rehman et al. 2023)

energy analytics platforms provide insights into energy usage patterns, enabling consumers to make informed decisions about their energy consumption and reduce their carbon footprint (Fig. 5.4).

One notable example of energy management in a smart city context can be seen in the City of Copenhagen, Denmark. Renowned for its commitment to sustainability, Copenhagen has implemented a comprehensive smart grid system to optimise energy consumption and reduce carbon emissions (Bjørner 2021). A key component of this system is the Copenhagen Energy Data Platform, which collects and analyses vast amounts of data from various sources including electricity metres, weather stations, and building management systems. By leveraging advanced analytics and machine learning algorithms, the platform enables real-time monitoring of energy usage patterns and identifies opportunities for efficiency improvements. As a result, Copenhagen has achieved remarkable results: according to official reports, the city has reduced its carbon emissions by 42% since 2005, surpassing its target of 40% by 2025 well ahead of schedule (Krähmer 2021). Additionally, Copenhagen has become a global leader in renewable energy adoption, with wind power alone accounting for over half of its electricity consumption (Van Doren et al. 2020). These achievements underscore the tangible benefits of smart energy management initiatives in driving sustainable urban development and combating climate change.

5.3.3 *Environmental Monitoring and Sustainability Initiatives in Smart Cities*

AI technologies are utilised in environmental monitoring and sustainability initiatives to mitigate pollution, conserve natural resources, and promote eco-friendly practices within smart cities. Sensor networks with AI algorithms monitor air and water quality, detect environmental hazards, and provide early warning systems for natural disasters. AI-driven predictive models enable climate forecasting, facilitating proactive measures to mitigate the impact of extreme weather events and reduce vulnerability to climate change (Blasi et al. 2022). Additionally, AI-powered precision agriculture techniques optimise resource usage and crop yield, promoting sustainable food production within urban environments.

One compelling example of environmental monitoring and sustainability initiatives in a smart city context can be found in Barcelona, Spain (Bibri and Krogstie 2020). The city has implemented a comprehensive network of sensors and data analytics platforms to monitor air quality, noise levels, temperature, and other environmental parameters in real time. Through its "Sentilo" platform, Barcelona collects and analyses vast amounts of data to gain insights into the city's environmental conditions and trends. As a result of these efforts, Barcelona has made significant strides in improving air quality and reducing pollution (Chikharev et al. 2021). According to data from the Barcelona City Council, air pollution levels in the city have decreased by nearly 25% over the past decade, surpassing European Union standards for air quality (Rodriguez-Rey et al. 2022). Additionally, the city has seen a marked decrease in noise pollution, with initiatives such as traffic management and the implementation of green spaces contributing to a more livable urban environment. Barcelona's commitment to environmental monitoring and sustainability not only enhances the quality of life for its residents but also serves as a model for other cities seeking to achieve similar goals.

5.3.4 Public Safety and Security in Smart City

AI-driven public safety and security systems enhance situational awareness, crime prevention, crime hotspot detection, and emergency response capabilities within smart cities (Amingad et al. 2023). Surveillance systems equipped with AI-powered video analytics detect suspicious activities, identify potential security threats, and provide real-time alerts to law enforcement agencies. AI-driven predictive policing models analyse crime data to identify high-risk areas and deploy resources more effectively to deter criminal activities. Furthermore, AI-powered emergency response systems facilitate rapid coordination and communication during disasters and emergencies, ensuring timely assistance and minimising casualties (McDaniel and Pease 2021) (Fig. 5.5).

One prominent example of public safety and security in a smart city is the deployment of video surveillance and analytics systems in New York City, USA. The city's Domain Awareness System (DAS) is a collaboration between the New York Police Department (NYPD) and technology companies like Microsoft (Worthington 2022). DAS integrates data from a network of cameras, license plate readers, radiation detectors, and other sensors to provide real-time situational awareness to law enforcement agencies. As of recent data, New York City operates over 18,000 cameras throughout the five boroughs, with plans for further expansion. The system utilises advanced analytics, including facial recognition technology, to identify and track individuals of interest and potential threats. According to the NYPD, DAS has

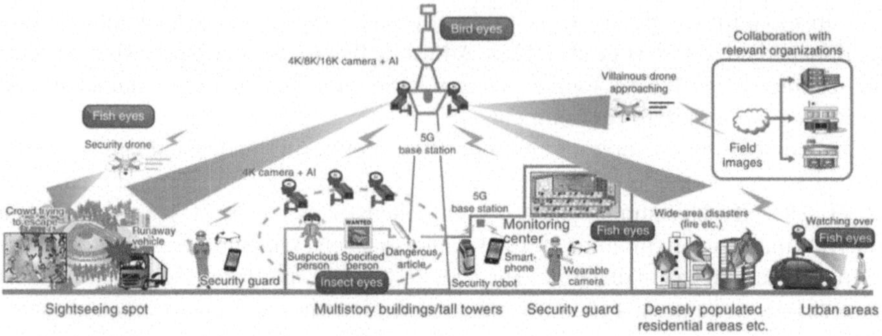

Fig. 5.5 Public safety in smart city (https://www.youtube.com/watch?v=StcEYJSfWiQ&t=369s&ab_channel=HotTalks)

played a significant role in crime prevention and response, with reported reductions in major crimes such as burglary and robbery. Additionally, the system has been instrumental in enhancing emergency response capabilities, enabling faster and more targeted responses to incidents (Brooks and Lopez 2020). Despite some controversies surrounding privacy concerns, proponents argue that DAS has been instrumental in enhancing public safety and security in one of the world's largest and most complex urban environments.

5.4 Data Management and Analytics in Smart Cities

Data serves as the foundation of smart city operations, providing insights into urban dynamics, citizen behaviour, and infrastructure performance. Data collected from e-governance systems and IoT devices, sensors, and other sources enable cities to monitor key metrics, identify trends, and make data-driven decisions to optimise resource allocation and service delivery to improve the welfare of articles. Additionally, open data initiatives promote transparency and citizen engagement by making urban data accessible to the public for analysis and innovation (Neves et al. 2020). Despite its importance, data management poses several challenges for smart cities, including data fragmentation, privacy concerns, and scalability issues. Cities must implement robust data governance frameworks to ensure data quality, security, and compliance with regulations (Kandt and Batty 2021). Cloud computing and edge computing technologies offer scalable solutions for data storage and processing, enabling cities to manage large volumes of data efficiently. Furthermore, advances in data analytics techniques, such as machine learning and deep learning, enable cities to extract actionable insights from complex datasets and improve decision-making processes in smart cities. AI algorithms play a crucial role in processing and deriving insights from urban data, enabling cities to extract valuable information and optimise various aspects of urban operations (Fig. 5.6).

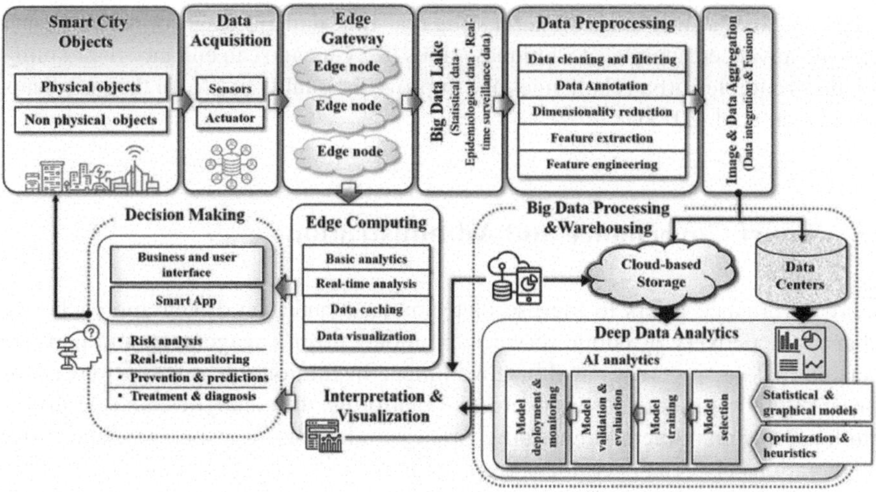

Fig. 5.6 Data management and analytics (Smart Cities after COVID-19: Building a Conceptual Framework through a Multidisciplinary Perspective - Scientific Figure on ResearchGate. Available from: https://www.researchgate.net/figure/Framework-of-the-smart-city-technical-dimension-data-pipeline-in-the-fight-against_fig7_363663080 [accessed 23 Apr, 2024])

One compelling example of data management and analytics in a smart city context can be observed in the city of Chicago, USA, through its Array of Things (AoT) project (Johnson et al. 2022). Launched in 2016, the AoT initiative involves the deployment of a network of sensor nodes throughout the city to collect real-time data on environmental factors such as air quality, temperature, humidity, and noise levels. These sensors generate a wealth of information, which is then aggregated, processed, and analysed by data management and analytics platforms.

According to data from the City of Chicago, the AoT project has deployed over 500 sensor nodes across various neighbourhoods, generating millions of data points every day. Through sophisticated analytics algorithms, city officials and urban planners gain insights into patterns and trends in environmental conditions, enabling them to make data-driven decisions to improve public health, safety, and quality of life (Lyu et al. 2022). AoT data has been instrumental in identifying pollution hotspots and informing targeted interventions to mitigate air quality issues. Moreover, it has enabled the city to monitor and respond to heat waves and other extreme weather events more effectively, reducing the risk of heat-related illnesses and fatalities. AoT project fosters collaboration between the city government, academic institutions, and the private sector, facilitating innovation and the development of new solutions to urban challenges. Researchers and technologists can access the anonymized data collected by the AoT sensors through an open data portal, enabling them to develop applications and tools that leverage this wealth of information for various purposes, from urban planning to public health initiatives. Overall, the Array of Things project in Chicago exemplifies the transformative potential of data management and analytics in the context of a smart city. By harnessing real-time data from sensor networks and applying advanced analytics techniques, cities like Chicago can enhance their ability to address complex urban challenges and improve the quality of life for their residents (Yigitcanlar et al. 2021).

5.5 Smart Governance and Administration

Smart governance refers to the use of technology and data-driven approaches to enhance the delivery of public services, promote citizen engagement, and improve decision-making processes within government institutions. It involves the adoption of digital tools, such as e-governance platforms, data analytics, and AI-driven solutions, to streamline administrative processes, increase transparency, and foster collaboration between government agencies and citizens (Nastjuk et al. 2022). Smart governance, propelled by digital transformation and artificial intelligence (AI), is reshaping administrative processes and decision-making in urban environments. Leveraging AI-driven platforms, municipalities worldwide are streamlining operations and enhancing citizen engagement. For instance, Barcelona's "CityOS" integrates data from various sources, enabling real-time monitoring of city services and resources (Fernandez-Monge et al. 2023). This approach has resulted in a 20% reduction in response time to citizen requests and a 25% increase in citizen satisfaction. Similarly, Singapore's "Virtual Singapore" platform utilises AI algorithms to simulate urban scenarios, enabling policymakers to test and optimise interventions for traffic management, urban planning, and disaster preparedness. Such initiatives have contributed to a 30% reduction in traffic congestion and a 15% decrease in carbon emissions (Yang et al. 2019). These examples underscore the transformative potential of smart governance in fostering responsive, efficient, and sustainable urban management.

5.5.1 Artificial Intelligence for Services and Assistance in Administration

AI-powered chatbots and virtual assistants are revolutionising citizen interaction in smart cities by providing personalised and efficient support across various government services and progress, etc. (Bullock et al. 2020). These conversational AI interfaces enable citizens to access information, report issues, and engage with government agencies through natural language conversations. For instance, chatbots can assist citizens in navigating bureaucratic processes, accessing public services, and obtaining real-time updates on city-related information (Devlin 2020). Virtual assistants can provide personalised recommendations and assistance based on individual

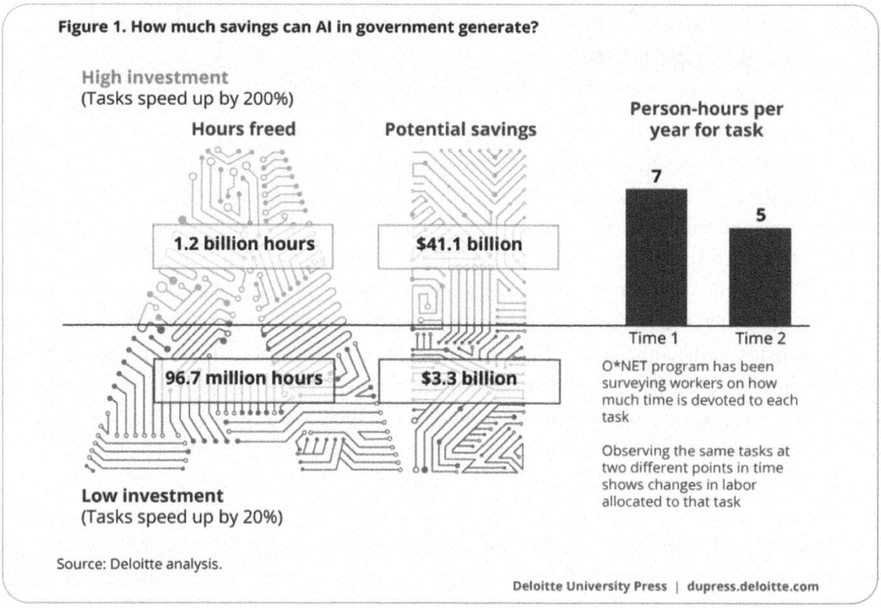

Fig. 5.7 AI in governance (https://www.v7labs.com/blog/ai-in-government)

preferences and historical interactions, enhancing the overall user experience and increasing citizen satisfaction (Chen et al. 2021) (Fig. 5.7).

AI-powered services and assistance are revolutionizing administrative tasks across various sectors by streamlining processes, improving efficiency, and enhancing decision-making. One notable example is the adoption of virtual assistants in administrative functions. Companies like IBM with their Watson Assistant and Microsoft with Cortana are providing AI-driven virtual assistants that can handle a wide range of administrative tasks, from scheduling meetings and managing emails to providing real-time data insights (Nirala et al. 2022).

In government administration, AI-powered chatbots are increasingly being used to handle citizen inquiries and provide information about public services. For instance, the Singapore government's virtual assistant, Ask Jamie, assists citizens in finding relevant government information quickly and efficiently, reducing the burden on human administrators and improving service delivery (Jeffares 2020).

In education administration, AI-powered systems are being used to personalise learning experiences for students by analysing their performance data and providing tailored recommendations for improvement. For instance, platforms like DreamBox Learning use AI algorithms to adapt learning content based on each student's strengths, weaknesses, and learning styles, thereby maximising learning outcomes (Owan et al. 2023).

5.5.2 *Personalised Services and Recommendations Based on AI Algorithms*

AI algorithms enable smart cities to deliver personalised services and recommendations tailored to the unique needs and preferences of individual citizens. By analysing vast amounts of data collected from various sources, including IoT devices, sensors, and citizen feedback, AI systems can infer patterns and preferences to anticipate user needs and deliver targeted recommendations. For example, AI-powered recommendation engines can suggest personalised transportation routes, local events and activities, and provide personalised healthcare recommendations based on individual health profiles (Alowais et al. 2023). These personalised services enhance citizen engagement, satisfaction, and overall quality of life in smart cities. Several cities worldwide have successfully implemented AI-driven solutions to enhance government operations and improve service delivery. For example, Singapore's Virtual Singapore project utilises AI and 3D modelling to create a digital twin of the city, enabling urban planners to simulate and optimise various scenarios for infrastructure development and resource management (Haley 1998). Similarly, Barcelona's CityOS platform integrates AI and IoT technologies to monitor and manage urban services, such as waste management, transportation, and energy usage, in real time. These case studies highlight the transformative potential of AI in optimising government operations and improving urban livability for cities (Smith and Martín 2022).

5.6 Ethical and Social Implications

5.6.1 *Privacy Concerns and Data Security in Smart Cities*

The widespread adoption of AI in smart cities raises significant concerns about privacy and data security. As AI systems collect and analyse vast amounts of data from citizens, sensors, and IoT devices, there is a risk of unauthorised access, data breaches, and misuse of personal information. Smart cities must implement robust data protection measures, such as encryption, anonymisation, and access controls, to safeguard citizen privacy and ensure compliance with data protection regulations. Additionally, transparent data governance frameworks and citizen engagement initiatives are essential to build trust and accountability in AI-enabled smart cities (Kitchin 2016) (Fig. 5.8).

One real-world example highlighting privacy concerns and data security in smart cities is the controversy surrounding the use of facial recognition technology by law enforcement agencies in various cities worldwide, including San Francisco, California, and Portland, Oregon (Caines 2021). In San Francisco, the city became the first in the United States to ban the use of facial recognition technology by government agencies, citing concerns over civil liberties and potential abuse of surveillance capabilities (Conger et al. 2019).

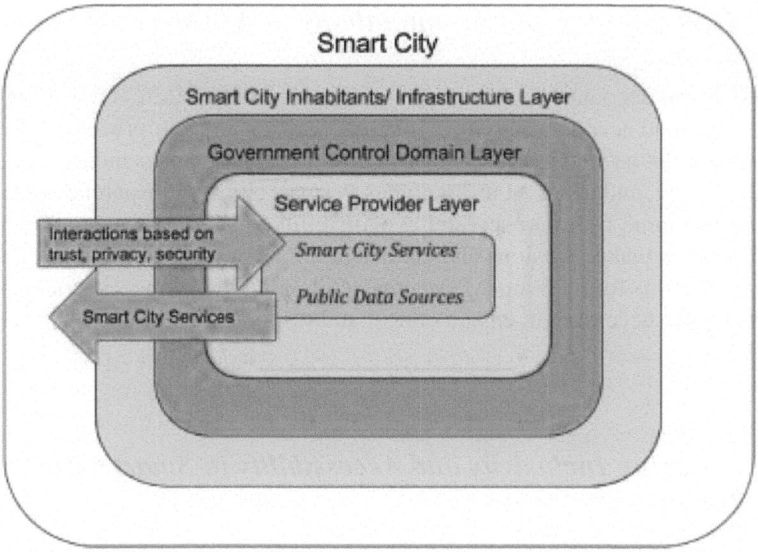

Fig. 5.8 Privacy concerns for smart cities with AI technology (Braun, T., Fung, B. C., Iqbal, F., & Shah, B. (2018). Security and privacy challenges in smart cities. *Sustainable cities and society*, *39*, 499–507)

These bans were driven by widespread concerns among residents, privacy advocates, and civil rights organisations regarding the indiscriminate collection and storage of biometric data without individuals' consent. Facial recognition systems, when deployed in public spaces such as streets, parks, and transportation hubs, have the potential to track individuals' movements and activities without their knowledge or consent, raising significant privacy and civil liberties concerns.

Moreover, studies have shown that facial recognition technology can exhibit biases, particularly against marginalised communities, leading to misidentifications and wrongful arrests. Concerns about the lack of transparency and accountability in the use of these technologies by law enforcement further exacerbate privacy concerns.

The controversy surrounding facial recognition technology in San Francisco, Portland, and other cities serves as a poignant reminder of the challenges associated with ensuring privacy and data security in the era of smart cities (Sookhak et al. 2018). It highlights the need for robust regulatory frameworks, ethical guidelines, and public engagement to address these concerns while harnessing the benefits of technological innovation for the betterment of urban life.

5.6.2 *Transparency and Accountability in AI Governance*

Transparent and accountable AI governance is essential to address concerns about bias, fairness, and accountability in AI-driven decision-making processes. Governments and regulatory bodies must establish clear guidelines and standards for developing, deploying, and using AI technologies in smart cities. Transparency measures, such as algorithmic transparency and explainability, enable citizens to understand how AI systems make decisions and challenge unfair or biased outcomes. Furthermore, mechanisms for auditing AI systems and holding developers accountable for their actions are necessary to ensure ethical and responsible AI governance (Koene et al. 2019).

5.6.3 *Ensuring Inclusivity and Accessibility in Smart City Initiatives*

Smart city initiatives must prioritise inclusivity and accessibility to ensure that AI-driven solutions benefit all members of society, including vulnerable and marginalised communities. Cities must address digital divides and ensure equitable access to technology and digital services for all citizens, regardless of socioeconomic status or demographic characteristics. Additionally, AI systems must be designed with accessibility features, such as voice recognition and screen reader support, to accommodate individuals with disabilities. Moreover, citizen engagement processes should be inclusive and participatory, allowing diverse voices to be heard in decision-making processes related to smart city development (Kolotouchkina et al. 2022).

5.7 Challenges and Future Directions

The adoption of AI in smart cities faces various regulatory and policy challenges, including concerns about data privacy, liability, and accountability. Governments must develop clear regulations and standards to govern the use of AI in urban environments, addressing issues such as data ownership, consent, and algorithmic transparency. Additionally, international cooperation and collaboration are essential to harmonise regulations and facilitate cross-border data sharing in AI-enabled smart cities. Technical hurdles and interoperability issues pose significant challenges to the widespread adoption of AI in smart cities. Integrating disparate systems and data sources from different vendors and platforms requires standardised protocols and interfaces. Additionally, ensuring interoperability between AI systems and legacy infrastructure is essential to maximise efficiency and effectiveness. Cities must invest in interoperability standards, open APIs, and data exchange platforms to enable seamless integration and collaboration across diverse stakeholders (Juma and Shaalan 2020).

5.8 Case Studies and Best Practices

Numerous cities worldwide have implemented AI-driven smart city projects to improve urban services and enhance citizen well-being. For example, Amsterdam's Smart City Initiative utilises AI and IoT technologies to optimise energy usage, reduce carbon emissions, and enhance sustainability (Noori et al. 2020). Similarly, Seoul's Smart Seoul 2030 initiative leverages AI and big data analytics to improve public safety, transportation, and healthcare services (Robinson and Ji 2022). These case studies demonstrate the diverse applications of AI in addressing urban challenges and achieving sustainable development goals.

Successful implementation of AI-driven smart city projects requires careful planning, stakeholder engagement, and capacity building. Cities must prioritise citizen engagement and co-creation processes to ensure that AI solutions address the real needs and priorities of residents. Additionally, fostering partnerships between government, industry, academia, and civil society is essential to leverage collective expertise and resources. Moreover, cities must invest in digital infrastructure, data literacy, and skills development to build a foundation for AI-driven innovation and transformation (Xia et al. 2023).

Measuring the impact of AI-driven smart city initiatives on citizen well-being and urban development is essential to evaluate their effectiveness and identify areas for improvement. Impact assessments should encompass various dimensions, including economic, social, environmental, and governance impacts. Key performance indicators (KPIs) such as citizen satisfaction, resource efficiency, and environmental quality can be used to evaluate the outcomes of AI-driven smart city projects. Additionally, qualitative assessments, such as case studies and stakeholder interviews, provide valuable insights into the lived experiences and perceptions of residents affected by smart city initiatives (Sector, S. FG-AI4EE D. WG2-04).

In conclusion, AI-driven smart cities hold immense potential to address urban challenges, enhance service delivery, and improve the quality of life for residents. By leveraging AI technologies, cities can optimise resource allocation, promote sustainability, and foster innovation in various sectors. However, realising the full benefits of AI in smart cities requires addressing ethical, regulatory, and technical challenges, and ensuring inclusivity and accessibility for all citizens. Policymakers, urban planners, and stakeholders must collaborate to develop clear regulations, standards, and governance frameworks for the responsible use of AI in smart cities. Additionally, investing in digital infrastructure, data literacy, and skills development is essential to build a foundation for AI-driven innovation and transformation. Moreover, prioritising citizen engagement, inclusivity, and accessibility is critical to ensure that AI-driven smart city initiatives benefit all members of society. Looking ahead, AI-driven smart cities have the potential to become more inclusive, sustainable, and resilient urban ecosystems. By harnessing the power of AI technologies, cities can address complex urban challenges and create thriving, livable environments for current and future generations. However, realising this vision requires collective action, collaboration, and a commitment to responsible innovation and governance in the digital age.

References

Abduljabbar R, Dia H, Liyanage S, Bagloee SA (2019) Applications of artificial intelligence in transport: an overview. Sustainability 11(1):189

Agarwal PK, Gurjar J, Agarwal AK, Birla R (2015) Application of artificial intelligence for development of intelligent transport systems in smart cities. J Traffic Transp Eng 1(1):20–30

Agarwal S, Koo KM (2016) Impact of electronic road pricing (ERP) changes on transport modal choice. Reg Sci Urban Econ 60:1–11

Al Marzouqi N, Bueti C, Menon M (2021) Digital transformation to build smart cities. In: Machine intelligence and data analytics for sustainable future smart cities. Springer International Publishing, Cham, pp 145–169

Alowais SA, Alghamdi SS, Alsuhebany N, Alqahtani T, Alshaya AI, Almohareb SN, ... Albekairy AM (2023) Revolutionizing healthcare: the role of artificial intelligence in clinical practice. BMC Med Educ 23(1):689

Amingad SC, Rahul M, Reddy PS, Gupta NS (2023, November). Enhancing public safety with AI-Powered intelligent surveillance: an examination of immediate incident detection and rapid response in urban settings. In: 2023 international conference on advances in computation, communication and information technology (ICAICCIT). IEEE, pp 205–210

Antonopoulos I, Robu V, Couraud B, Kirli D, Norbu S, Kiprakis A, ... Wattam S (2020) Artificial intelligence and machine learning approach to energy demand-side response: a systematic review. Renew Sustain Energy Rev 130:109899

Bibri SE, Krogstie J (2020) The emerging data–driven smart city and its innovative applied solutions for sustainability: the cases of London and Barcelona. Energy Inform 3(1):5

Bjørner T (2021) The advantages of and barriers to being smart in a smart city: the perceptions of project managers within a smart city cluster project in Greater Copenhagen. Cities 114:103187

Blasi S, Ganzaroli A, De Noni I (2022) Smartening sustainable development in cities: strengthening the theoretical linkage between smart cities and SDGs. Sustain Cities Soc 80:103793

Brooks R, Lopez C (2020) Policing in a time of pandemic: recommendations for law enforcement. COVID-19 rapid response impact initiative

Bullock J, Young MM, Wang YF (2020) Artificial intelligence, bureaucratic form, and discretion in public service. Inf Polity 25(4):491–506

Caines S (2021) The many faces of facial recognition. In: Research handbook on big data law. Edward Elgar Publishing, pp 29–56

Chen T, Guo W, Gao X, Liang Z (2021) AI-based self-service technology in public service delivery: user experience and influencing factors. Gov Inf Q 38(4):101520

Chikharev IA, Tikunova IN, Fedorova EA (2021, April) Mediterranean city: constructing a social attractor (the example of Barcelona). In: IOP conference series: earth and environmental science, vol 740, No 1. IOP Publishing, p 012009

Conger K, Fausset R, Kovaleski SF (2019) San Francisco Bans facial recognition technology. https://www.nytimes.com/2019/05/14/us/facial-recognition-ban-san-francisco.html

Devlin C (2020) Digital social innovation and the adoption of# PlanTech: the case of coventry city council. Urban Plann 5(4):59–67

Fernandez-Monge F, Barns S, Kattel R, Bria F (2023) Reclaiming data for improved city governance: Barcelona's new data deal. Urban Stud. 00420980231204835

Haley UC (1998) Virtual Singapores: shaping international competitive environments through business-government partnerships. J Organ Chang Manag 11(4):338–356

Jagatheesaperumal SK, Rahouti M, Ahmad K, Al-Fuqaha A, Guizani M (2021) The duo of artificial intelligence and big data for industry 4.0: applications, techniques, challenges, and future research directions. IEEE Internet of Things J 9(15):12861–12885

Jeffares S (2020) The virtual public servant: artificial intelligence and frontline work. Springer Nature

Johnson J, Hevia A, Yergin R, Karbassi S, Levine A, Ortiz J (2022) Data governance frameworks for smart cities: key considerations for data management and use. JL & Mobility 1

Juma M, Shaalan K (2020) Cyber-physical systems in the smart city: challenges and future trends for strategic research. In: Swarm intelligence for resource management in the Internet of things. Academic Press pp 65–85

Kandt J, Batty M (2021) Smart cities, big data and urban policy: towards urban analytics for the long run. Cities 109:102992

Kitchin R (2016) Getting smarter about smart cities: improving data privacy and data security

Koene A, Clifton C, Hatada Y, Webb H, Richardson R (2019) A governance framework for algorithmic accountability and transparency

Kolotouchkina O, Barroso CL, Sánchez JLM (2022) Smart cities, the digital divide, and people with disabilities. Cities 123:103613

Krähmer K (2021) Are green cities sustainable? A degrowth critique of sustainable urban development in Copenhagen. Eur Plan Stud 29(7):1272–1289

Le TT, Priya JC, Le HC, Le NVL, Duong MT, Cao DN (2024) Harnessing artificial intelligence for data-driven energy predictive analytics: a systematic survey towards enhancing sustainability. Int J Renew Energy Dev 13(2):270–293

Lyu F, Wang S, Han SY, Catlett C, Wang S (2022) An integrated cyberGIS and machine learning framework for fine-scale prediction of urban heat island using satellite remote sensing and urban sensor network data. Urban Inform 1(1):6

Mahmoud MA, Md Nasir NR, Gurunathan M, Raj P, Mostafa SA (2021) The current state of the art in research on predictive maintenance in smart grid distribution network: Fault's types, causes, and prediction methods—A systematic review. Energies 14(16):5078

McDaniel JL, Pease K (eds).(2021) Predictive policing and artificial intelligence. Routledge, Taylor & Francis Group

Menon G, Guttikunda S (2010) Electronic road pricing: experience & lessons from Singapore. SIM Air Work Pap Series 33:1–15

Nastjuk I, Trang S, Papageorgiou EI (2022) Smart cities and smart governance models for future cities: current research and future directions. Electron Mark 32(4):1917–1924

Neves FT, de Castro Neto M, Aparicio M (2020) The impacts of open data initiatives on smart cities: a framework for evaluation and monitoring. Cities 106:102860

Nirala KK, Singh NK, Purani VS (2022) A survey on providing customer and public administration-based services using AI: chatbot. Multim Tools Appl 81(16):22215–22246

Noori N, Hoppe T, de Jong M (2020) Classifying pathways for smart city development: comparing design, governance and implementation in Amsterdam, Barcelona, Dubai, and Abu Dhabi. Sustainability 12(10):4030

Owan VJ, Abang KB, Idika DO, Etta EO, Bassey BA (2023) Exploring the potential of artificial intelligence tools in educational measurement and assessment. EURASIA J Math, Sci Technol Educ 19(8):em2307

Robinson T, Ji M (2022) Smart city Seoul: solving the urban puzzle. Sustainable, smart and solidary Seoul: transforming an asian megacity. Springer International Publishing, Cham, pp 99–134

Rodriguez-Rey D, Guevara M, Linares MP, Casanovas J, Armengol JM, Benavides J, ... García-Pando CP (2022) To what extent the traffic restriction policies applied in Barcelona city can improve its air quality? Sci Total Environ 807:150743

Sagayaraj AS, Kabilesh SK, Devi TK, Chhabra V (2024) Strategies for the sustainable development of the smart cities by implementing AI. In: Handbook of artificial intelligence for smart city development. CRC Press, pp 209–227

Sanghavi K (2024) Revolutionizing transportation with AI: benefits, use cases and examples. https://syndelltech.com/ai-in-transportation/#:~:text=A%20study%20by%20McKinsey%20%26%20Company,significant%20economic%20and%20environmental%20benefits. Accessed 05 April 2024

Sector, S. FG-AI4EE D. WG2-04 Effective use cases on employing artificial intelligence for achieving sustainable development goals and their applications in smart sustainable cities

Silva BN, Khan M, Han K (2018) Towards sustainable smart cities: a review of trends, architectures, components, and open challenges in smart cities. Sustain Cities Soc 38:697–713

Smith A, Martín PP (2022) Going beyond the smart city? Implementing technopolitical platforms for urban democracy in Madrid and Barcelona. In: Sustainable smart city transitions. Routledge, pp 280–299

Sookhak M, Tang H, He Y, Yu FR (2018) Security and privacy of smart cities: a survey, research issues and challenges. IEEE Commun Surv Tutor 21(2):1718–1743

ur Rehman U, Faria P, Gomes L, Vale Z (2023) Future of energy management systems in smart cities: a systematic literature review. Sustain Cities Soc 104720

van Doren D, Driessen PP, Runhaar HA, Giezen M (2020) Learning within local government to promote the scaling-up of low-carbon initiatives: a case study in the City of Copenhagen. Energy Policy 136:111030

Worthington C (2022) Safety as a smokescreen: the new york police department, surveillance technology, and necropower. Doctoral dissertation, Columbia University

Xia L, Semirumi DT, Rezaei R (2023) A thorough examination of smart city applications: exploring challenges and solutions throughout the life cycle with emphasis on safeguarding citizen privacy. Sustain Cities Soc 98:104771

Yang S, Ji Y, Zhang D, Fu J (2019) Equilibrium between road traffic congestion and low-carbon economy: a case study from Beijing, China. Sustainability 11(1):219

Yigitcanlar T, Corchado JM, Mehmood R, Li RYM, Mossberger K, Desouza K (2021) Responsible urban innovation with local government artificial intelligence (AI): a conceptual framework and research agenda. J Open Innov: Technol, Mark Complex 7(1):71

Chapter 6
Artificial Intelligence and Intelligent Factories for the Future

Abstract This chapter explores the future of artificial intelligence (AI) in the context of intelligent factories. It delves into the transformative potential of AI technologies in revolutionising manufacturing processes, optimising production, and creating highly efficient and adaptive factory environments. This chapter discusses the key components of intelligent factories, including AI-powered automation, machine learning algorithms, and the integration of the Internet of Things (IoT) and big data analytics. It explores how these technologies work together to enhance productivity, quality control, and responsiveness in manufacturing operations. This chapter emphasises the need for a holistic approach, considering the technical, economic, and societal implications of AI implementation in factories. The future of AI and intelligent factories is one of collaboration and augmentation, where human expertise and creativity intersect with AI capabilities to drive the next wave of the industrial revolution.

Keywords Artificial intelligence · Intelligent factory · Skills · IoT · Cyber-physical systems

6.1 Introduction to AI in Manufacturing

Manufacturing industries, the backbone of economies worldwide, have traditionally relied on human labour and conventional automation methods to drive the production of several types of products. However, the landscape is rapidly evolving with the advent of digitalization and now with artificial intelligence (AI), marking a profound transformation in how products are made, managed, recorded, delivered serviced and maintained (Śledziewska and Włoch 2021). Once confined to the realm of science fiction, AI has now become a tangible and transformative force reshaping the manufacturing sector, promising to revolutionise manufacturing processes, optimise resources such as raw and finished with efficiency, and drive innovation with available previous experiences and experiments recorded in the form of data (Arinez et al. 2020). To appreciate the potential impact of AI in manufacturing, it's essential to understand the current state of the industry. Traditionally,

S. Kumar et al., *Digital Transformation, Artificial Intelligence and Society*, Frontiers of Artificial Intelligence, Ethics and Multidisciplinary Applications,
https://doi.org/10.1007/978-981-97-5656-8_6

manufacturing processes have been characterised by rigid workflows, standardised production lines, and heavy reliance on manual labour (Williams et al. 1992). While automation has undoubtedly improved efficiency and reduced labour costs, it has limitations in terms of adaptability and intelligence. Traditional automation systems follow pre-programmed instructions and cannot learn and adapt to changing conditions autonomously. The introduction of AI into manufacturing heralds a new era. Unlike traditional automation, AI-enabled systems possess the ability to learn from real-time data, adapt to changing conditions and scenarios, and make autonomous decisions for improving production and resource optimization as per present and future needs. This transformative capability opens up a myriad of possibilities for optimising production processes, enhancing quality control, driving innovation, and improving product portfolio (Huang et al. 2021). AI systems can analyse vast amounts of data to identify patterns, make predictions, and optimise processes in ways that were previously unimaginable. From predictive maintenance to demand forecasting, AI has the potential to revolutionise every aspect of the manufacturing sector (Javaid et al. 2022).

Several factors are driving the rapid adoption of AI in manufacturing. One of the primary drivers is the increasing demand for customization and personalization. In today's consumer-driven market, customers expect products that are tailored to their individual needs and preferences. This necessitates more flexible and agile production processes that can quickly adapt to changing demands (Mourtzis et al. 2024). Additionally, the need to improve operational efficiency and productivity is pushing manufacturers to explore new technologies such as AI. By automating repetitive tasks and streamlining workflows, AI can significantly enhance productivity and reduce production and inventory costs (Javaid et al. 2022).

Initiatives like Industry 4.0 are also accelerating the adoption of AI across the manufacturing industry. Industry 4.0 advocates for the integration of digital technologies, including AI, IoT, big data analytics, and cloud computing, into manufacturing processes (Nath et al. 2020). These technologies enable the creation of "smart factories" that are interconnected, adaptive, and highly efficient. By leveraging AI and other digital technologies and IoT, manufacturers can achieve unprecedented levels of intelligent automation, optimization, and responsiveness, paving the way for the transformative and sustainable future of manufacturing. The integration of AI into manufacturing represents a paradigm shift that promises to revolutionise the industry majorly depending on the manufacturing sector. By harnessing the power of AI, manufacturers can unlock new levels of efficiency, productivity, and innovation. However, realising the full potential of AI in manufacturing requires a concerted effort to overcome technical, organisational, and cultural barriers (Kinkel et al. 2022). With the right approach, AI has the potential to transform manufacturing processes and drive the next wave of industrial revolution.

6.2 Key Components of Intelligent Factories

At the heart of intelligent factories lies AI-powered automation, representing a fundamental shift in manufacturing paradigms. These systems leverage advanced AI algorithms to control and optimise various manufacturing processes, ranging from assembly line operations to logistics management (Plathottam et al. 2023). Perhaps one of the most striking examples of AI-powered automation is the deployment of robotic arms endowed with AI capabilities. These robotic systems possess human-like dexterity and accuracy, enabling them to perform intricate tasks with precision and efficiency. By replacing manual labour with AI-powered robotics, manufacturers can significantly reduce production costs, enhance productivity, and improve overall quality control (Pillai et al. 2022). The integration of AI into automation processes enables factories to achieve unprecedented levels of adaptability and responsiveness. Unlike traditional automation systems that operate on fixed rules and predefined instructions, AI-powered automation systems can learn from data, adapt to changing conditions, and make autonomous decisions. For instance, AI algorithms can analyse real-time production data to identify inefficiencies or bottlenecks in the manufacturing process. Based on these insights, AI-powered systems can dynamically adjust production schedules, allocate resources more efficiently, and optimise overall performance (Aldoseri et al. 2023). AI-powered automation facilitates the seamless integration of disparate manufacturing processes, creating a cohesive and interconnected production ecosystem (Wan et al. 2020). By leveraging AI-driven optimization algorithms, manufacturers can synchronise various operations across different departments, suppliers, and distribution channels. This level of integration not only streamlines workflows but also enhances communication and collaboration throughout the manufacturing value chain, leading to improved efficiency and agility. AI-powered automation represents a cornerstone of intelligent factories, enabling manufacturers to achieve unparalleled levels of efficiency, flexibility, and competitiveness. By harnessing the power of AI, manufacturers can optimise their production processes, reduce costs, and stay ahead of the curve in today's rapidly evolving market landscape (Fig. 6.1).

Machine learning algorithms serve as the backbone of AI-enabled systems in manufacturing, playing a pivotal role in driving innovation and optimization across various operational domains (Huang et al. 2021). These algorithms analyse vast amounts of data to identify patterns, make predictions, and optimise processes, thereby enabling manufacturers to operate more efficiently and effectively. One of the key applications of machine learning in manufacturing is demand forecasting. By analysing historical sales data, market trends, and other relevant factors, machine learning models can accurately predict future demand for products. This enables manufacturers to optimise inventory levels, reduce stockouts, and minimise excess inventory, leading to improved supply chain management and cost savings.

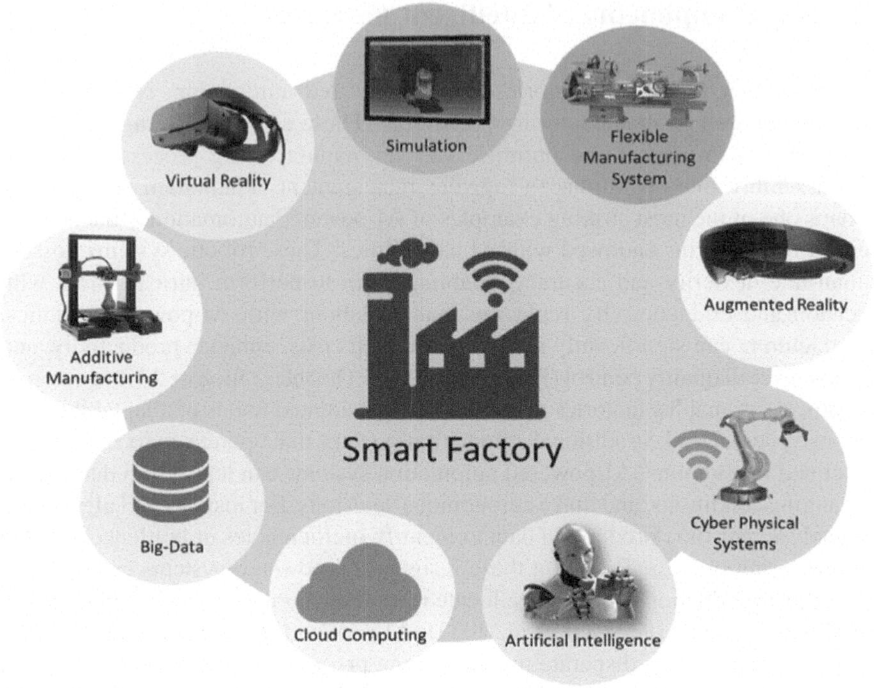

Fig. 6.1 Components of smart manufacturing system. https://www.researchgate.net/figure/Components-of-Smart-Manufacturing-System_fig1_341069796

Additionally, machine learning algorithms are instrumental in optimising production processes to maximise efficiency and minimise waste. For example, these algorithms can analyse production data to identify opportunities for process optimization, such as reducing cycle times, improving yield rates, or optimising energy consumption (Weichert et al. 2019). By continuously learning from data and refining their models, machine learning algorithms can drive continuous improvement in manufacturing operations, leading to increased productivity and profitability.

6.3 Integration of IoT and Big Data Analytics

The integration of the Internet of Things (IoT) and big data analytics is a critical component of intelligent factories, enabling manufacturers to harness the power of data to drive decision-making and optimization. IoT devices, such as sensors and actuators, collect data from machines, equipment, and production processes, while big data analytics platforms process and analyse this data to extract valuable insights (Li et al. 2022). One of the key benefits of IoT and big data analytics in manufacturing is real-time monitoring and analysis of production processes. By collecting data from sensors embedded in equipment and machinery, manufacturers can gain visibility into various aspects of their operations, such as temperature, pressure, speed, and throughput. This real-time data allows manufacturers to identify inefficiencies, detect anomalies, and troubleshoot issues before they escalate, thereby minimising downtime and improving overall equipment effectiveness (OEE) (Elsawaf 2023). It can also help in creating digital replicas of physical processes and help in real-time monitoring. Furthermore, IoT and big data analytics enable predictive maintenance, a proactive approach to maintenance that aims to prevent equipment failures before they occur (Mourtzis et al. 2016). By analysing data from sensors and other sources, manufacturers can detect early signs of equipment degradation or impending failures and take preventive action, such as scheduling maintenance or replacing components, to avoid costly unplanned downtime. Additionally, IoT and big data analytics facilitate continuous improvement and optimization of manufacturing processes. By collecting and analysing data from various sources, including production equipment, supply chain systems, and customer feedback, manufacturers can gain insights into their operations and identify opportunities for optimization.

6.4 Transformative Potential of AI Technologies

The transformative potential of AI in manufacturing processes cannot be overstated. It represents a paradigm shift from conventional methods to intelligent systems capable of optimising operations at an unprecedented scale. One of the most compelling applications of AI in manufacturing is predictive maintenance (Hrnjica and Softic 2020). Traditional maintenance practices often rely on scheduled inspections or reactive responses to equipment failures, leading to costly downtime and production disruptions. AI-powered predictive maintenance, on the other hand, leverages machine learning algorithms to analyse vast amounts of sensor data in real-time. By identifying patterns indicative of impending equipment failures, AI systems can predict maintenance needs before they occur, allowing for timely interventions that prevent costly breakdowns and extend the lifespan of machinery (Rauch 2020). This proactive approach not only minimises downtime but also contributes to significant cost savings and increased productivity. By maximising the operational efficiency of manufacturing equipment, AI-driven predictive maintenance enables manufacturers to maintain a competitive edge in today's fast-paced market. Another hallmark of AI in manufacturing is its ability to create adaptable and responsive systems that can swiftly adjust to changing conditions. Traditional manufacturing systems often operate on fixed schedules and predefined workflows, leaving little room for flexibility or agility. In contrast, AI-enabled systems can dynamically adapt production schedules, inventory levels, and resource allocations based on real-time data and market dynamics (Wan et al. 2020). This agility is particularly valuable in industries characterised by high demand variability, supply chain disruptions, or seasonal fluctuations. By continuously analysing incoming data streams, AI systems can anticipate changes in demand, identify potential bottlenecks, and optimise production processes accordingly. This not only minimises disruptions but also maximises efficiency and resource utilisation, ultimately driving cost savings and enhancing competitiveness (Rauch 2020).

6.4.1 Enhancing Productivity

AI's ability to automate repetitive tasks and streamline workflows is a game-changer for productivity in manufacturing. AI-powered robotic systems, for instance, can perform complex assembly tasks with speed and precision, surpassing human capabilities in terms of speed, accuracy, and consistency. By integrating AI into production lines, manufacturers can significantly increase throughput, reduce cycle times, and scale operations to meet growing demand. Moreover, AI-driven optimization algorithms can fine-tune production processes to achieve optimal efficiency levels. By analysing historical production data and identifying areas for improvement, AI systems can eliminate waste, minimise downtime, and maximise the utilisation of resources (Shahin et al. 2023). This not only boosts productivity but also improves overall operational efficiency, contributing to long-term sustainability and growth.

6.4.2 Quality Control

Ensuring product quality and consistency is paramount in manufacturing, and AI technologies are instrumental in achieving manufacturing quality standards and goals. Machine learning algorithms can analyse sensor data from production processes to detect anomalies and defects that may compromise product quality. For example, AI-powered visual inspection systems can identify minute defects or deviations from quality standards that may not be discernible to the human eye (Miski 2021). By flagging potential issues in real-time, AI-driven quality control systems enable manufacturers to take corrective actions promptly, preventing defective products from reaching the market (Soori et al. 2023). This not only safeguards brand reputation and customer satisfaction but also reduces the likelihood of costly recalls or warranty claims. Additionally, by continuously learning from past inspections and feedback, AI systems can refine their algorithms over time, further enhancing the accuracy and effectiveness of quality control measures. For example, Siemens reported a 10% increase in productivity and a 20% reduction in maintenance costs (Rüßmann et al. 2015). BMW reported a 5% improvement in product quality and a 10% reduction in inspection time (Ramvishvas Kumar 2024). Foxconn reported a 30% increase in production efficiency and a 20% decrease in defects (WEF 2023). Foxconn, a major electronics manufacturer, integrated AI technologies into their assembly lines (Lee 2020). AI-driven robotics and automation optimise the production process, reducing human error and increasing throughput. This has resulted in higher productivity and improved product quality, contributing to overall cost savings.

6.4.3 Predictive Maintenance

Predictive maintenance is a prime example of how the interconnected components of intelligent factories work synergistically to optimise operations and reduce downtime. IoT sensors embedded in manufacturing equipment continuously collect data on various parameters such as temperature, vibration, and energy consumption. This data is then transmitted to AI-powered predictive maintenance algorithms, which analyse it to detect patterns indicative of potential equipment failures. By leveraging machine learning techniques, these algorithms can predict maintenance needs with high accuracy, allowing manufacturers to take proactive measures to prevent costly downtime and disruptions (Aksa et al. 2021). For example, if abnormal patterns are detected in the data, such as an increase in vibration levels or a drop in temperature, the predictive maintenance system can alert maintenance personnel to investigate and address the issue before it escalates into a major equipment failure. Furthermore, predictive maintenance systems can optimise maintenance schedules based on factors such as equipment usage, operating conditions, and historical performance data. By analysing this data, the system can determine the optimal time for maintenance activities to minimise disruption to production schedules while ensuring the reliability and longevity of equipment.

For example, the implementation of predictive maintenance significantly reduced unplanned downtime for Schindler's elevators and escalators. They reported a decrease in downtime by 25%. Proactive maintenance led to cost savings for Schindler Group. They reported a reduction in maintenance costs by 20% due to fewer emergency repairs and optimised maintenance schedules (Weiss, E. N).

6.4.4 Optimised Production

By integrating data from IoT sensors, machine learning algorithms can dynamically adjust production schedules based on factors such as equipment availability, material availability, and demand forecasts. For example, if a critical piece of equipment malfunctions or experiences unexpected downtime, the production schedule can be automatically adjusted to allocate resources to other production lines or prioritise orders based on urgency. Similarly, if demand suddenly spikes or drops, the production schedule can be quickly recalibrated to meet changing market conditions. Additionally, real-time monitoring and analysis enable manufacturers to identify bottlenecks and optimise workflows to improve efficiency and performance (Li et al. 2009). By continuously analysing production data and identifying areas for improvement, manufacturers can streamline processes, reduce cycle times, and minimise waste, ultimately enhancing overall productivity and competitiveness. The interconnected components of intelligent factories work together seamlessly to drive continuous optimization and innovation. By leveraging the power of AI, machine learning, IoT, and big data analytics, manufacturers can achieve unprecedented levels of efficiency, flexibility, and responsiveness, paving the way for the future of manufacturing. For example, The impact of Toyota's optimised production practices is evident in its performance metrics. Toyota reported a 50% reduction in lead times, enabling faster response to market demands and improved customer satisfaction (Ford et al. 2012).

6.5 Holistic Approach to AI Implementation

The integration of AI into manufacturing brings forth significant economic implications that necessitate a comprehensive assessment. While AI adoption promises to reduce costs, enhance efficiency, and spur innovation, it also entails upfront investment costs associated with implementing AI-enabled systems. Manufacturers need to invest in AI infrastructure, hardware, software, and human resources training to fully leverage its benefits (Wamba-Taguimdje et al. 2020). However, studies indicate that the long-term benefits of AI adoption, such as increased productivity, competitiveness, and revenue growth, often outweigh these initial investment costs. Furthermore, AI adoption can lead to a restructuring of the labour force, raising concerns about job displacement and income inequality. While some routine and repetitive tasks may be automated, new job opportunities may emerge in areas such as AI programming, data analysis, and system maintenance. Therefore, manufacturers must invest in reskilling and upskilling programmes to ensure that workers can adapt to the evolving demands of the digital economy. By investing in human capital development, manufacturers can mitigate the negative impacts of automation and empower their workforce to thrive in the AI-driven future (Tschang and Almirall 2021).

Additionally, the economic benefits of AI adoption extend beyond individual firms to the broader economy. AI-enabled manufacturing ecosystems can spur innovation, attract investment, and create new business opportunities, driving economic growth and prosperity. Therefore, policymakers need to create an enabling environment that encourages AI adoption while addressing potential challenges such as data privacy, intellectual property rights, and regulatory compliance.

6.6 Societal Implications

In addition to economic considerations, the integration of AI into manufacturing raises important societal implications that warrant careful consideration. One of the primary concerns is the impact of automation on employment opportunities. While AI adoption may lead to job displacement in certain sectors, it can also create new job opportunities in high-skilled, knowledge-intensive roles (Oluwaseyi and Cena

2024). However, there is a risk of exacerbating income inequality if the benefits of AI adoption are not equitably distributed. To address these concerns, manufacturers must prioritise workforce development initiatives that focus on reskilling and upskilling workers for the jobs of the future. By investing in lifelong learning programmes, vocational training, and apprenticeships, manufacturers can ensure that their workforce remains competitive and adaptable in the face of technological change. Moreover, a collaboration between industry, government, and educational institutions is essential to aligning education and training programmes with the evolving needs of the labour market. Additionally, there are ethical considerations surrounding the use of AI in manufacturing, particularly concerning issues such as data privacy, algorithmic bias, and the use of AI in autonomous decision-making. Manufacturers must adhere to ethical principles and best practices to ensure that AI is deployed responsibly and transparently (De Laat 2021). This may involve implementing robust data governance frameworks, conducting regular audits of AI systems, and providing transparency and accountability in decision-making processes. In summary, addressing the societal implications of AI implementation in manufacturing requires a collaborative effort between industry stakeholders, policymakers, and the broader community. By prioritising workforce development, promoting ethical AI practices, and fostering inclusive growth, manufacturers can harness the full potential of AI while ensuring that its benefits are shared equitably across society.

6.7 Collaboration, Augmentation, and Creativity

Rather than displacing human workers, AI is poised to augment human capabilities and expertise, leading to a synergistic partnership that drives innovation in manufacturing. AI-enabled systems have the potential to assist workers in complex decision-making tasks by providing real-time insights and recommendations based on data analysis (Jarrahi 2018). For example, AI-powered analytics platforms can analyse production data to identify trends, anomalies, and optimization opportunities, empowering workers to make informed decisions that drive efficiency and productivity. Moreover, AI can enhance human creativity by automating routine tasks and freeing up time for more creative endeavours. For instance, AI-powered design tools can generate innovative product concepts based on input from designers, enabling them to explore a wider range of design options and iterate more quickly (Verganti et al. 2020). This not only accelerates the product development process but also fosters a culture of innovation within organisations, driving continuous improvement and competitiveness. Furthermore, AI can augment human capabilities in areas such as safety, quality control, and maintenance. AI-enabled sensors and predictive analytics systems can monitor equipment performance in real-time, detect potential issues before they escalate, and recommend preventive actions to minimise downtime and ensure worker safety. By leveraging AI-driven insights, manufacturers can create safer, more efficient, and more sustainable workplaces that prioritise worker well-being and operational excellence.

AI has the potential to enhance human creativity by automating routine tasks and providing inspiration and insights that fuel innovation. For example, AI-powered generative design tools can explore a vast design space and generate novel design concepts that push the boundaries of creativity (Ghorbani 2023). By automating repetitive tasks such as modelling, simulation, and optimization, these tools enable designers to focus on higher-level creative tasks such as ideation, conceptualization, and experimentation. Moreover, AI can facilitate interdisciplinary collaboration by providing a common platform for data sharing, analysis, and visualisation. For instance, AI-powered analytics platforms can integrate data from various sources such as production systems, supply chain networks, and customer feedback channels, enabling cross-functional teams to collaborate on problem-solving and decision-making (Akter et al. 2023). By breaking down silos and fostering collaboration, AI can accelerate innovation and drive breakthroughs in product design, process optimization, and business strategy. In conclusion, the collaboration between humans and AI holds immense potential for driving innovation and competitiveness in manufacturing. By harnessing the complementary strengths of humans and machines, manufacturers can unlock new possibilities and create value in ways that were previously unimaginable. However, realising this potential requires a cultural shift towards embracing AI as a partner rather than a replacement, fostering a collaborative and inclusive work environment where human creativity and expertise are augmented by AI-driven insights and capabilities.

References

Aksa K, Aitouche S, Bentoumi H, Sersa I (2021) Developing a web platform for the management of predictive maintenance in smart factories. Wirel Pers Commun 119(2):1469–1497

Akter S, Hossain MA, Sajib S, Sultana S, Rahman M, Vrontis D, McCarthy G (2023) A framework for AI-powered service innovation capability: review and agenda for future research. Technovation 125:102768

Aldoseri A, Al-Khalifa K, Hamouda A (2023) A roadmap for integrating automation with process optimization for AI-powered digital transformation

Arinez JF, Chang Q, Gao RX, Xu C, Zhang J (2020) Artificial intelligence in advanced manufacturing: current status and future outlook. J Manuf Sci Eng 142(11):110804

de Laat PB (2021) Companies committed to responsible AI: from principles towards implementation and regulation? Philos Technol 34(4):1135–1193

Elsawaf A (2023) Unlocking operational efficiency through reliable asset data: a case study of maintenance strategies in Company X. Bachelor's thesis, University of Twente

Ford AL, Williams JA, Spencer M, McCammon C, Khoury N, Sampson TR, ... Lee JM (2012) Reducing door-to-needle times using Toyota's lean manufacturing principles and value stream analysis. Stroke 43(12):3395–3398

Ghorbani MA (2023) AI tools to support design activities and innovation processes

Hrnjica B, Softic S (2020, August) Explainable AI in manufacturing: a predictive maintenance case study. In: *IFIP* international conference on advances in production management systems. Springer International Publishing, Cham, pp 66–73

Huang Z, Shen Y, Li J, Fey M, Brecher C (2021) A survey on AI-driven digital twins in industry 4.0: smart manufacturing and advanced robotics. Sensors 21(19):6340

Jarrahi MH (2018) Artificial intelligence and the future of work: human-AI symbiosis in organizational decision making. Bus Horiz 61(4):577–586

Javaid M, Haleem A, Singh RP, Suman R (2022) Artificial intelligence applications for industry 4.0: a literature-based study. J Ind Integr Manag 7(1):83–111

Kinkel S, Baumgartner M, Cherubini E (2022) Prerequisites for the adoption of AI technologies in manufacturing—Evidence from a worldwide sample of manufacturing companies. Technovation 110:102375

Lee J (2020) Industrial ai. Applications with sustainable performance

Li C, Chen Y, Shang Y (2022) A review of industrial big data for decision making in intelligent manufacturing. Eng Sci Technol Int J 29:101021

Li L, Chang Q, Ni J, Biller S (2009) Real-time production improvement through bottleneck control. Int J Prod Res 47(21):6145–6158

Miski AG (2021) Automated surface anomaly detection system for quality inspection of small parts using computer vision and convolutional neural networks. Doctoral dissertation, University of Miami

Mourtzis D, Panopoulos N, Stavropoulos P, Papakostas N (2024) Artificial intelligence for production management and control towards mass personalization of global networks. In: CIRP novel topics in production engineering: Volume 1. Springer Nature Switzerland, Cham, pp 267–312

Mourtzis D, Vlachou E, Milas NJPC (2016) Industrial big data as a result of IoT adoption in manufacturing. Procedia Cirp 55:290–295

Nath SV, Dunkin A, Chowdhary M, Patel N (2020) Industrial digital transformation: accelerate digital transformation with business optimization, AI, and Industry 4.0. Packt Publishing Ltd

Oluwaseyi J, Cena J (2024) Analyzing the impact of artificial intelligence on job. Statistics 14(1):150–155

Pillai R, Sivathanu B, Mariani M, Rana NP, Yang B, Dwivedi YK (2022) Adoption of AI-empowered industrial robots in auto component manufacturing companies. Prod Plann Control 33(16):1517–1533

Plathottam SJ, Rzonca A, Lakhnori R, Iloeje CO (2023) A review of artificial intelligence applications in manufacturing operations. J Adv Manuf Process 5(3):e10159

Ramvishvas Kumar (2024) AI manufacturing: revolutionizing process optimization and predictive maintenance. https://primathon.in/blog/ai-manufacturing-revolutionizing-process-optimization-and-predictive-maintenance/. Accessed 05 April 2024

Rauch E (2020) Industry 4.0+: the next level of intelligent and self-optimizing factories. In: Advances in design, simulation and manufacturing III: proceedings of the 3rd international conference on design, simulation, manufacturing: the innovation exchange, DSMIE-2020, June 9–12, 2020, Kharkiv, Ukraine–Volume 1: Manufacturing and Materials Engineering. Springer International Publishing, pp 176–186

Rüßmann M, Lorenz M, Gerbert P, Waldner M, Justus J, Engel P, Harnisch M (2015) Industry 4.0: The future of productivity and growth in manufacturing industries. Boston Consulting Group 9(1):54–89

Shahin M, Chen FF, Hosseinzadeh A, Zand N (2023) Using machine learning and deep learning algorithms for downtime minimization in manufacturing systems: an early failure detection diagnostic service. Int J Adv Manuf Technol 128(9–10):3857–3883

Śledziewska K, Włoch R (2021) How is production changing? In: The economics of digital transformation. Taylor & Francis

Soori M, Arezoo B, Dastres R (2023) Internet of things for smart factories in industry 4.0, a review. In: Internet of Things and cyber-physical systems

Tschang FT, Almirall E (2021) Artificial intelligence as augmenting automation: implications for employment. Acad Manag Perspect 35(4):642–659

Verganti R, Vendraminelli L, Iansiti M (2020) Innovation and design in the age of artificial intelligence. J Prod Innov Manag 37(3):212–227

Wamba-Taguimdje SL, Fosso Wamba S, Kala Kamdjoug JR, Tchatchouang Wanko CE (2020) Influence of artificial intelligence (AI) on firm performance: the business value of AI-based transformation projects. Bus Process Manag J 26(7):1893–1924

Wan J, Li X, Dai HN, Kusiak A, Martinez-Garcia M, Li D (2020) Artificial-intelligence-driven customized manufacturing factory: key technologies, applications, and challenges. Proc IEEE 109(4):377–398

WEF (2023) Factories of the future show how to apply AI to benefit people, planet and performance. https://www.weforum.org/press/2023/12/factories-of-the-future-show-how-to-apply-ai-to-benefit-people-planet-and-performance/. Accessed 04 April 2024

Weichert D, Link P, Stoll A, Rüping S, Ihlenfeldt S, Wrobel S (2019) A review of machine learning for the optimization of production processes. Int J Adv Manuf Technol 104(5):1889–1902

Williams K, Haslam C, Williams J (1992) Ford versus Fordism': the beginning of mass production? Work Employ Soc 6(4):517–555

Chapter 7
Opportunities and Challenges for Data-Driven and Circular Economy

Abstract The circular economy aims to decouple economic growth from resource consumption by promoting the reuse, recycling, and regeneration of materials and products. This chapter discusses how data-driven technologies, such as the Internet of Things (IoT), big data analytics, and machine learning, can enable the optimization of resource flows, facilitate the tracking and tracing of materials, and support decision-making for sustainable production and consumption. The chapter explores the role of policy and regulatory frameworks in promoting data-driven and circular economy practices. It discusses the need for supportive policies that incentivize data sharing, promote eco-design, and encourage collaboration among businesses, governments, and civil society.

Keywords Circular economy · Data-driven systems · Resources usage · Recycle · Policy

7.1 Introduction

The circular economy has gained increasing attention as a viable alternative to the traditional linear model of production and consumption. In the linear economy, resources are extracted, used to manufacture products, and then disposed of as waste after their intended use (Sariatli 2017). This linear model is inherently unsustainable, leading to resource depletion, environmental degradation, and economic inefficiency (Geissdoerfer et al. 2017). In contrast, the circular economy aims to decouple economic growth from resource consumption by promoting strategies such as reuse, recycling, and regeneration. Data-driven technologies play a crucial role in advancing the principles of the circular economy. These technologies, including the Internet of Things (IoT), big data analytics, and machine learning, enable the optimization of resource flows, facilitate the tracking and tracing of materials, and support decision-making for sustainable production and consumption (Tseng et al. 2022). By harnessing the power of real-time data and predictive analytics, data-driven approaches help businesses, governments, and other stakeholders transition towards

S. Kumar et al., *Digital Transformation, Artificial Intelligence and Society*, Frontiers of Artificial Intelligence, Ethics and Multidisciplinary Applications,
https://doi.org/10.1007/978-981-97-5656-8_7

more sustainable and resource-efficient practices. Numerous studies have highlighted the potential of data-driven technologies to drive the circular economy forward. For example, research published explores the role of digital technologies in enabling circular business models (Geissdoerfer et al. 2020). The authors argue that digitalization, including IoT sensors and data analytics, can enable the efficient management of material flows and facilitate the implementation of circular strategies such as product-as-a-service and closed-loop recycling. Furthermore, a study by Geng et al. (2019) published in the Journal of Industrial Ecology examines the application of big data analytics in optimising material flows within industrial ecosystems. The authors demonstrate how advanced analytics techniques can uncover hidden patterns and inefficiencies in material usage, leading to more sustainable resource management practices. Overall, the introduction sets the stage for the subsequent sections of the chapter by providing an overview of the circular economy and highlighting the transformative potential of data-driven technologies in advancing circular economy principles (Fig. 7.1).

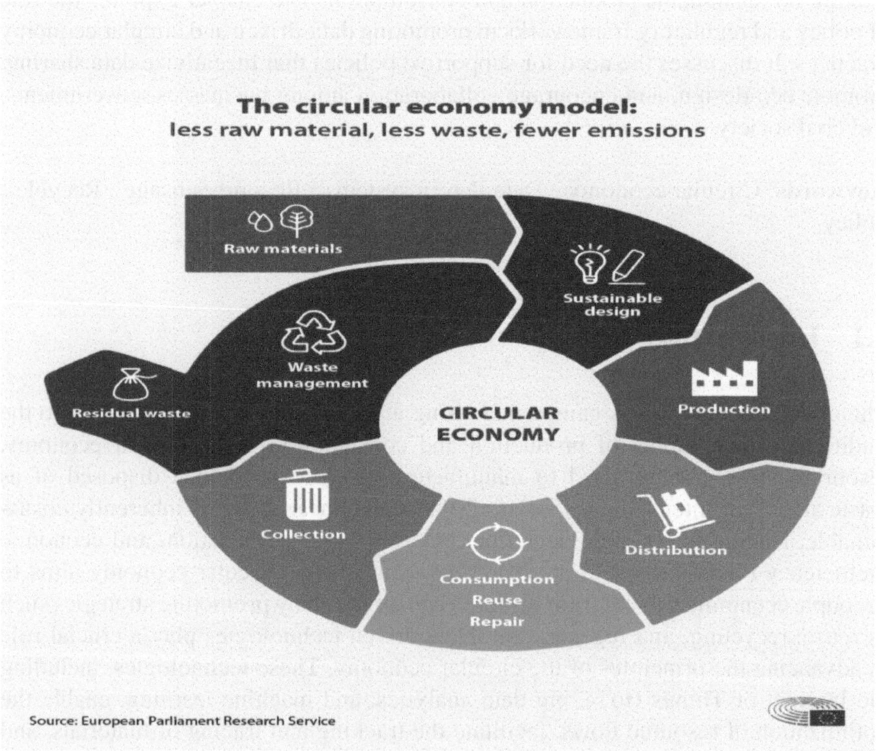

Fig. 7.1 Circular economy concept representation (https://www.europarl.europa.eu/topics/en/article/20151201STO05603/circular-economy-definition-importance-and-benefits)

7.2 Optimising Resource Flows

Optimising resource flows is a fundamental aspect of the circular economy, aiming to ensure that materials and products are utilised efficiently throughout their life cycles. Data-driven technologies play a crucial role in this optimization process by providing insights into resource usage, identifying inefficiencies, and facilitating informed decision-making (Wilkin et al. 2020). The Internet of Things (IoT) has emerged as a powerful tool for optimising resource flows in various industries. IoT sensors can be deployed throughout supply chains to monitor and track the movement of materials in real time. These sensors collect data on factors such as inventory levels, production rates, and energy consumption, allowing businesses to identify areas where resources are being underutilised or wasted. A study examines the application of IoT technology in optimising resource flows within manufacturing environments (da Silva et al. 2021). The authors demonstrate how IoT-enabled sensors can provide real-time visibility into production processes, enabling proactive maintenance and resource allocation decisions. In addition to IoT, big data analytics and machine learning offer advanced capabilities for optimising resource flows. Big data analytics techniques can process large volumes of data to identify patterns and trends, uncovering opportunities for resource optimization. Machine learning algorithms can then leverage this data to make predictive recommendations for improving resource efficiency (Fig. 7.2).

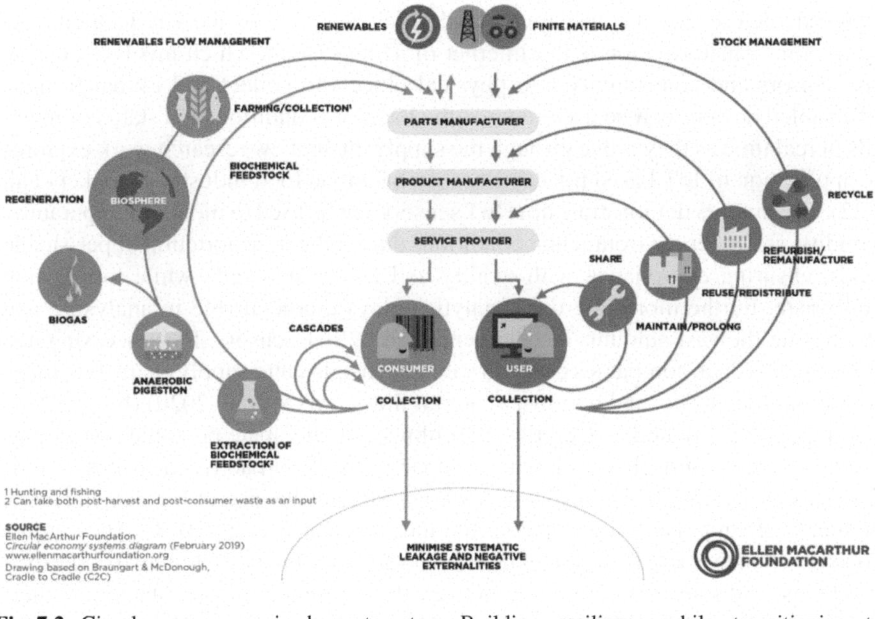

Fig. 7.2 Circular economy is here to stay—Building resilience while transitioning to circularity (https://inchainge.com/resources/blogs/circular-economy-is-here-to-stay-building-resilience-while-transitioning-to-circularity/)

Similalr type of research published investigates the use of machine learning algorithms for optimising inventory management in supply chains (Cavalcante et al. 2019). The authors propose a predictive model that uses historical data to forecast demand and optimise inventory levels, reducing waste and improving resource utilisation. Overall, data-driven technologies such as IoT, big data analytics, and machine learning offer powerful tools for optimising resource flows in the circular economy. By providing real-time insights and predictive capabilities, these technologies enable businesses to minimise waste, reduce costs, and enhance sustainability across their operations (Bressanelli et al. 2018).

7.3 Tracking and Tracing Materials

In a globalised economy where supply chains span across continents, ensuring the traceability of materials is paramount for promoting sustainability and accountability. Traceability refers to the ability to track the movement of materials or products throughout the supply chain, from raw material extraction to end-of-life disposal or recycling (Rusinek et al. 2018). By implementing robust traceability systems, companies can better understand the environmental and social impacts associated with their products, identify areas for improvement, and mitigate risks such as unethical sourcing or counterfeit products (Gayialis et al. 2022). The adoption of data-driven technologies has revolutionised the tracking and tracing of materials, offering unprecedented levels of transparency and efficiency. One of the key technologies driving this transformation is the Internet of Things (IoT), which involves embedding sensors and connectivity into physical objects to collect and exchange data. IoT-enabled devices can be used to track the location, condition, and status of materials in real time as they move through the supply chain. Few research work explores the application of IoT-based traceability systems in the food industry (Kayikci et al. 2022). The authors demonstrate how IoT sensors can be used to monitor temperature, humidity, and other environmental conditions during the transportation of perishable goods, ensuring compliance with quality and safety standards while minimising food waste. Furthermore, big data analytics plays a crucial role in analysing and interpreting the vast amounts of data generated by IoT sensors. By processing and analysing this data, companies can gain valuable insights into supply chain dynamics, identify inefficiencies, and optimise material flows (Aryal et al. 2020) (Fig. 7.3).

For example, predictive analytics algorithms can anticipate potential disruptions or delays in the supply chain, allowing companies to take proactive measures to mitigate risks (Aljohani 2023). Research work investigates the use of big data analytics for supply chain traceability in the textile industry (Zhou et al. 2024). The authors propose a framework that integrates data from various sources, including IoT sensors, RFID tags, and transaction records, to track the movement of raw materials, intermediate products, and finished goods. By leveraging big data analytics, companies can improve visibility and transparency across their supply chains, leading to more sustainable and ethical practices. Machine learning algorithms also play a significant

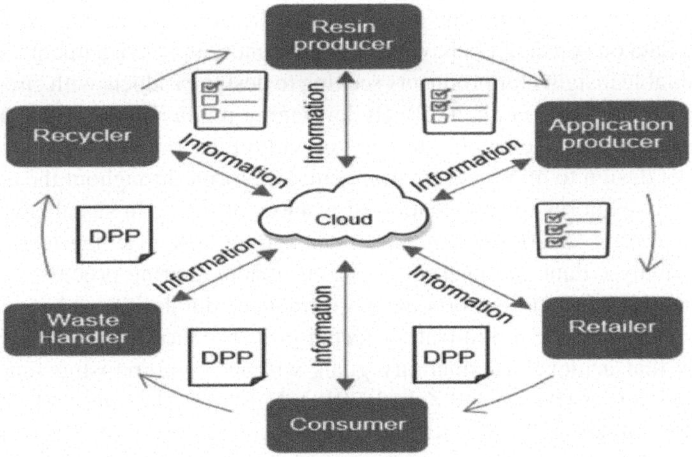

Fig. 7.3 Tracking of material (Pixabay GmbH. Pixabay—Kostenlose and Lizenzfreie Bilder. Available online: https://pixabay.com/de/ (accessed on 4 February 2023))

role in enhancing traceability and transparency in supply chains. These algorithms can analyse historical data to identify patterns and anomalies, detect fraudulent activities, and optimise routing and logistics operations. By continuously learning from new data, machine learning models can adapt to changing supply chain dynamics and improve performance over time. A study by (Wang et al. 2022) published in the Journal of Operations Management examines the use of machine learning algorithms for traceability and risk management in the automotive industry. The authors develop a predictive model that uses historical data on supplier performance, production processes, and quality control to identify potential risks and vulnerabilities in the supply chain. By proactively addressing these risks, companies can reduce the likelihood of disruptions and ensure the integrity and sustainability of their supply chains. Overall, data-driven technologies such as IoT, big data analytics, and machine learning offer powerful tools for enhancing traceability and transparency in supply chains. By providing real-time visibility into material flows, identifying risks and opportunities, and enabling proactive decision-making, these technologies empower companies to build more sustainable and resilient supply chains (Pessot et al. 2023).

7.4 Decision-Making for Sustainable Production and Consumption

In the pursuit of sustainable production and consumption, data-driven technologies play a pivotal role in shaping decision-making processes for both producers and consumers. Machine learning algorithms, in particular, have emerged as powerful tools for informing sustainable product design and influencing consumer behaviour towards more eco-conscious choices. Machine learning algorithms analyse vast amounts of data on consumer behaviour, market trends, and environmental impact to provide valuable insights for producers seeking to design products with circular principles in mind (Volkmar et al. 2022). By leveraging predictive analytics, producers can anticipate market demands, identify opportunities for innovation, and optimise product design to minimise environmental footprint throughout the entire lifecycle. A study explores the application of machine learning in sustainable product design (Tayal et al. 2020). The authors demonstrate how machine learning algorithms can analyse data on material properties, manufacturing processes, and end-of-life scenarios to optimise product performance, durability, and recyclability. Through simulation and optimization techniques, producers can identify design alternatives that achieve sustainability goals without compromising functionality or cost-effectiveness (Bazmi and Zahedi 2011). Moreover, data-driven technologies empower consumers with information on the sustainability footprint of products, thereby influencing purchasing decisions towards more environmentally friendly options. For instance, mobile apps and online platforms equipped with machine learning algorithms can provide consumers with real-time information on the environmental impact of products, such as carbon footprint, water usage, and waste generation (Chadoulos et al. 2020). Armed with such knowledge, consumers can make informed choices that align with their values and contribute to the circular economy (Fig. 7.4).

Research studies examine the role of information and communication technologies (ICT) in promoting sustainable consumption behaviour. The study highlights how ICT tools, including mobile apps and social media platforms, can raise awareness about the environmental and social implications of consumption choices, leading to shifts towards more sustainable lifestyles (Matharu et al. 2020). By

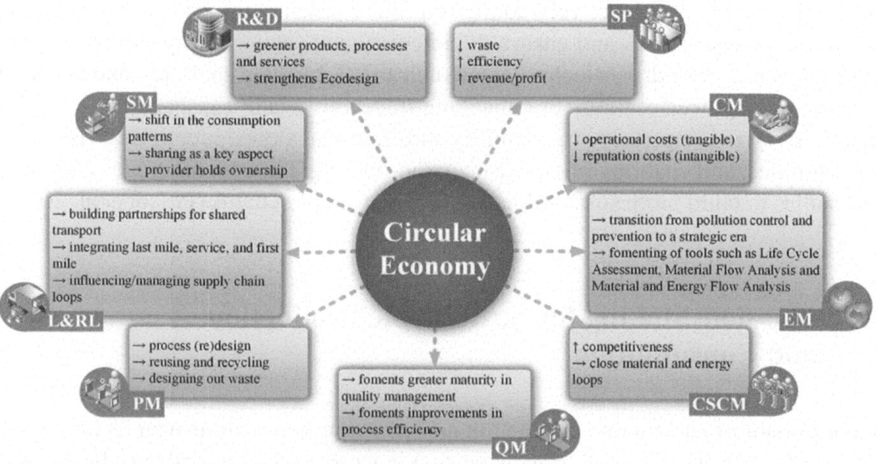

Fig. 7.4 Circular economy and decision-making for sustainable production and consumption (Barros et al. 2021)

leveraging data-driven insights, these technologies empower consumers to make conscious decisions that support circular economy principles. Furthermore, case studies provide concrete examples of how data-driven decision-making can promote sustainable production and consumption. For instance, Patagonia, a leading outdoor apparel company, employs machine learning algorithms to analyse customer feedback, product performance data, and supply chain information to drive sustainability initiatives (Sharma et al. 2023). By incorporating insights from data analytics into product design and marketing strategies, Patagonia has successfully cultivated a loyal customer base committed to sustainability (Grant 2020). In conclusion, data-driven technologies, particularly machine learning algorithms, have the potential to revolutionise decision-making processes for sustainable production and consumption. By providing actionable insights into market dynamics, consumer preferences, and environmental impacts, these technologies empower producers and consumers to drive positive change towards a circular economy (de Oliveira et al. 2023).

7.5 Role of Policy and Regulatory Frameworks

The integration of data-driven technologies into the circular economy requires a supportive policy and regulatory environment to realise its full potential (Fitch-Roy et al. 2021). Policy measures play a crucial role in incentivizing data sharing, promoting eco-design principles, and fostering collaboration among stakeholders. One key aspect of supportive policies is incentivizing data sharing among businesses, governments, and other stakeholders to facilitate transparency and collaboration. By encouraging the sharing of data on material flows, supply chain processes, and environmental impacts, policymakers can enable more informed decision-making and promote greater efficiency in resource use. A study examines the role of policy frameworks in promoting data sharing for sustainability (Hossain et al. 2020). The authors highlight the importance of regulatory measures such as data standardisation, interoperability, and privacy protection to overcome barriers to data sharing and promote collaboration among stakeholders. Additionally, policy measures can promote eco-design principles by incentivizing product innovation towards sustainability. Regulations such as extended producer responsibility (EPR) and eco-labelling schemes encourage manufacturers to design products with circularity in mind, considering factors such as material recyclability, product durability, and end-of-life management (de Souza Corrêa et al. 2022).

Several research works have explored the effectiveness of eco-design policies in promoting sustainable product development (Dahmani et al. 2021). The study evaluates the impact of regulatory measures such as the EU Eco-design Directive on the environmental performance of consumer products and highlights the importance of integrating eco-design principles into product design processes. Furthermore, policy frameworks can foster collaboration among businesses, governments, and civil society to address common challenges and promote best practices in the circular economy. Initiatives such as public–private partnerships, industry consortia,

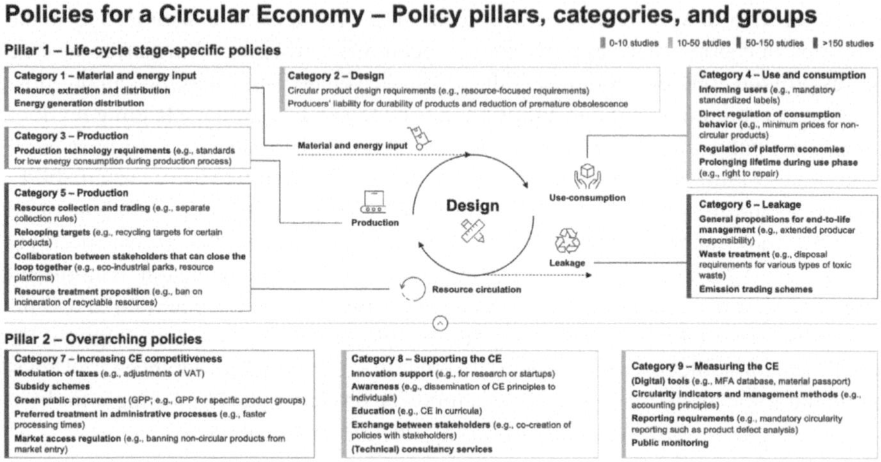

Fig. 7.5 Policies and regulation for circular economy (Hartley et al. 2023)

and multi-stakeholder platforms create opportunities for knowledge sharing, capacity building, and collective action towards sustainability goals (Fig. 7.5).

An article by Hartley, K., Schülzchen discusses the role of policy frameworks in advancing the circular economy transition. The article emphasises the importance of regulatory measures that incentivize collaboration and innovation, citing examples of successful policy initiatives from different regions, including the European Union, China, and Japan (Hartley et al. 2023).

Overall, supportive policy and regulatory frameworks are essential for integrating data-driven technologies into the circular economy. By incentivizing data sharing, promoting eco-design principles, and fostering collaboration, policymakers can create an enabling environment for sustainable innovation and accelerate the transition towards a circular economy.

7.6 Challenges and Limitations

While data-driven technologies offer tremendous potential for advancing the circular economy, their implementation is not without challenges and limitations. Identifying and addressing these obstacles is essential to maximising the benefits of data-driven approaches and overcoming barriers to adoption (Huo et al. 2024). One of the primary challenges is data privacy and security concerns associated with the collection, storage, and sharing of sensitive information. In the context of the circular economy, data on material flows, supply chain processes, and environmental impacts may contain proprietary or confidential information that needs to be protected from unauthorised access or misuse. A study explores the ecological ethics implications of data-driven approaches in the circular economy (Hoyng 2023). The authors highlight the need for robust data governance frameworks, encryption techniques, and access controls to safeguard sensitive information and ensure compliance with privacy regulations. Moreover, technological barriers such as interoperability, data quality, and scalability can hinder the effective implementation of data-driven technologies in the circular economy. Integrating diverse data sources, formats, and systems requires interoperable standards and protocols to ensure seamless data exchange and integration. There are technical challenges to implementing data-driven approaches for resource efficiency. Issues such as data fragmentation, inconsistency, and compatibility and propose strategies for overcoming these barriers through data standardisation and harmonisation efforts (Seng et al. 2021). In addition to technical challenges, resistance to change and organisational inertia can impede the adoption of data-driven technologies in traditional business models. Cultural barriers, lack of awareness, and perceived risks may deter companies from investing in new technologies or changing established practices. Several research studies also investigate the organisational barriers to data-driven innovation in the circular economy. The authors identify factors such as management support, employee skills, and organisational culture as critical determinants of successful technology adoption and suggest strategies for overcoming resistance to change. (Awan et al. 2021a, b).

Overall, addressing the challenges and limitations of data-driven technologies in the circular economy requires a holistic approach that encompasses technical, organisational, and regulatory dimensions. By implementing robust data governance frameworks, fostering collaboration and knowledge sharing, and promoting a culture of innovation and openness, stakeholders can unlock the full potential of data-driven approaches for sustainability.

7.7 Case Studies

Real-world case studies provide tangible examples of how data-driven technologies are being successfully applied to promote circular economy practices across various industries and sectors. These case studies offer insights into the key factors contributing to success, lessons learned, and implications for future implementation. One notable case study is the adoption of blockchain technology to enhance traceability and transparency in global supply chains. Blockchain, a decentralised and immutable ledger system, enables secure and transparent recording of transactions and data exchanges, making it ideal for tracking the movement of materials and products across complex supply networks. Research examines the use of blockchain-based traceability systems in the food and beverage industry. The authors highlight how blockchain technology enables real-time tracking of products from farm to fork, providing consumers with verifiable information on product origin, production methods, and supply chain integrity (Bosona and Gebresenbet 2023). Another compelling case study is the application of predictive analytics and machine learning algorithms to optimise waste management and resource recovery processes.

By analysing data on waste generation, composition, and disposal patterns, municipalities and waste management companies can identify opportunities for recycling, reuse, and recovery of valuable resources from waste streams. Research investigates the use of predictive analytics for municipal solid waste management. The authors develop a predictive model that analyses historical data on waste generation, demographic trends, and environmental factors to forecast future waste generation and plan resource allocation and infrastructure investments accordingly (Araiza-Aguilar et al. 2020). Furthermore, case studies from the manufacturing sector demonstrate how data-driven approaches are transforming traditional linear production systems into closed-loop, circular models. By leveraging IoT sensors, big data analytics, and machine learning algorithms, manufacturers can optimise material flows, improve resource efficiency, and reduce waste throughout the product life cycle.

Research studies of companies implementing circular business models enabled by data-driven technologies. The authors highlight examples from industries such as automotive, electronics, and textiles, illustrating how data analytics and digital platforms are driving innovation and sustainability across value chains. In conclusion, case studies provide concrete evidence of the transformative potential of data-driven technologies in promoting circular economy practices (Islam et al. 2022). By showcasing successful applications across different industries and sectors, these case studies inspire and inform future initiatives, driving continued progress towards a more sustainable and resource-efficient economy.

7.8 Future Directions

The future of the circular economy is intertwined with the evolution of data-driven technologies, presenting a myriad of opportunities for innovation and sustainable development (Chauhan et al. 2022). As we look ahead, several emerging trends and advancements are poised to further advance the circular economy, reshaping industries and driving transformative change. One of the key trends on the horizon is the convergence of data-driven technologies with emerging fields such as artificial intelligence (AI) and blockchain. AI holds immense potential for optimising resource flows and enhancing decision-making in the circular economy. By leveraging machine learning algorithms, AI systems can analyse vast amounts of data to identify patterns, predict future trends, and optimise processes for maximum efficiency. Blockchain technology, with its decentralised and immutable ledger system, offers new possibilities for enhancing transparency and traceability in supply chains (Cole et al. 2019). By recording transactions and tracking the movement of materials securely and transparently, blockchain can help verify the authenticity of products, prevent counterfeiting, and promote ethical sourcing practices. Research discusses the potential of blockchain to transform supply chains, emphasising its role in fostering trust and accountability in global trade (Chang et al. 2020). Furthermore, the Internet of Things (IoT) is expected to continue playing a pivotal role in shaping the future of the circular economy (Nobre and Tavares 2017). With the proliferation of connected devices and sensors, IoT technologies will enable unprecedented levels of visibility and control over material flows, production processes, and consumption patterns.

In addition to technological advancements, future developments in policy and regulation will also play a critical role in shaping the trajectory of the circular economy. Governments and regulatory bodies around the world are increasingly recognising the importance of sustainability and circularity, leading to the introduction of new policies and initiatives to support these objectives (Velenturf et al. 2018). For instance, the European Union's Circular Economy Action Plan sets ambitious targets for waste reduction, recycling, and resource efficiency, signalling a growing commitment to circularity at the legislative level (Domenech and Bahn-Walkowiak 2019).

As we explore future directions for the circular economy, it is essential to consider the broader societal and environmental implications of continued technological development. While data-driven technologies offer immense opportunities for innovation and efficiency, they also raise concerns about data privacy, the digital divide, and environmental impact (Bachmann et al. 2022). It is crucial to ensure that technological advancements are guided by principles of sustainability, equity, and social responsibility to avoid exacerbating existing inequalities and environmental degradation.

In light of these insights, a call to action is issued for policymakers, businesses, and stakeholders to collaborate in realising the full potential of data-driven approaches in advancing the circular economy (Awan et al. 2021a, b). By fostering innovation, promoting collaboration, and enacting supportive policies, we can accelerate the transition towards a more circular and regenerative economic model that benefits both people, the community and the planet. In closing, the convergence of data-driven technologies and the circular economy offers unprecedented opportunities for sustainable development and prosperity. By embracing this synergy and working together towards common goals, we can build a more resilient, equitable, and sustainable future for generations to come (Paniagua and Niembro-Garcia 2024).

References

Aljohani A (2023) Predictive analytics and machine learning for real-time supply chain risk mitigation and agility. Sustainability 15(20):15088

Araiza-Aguilar JA, Rojas-Valencia MN, Aguilar-Vera RA (2020) Forecast generation model of municipal solid waste using multiple linear regression. Global J Environ Sci Manag 6(1):1–14

Aryal A, Liao Y, Nattuthurai P, Li B (2020) The emerging big data analytics and IoT in supply chain management: a systematic review. Supply Chain Manag: Int J 25(2):141–156

Awan U, Shamim S, Khan Z, Zia NU, Shariq SM, Khan MN (2021a) Big data analytics capability and decision-making: The role of data-driven insight on circular economy performance. Technol Forecast Soc Chang 168:120766

Awan U, Sroufe R, Shahbaz M (2021b) Industry 4.0 and the circular economy: a literature review and recommendations for future research. Bus Strategy Environ 30(4):2038–2060

Bachmann N, Tripathi S, Brunner M, Jodlbauer H (2022) The contribution of data-driven technologies in achieving the sustainable development goals. Sustainability 14(5):2497

Barros MV, Salvador R, do Prado GF, de Francisco AC, Piekarski CM (2021) Circular economy as a driver to sustainable businesses. Clean Environ Syst 2:100006

Bazmi AA, Zahedi G (2011) Sustainable energy systems: role of optimization modelling techniques in power generation and supply—A review. Renew Sustain Energy Rev 15(8):3480–3500

Bosona T, Gebresenbet G (2023) The role of blockchain technology in promoting traceability systems in agri-food production and supply chains. Sensors 23(11):5342

Bressanelli G, Adrodegari F, Perona M, Saccani N (2018) Exploring how usage-focused business models enable circular economy through digital technologies. Sustainability 10(3):639

Cavalcante IM, Frazzon EM, Forcellini FA, Ivanov D (2019) A supervised machine learning approach to data-driven simulation of resilient supplier selection in digital manufacturing. Int J Inf Manag 49:86–97

Chadoulos S, Koutsopoulos I, Polyzos GC (2020) Mobile apps meet the smart energy grid: a survey on consumer engagement and machine learning applications. IEEE Access 8:219632–219655

Chang Y, Iakovou E, Shi W (2020) Blockchain in global supply chains and cross border trade: a critical synthesis of the state-of-the-art, challenges and opportunities. Int J Prod Res 58(7):2082–2099

Chauhan C, Parida V, Dhir A (2022) Linking circular economy and digitalisation technologies: a systematic literature review of past achievements and future promises. Technol Forecast Soc Chang 177:121508

Cole R, Stevenson M, Aitken J (2019) Blockchain technology: implications for operations and supply chain management. Supply Chain Manag: Int J 24(4):469–483

da Silva PC, de Oliveira Neto GC, Correia JMF, Tucci HNP (2021) Evaluation of economic, environmental and operational performance of the adoption of cleaner production: survey in large textile industries. J Clean Prod 278:123855

Dahmani N, Benhida K, Belhadi A, Kamble S, Elfezazi S, Jauhar SK (2021) Smart circular product design strategies towards eco-effective production systems: a lean eco-design industry 4.0 framework. J Clean Prod 320:128847

de Oliveira RT, Ghobakhloo M, Figueira S (2023) Industry 4.0 towards social and environmental sustainability in multinationals: enabling circular economy, organizational social practices, and corporate purpose. J Clean Prod 139712

de Souza Corrêa R, de Oliveira UR, Abdalla MM, Fernandes VA (2022) Systematic literature review on sustainable products: impact on organizations, research opportunities and future perspectives. Clean Waste Syst 1:100003

Domenech T, Bahn-Walkowiak B (2019) The transition towards a resource-efficient circular economy in Europe: policy lessons from the EU and the member states. Ecol Econ 155:7–19

Fitch-Roy O, Benson D, Monciardini D (2021) All around the world: assessing optimality in comparative circular economy policy packages. J Clean Prod 286:125493

Gayialis SP, Kechagias EP, Papadopoulos GA, Masouras D (2022) A review and classification framework of traceability approaches for identifying product supply chain counterfeiting. Sustainability 14(11):6666

Geissdoerfer M, Pieroni MP, Pigosso DC, Soufani K (2020) Circular business models: a review. J Clean Prod 277:123741

Geissdoerfer M, Savaget P, Bocken NM, Hultink EJ (2017) The circular economy—A new sustainability paradigm? J Clean Prod 143:757–768

Geng D, Zhang C, Xia C, Xia X, Liu Q, Fu X (2019) Big data-based improved data acquisition and storage system for designing industrial data platforms. IEEE Access 7:44574–44582

Grant J (2020) Greener marketing. John Wiley & Sons

Hartley K, Schülzchen S, Bakker CA, Kirchherr J (2023) A policy framework for the circular economy: lessons from the EU. J Clean Prod 412:137176

Hossain MU, Ng ST, Antwi-Afari P, Amor B (2020) Circular economy and the construction industry: existing trends, challenges and prospective framework for sustainable construction. Renew Sustain Energy Rev 130:109948

Hoyng R (2023) Ecological ethics and the smart circular economy. Big Data Soc 10(1):20539517231158996

Huo D, Malik AW, Ravana SD, Rahman AU, Ahmedy I (2024) Mapping smart farming: addressing agricultural challenges in a data-driven era. Renew Sustain Energy Rev 189:113858

Islam MT, Iyer-Raniga U, Trewick S (2022) Recycling perspectives of circular business models: a review. Recycling 7(5):79

Kayikci Y, Subramanian N, Dora M, Bhatia MS (2022) Food supply chain in the era of Industry 4.0: Blockchain technology implementation opportunities and impediments from the perspective of people, process, performance, and technology. Prod Plann Control 33(2–3):301–321

Matharu M, Jain R, Kamboj S (2020) Understanding the impact of lifestyle on sustainable consumption behaviour: a sharing economy perspective. Manag Environ Qual: Int J 32(1):20–40

Nobre GC, Tavares E (2017) Scientific literature analysis on big data and internet of things applications on circular economy: a bibliometric study. Scientometrics 111:463–492

Paniagua KL, Niembro-Garcia J (2024) Exploring the connection between digital systems and sustainability: synergy for a brighter future. In: Data-driven innovation for intelligent technology: perspectives and applications in ICT, pp 77–110

Pessot E, Zangiacomi A, Marchiori I, Fornasiero R (2023) Empowering supply chains with Industry 4.0 technologies to face megatrends. J Bus Logist 44(4):609–640

Rusinek MJ, Zhang H, Radziwill N (2018) Blockchain for a traceable, circular textile supply chain: a requirements approach. Softw Qual Prof 21(1)

Sariatli F (2017) Linear economy versus circular economy: a comparative and analyzer study for optimization of economy for sustainability. Visegrad J Bioecon Sustain Dev 6(1):31–34

Sharma A, Gaikwad A, Singh DP, Kalra R, Keerthi SS, Raj VH, Shaghnab ML (2023) Reshaping industry: adoption of sustainable techniques providing remanufacturing solutions in high-tech industries. In: E3S web of conferences, vol 453. EDP Sciences, p 01028

Tayal A, Solanki A, Singh SP (2020) Integrated framework for identifying sustainable manufacturing layouts based on big data, machine learning, meta-heuristic and data envelopment analysis. Sustain Cities Soc 62:102383

Tseng ML, Ha HM, Tran TPT, Bui TD, Chen CC, Lin CW (2022) Building a data-driven circular supply chain hierarchical structure: resource recovery implementation drives circular business strategy. Bus Strateg Environ 31(5):2082–2106

Velenturf AP, Purnell P, Tregent M, Ferguson J, Holmes A (2018) Co-producing a vision and approach for the transition towards a circular economy: perspectives from government partners. Sustainability 10(5):1401

Volkmar G, Fischer PM, Reinecke S (2022) Artificial intelligence and machine learning: exploring drivers, barriers, and future developments in marketing management. J Bus Res 149:599–614

Wang X, Bouzembrak Y, Lansink AO, van der Fels-Klerx HJ (2022) Application of machine learning to the monitoring and prediction of food safety: a review. Compr Rev Food Sci Food Saf 21(1):416–434

Wilkin C, Ferreira A, Rotaru K, Gaerlan LR (2020) Big data prioritization in SCM decision-making: its role and performance implications. Int J Account Inf Syst 38:100470

Zhou X, Lu H, Kumar Mangla S (2024) The impact of digital traceability on sustainability performance: investigating the roles of sustainability-oriented innovation and supply chain learning. Supply Chain Manag: Int J

Chapter 8
Industry 4.0 and International Relations Leading to Globalisation 4.0

Abstract This chapter examines the relationship between Industry 4.0 and international relations, with a focus on their role in shaping Globalisation 4.0. It explores how the Fourth Industrial Revolution, characterised by the integration of digital technologies and automation in manufacturing and other industries, is reshaping global economic, social, and political dynamics. It discusses how the digitalisation of industries is enabling global connectivity, cross-border collaboration, and the emergence of new economic and trade patterns. It examines the impact of Industry 4.0 on global value chains, labour markets, and the distribution of economic power. It examines how the digital transformation of industries and the increased interconnectivity of economies are shaping global governance, diplomatic relations, and international cooperation. In conclusion, Industry 4.0 and international relations are intricately linked, influencing and shaping Globalisation 4.0.

Keywords Industry 4.0 · International relations · Globalisation 4.0 · Digital technologies · Artificial intelligence · Diplomacy · Multilateral institutions

8.1 Industry 4.0 and Globalisation 4.0

In recent decades, the world has witnessed significant transformations driven by technological advancements and globalisation. Among these transformative forces, Industry 4.0 and Globalisation 4.0 stand out as pivotal paradigms reshaping the contemporary global landscape. Industry 4.0, often referred to as the Fourth Industrial Revolution, encompasses the integration of digital technologies into manufacturing and industrial processes (Voronkova et al. 2020). It represents a shift towards smart, interconnected systems that leverage automation, data analytics, artificial intelligence (AI), and the Internet of Things (IoT) to optimise production processes and enhance efficiency. Globalisation 4.0, on the other hand, reflects the evolving nature of globalisation in the digital age, characterised by increased interconnectedness, and cross-border flows of goods, services, capital, and information, facilitated by digital

S. Kumar et al., *Digital Transformation, Artificial Intelligence and Society*, Frontiers of Artificial Intelligence, Ethics and Multidisciplinary Applications,
https://doi.org/10.1007/978-981-97-5656-8_8

technologies (Chen and Martincus 2022). Scholars have highlighted the interconnectedness between Industry 4.0 and Globalisation 4.0, emphasising how technological advancements drive and shape global economic, social, and political dynamics (Castellani et al. 2022). For instance, Klaus Schwab, the founder and executive chairman of the World Economic Forum, argues that the Fourth Industrial Revolution is not occurring in isolation but is deeply intertwined with globalisation, leading to what he terms "Globalisation 4.0," where digital technologies are redefining the nature of economic activities and international relations (World Economic Forum 2016). To understand the profound implications of Industry 4.0 and Globalisation 4.0, it is essential to explore their interplay and how they collectively contribute to shaping the future of industries, economies, and societies on a global scale. We need to delve into these interconnected phenomena, examining their implications for manufacturing, industries, and international relations, and elucidating the transformative potential they hold for the global community.

8.2 Overview of Industry 4.0

Industry 4.0 represents a paradigm shift in manufacturing and industrial processes, driven by advancements in digital technologies. At its core, Industry 4.0 harnesses the power of connectivity, automation, and data analytics to create smart, efficient, and agile production systems. Key factors of Industry 4.0 include the following:

- Digital Transformation: Industry 4.0 is characterised by the digital transformation of manufacturing processes, enabled by technologies such as the Internet of Things (IoT), artificial intelligence (AI), and advanced robotics. According to a report by McKinsey, by 2025, Industry 4.0 could create between $3.7 trillion and $6.7 trillion in value globally in various industries (Schmitz et al. 2019). For example, the German manufacturing company, Siemens, utilises IoT sensors and AI algorithms to optimise production processes. Their "Factory of the Future" initiative has reduced downtime by 50% and increased productivity by 10% (Koren 2021).
- Artificial Intelligence (AI): AI technologies, such as machine learning and cognitive computing, enable machines to mimic human cognitive functions, including learning, reasoning, and problem-solving (Konar 2018). In manufacturing, AI-driven systems can optimise production processes, predict maintenance needs, and automate tasks, leading to increased efficiency and productivity (Javaid et al. 2022).
- Internet of Things (IoT): The IoT enables the interconnection of physical devices and objects embedded with sensors, software, and connectivity, facilitating real-time data exchange and communication between machines, systems, and humans (Borgia 2014). This interconnectedness enhances visibility, control, and decision-making in manufacturing environments. The number of connected IoT devices is projected to reach 41.6 billion by 2025, according to a report by Statista (Kolny 2021). In the automotive industry, Tesla utilises IoT sensors in its vehicles to

gather data on performance, driving habits, and maintenance needs. This data is used to improve vehicle functionality and provide predictive maintenance services (Vermesan et al. 2022).

- Big Data Analytics: Big data analytics involves the collection, processing, and analysis of large volumes of data to extract actionable insights and patterns (Saggi and Jain 2018). By leveraging advanced analytics techniques, manufacturers can gain valuable insights into production processes, customer preferences, and market trends, enabling data-driven decision-making and personalised customization (Ren et al. 2019). Industry 4.0 generates vast amounts of data, which is analysed to extract valuable insights for decision-making and process optimization. The global big data analytics market size is expected to reach $103 billion by 2027, growing at a compound annual growth rate (CAGR) of 10.9%, according to a report by Grand View Research (2024). For instance, General Electric (GE) uses big data analytics in its aviation division to analyse data from aircraft engines and predict maintenance needs. This proactive approach has led to a 20% reduction in maintenance costs (Bumblauskas et al. 2017).
- Robotics: Industry 4.0 incorporates advanced robotics systems capable of performing complex tasks autonomously. As per reports, The global industrial robotics market size is expected to reach $77.6 billion by 2027, growing at a CAGR of 14.5%, according to a report by Fortune Business Insights (2024). To understand this, we need to see that Amazon employs over 200,000 robotic systems in its fulfilment centres worldwide (Anh 2019). These robots work alongside human employees to automate tasks such as picking, packing, and sorting. Robotics plays a crucial role in Industry 4.0, encompassing a wide range of automated machines and systems capable of performing tasks traditionally performed by humans. Collaborative robots (cobots), autonomous drones, and robotic arms are among the innovative robotic technologies transforming manufacturing operations, and enhancing precision, speed, and safety (Goel and Gupta 2020).
- 3D Printing/Additive Manufacturing: Additive manufacturing technologies, such as 3D printing, enable layer-by-layer fabrication of complex three-dimensional objects from digital designs. This disruptive technology offers numerous benefits, including rapid prototyping, on-demand production, design flexibility, and waste reduction, revolutionising traditional manufacturing processes (Murr 2016). Additive manufacturing technologies enable the on-demand production of complex parts and prototypes. The global 3D printing market size is projected to reach $51.77 billion by 2026, growing at a CAGR of 21.8%, according to a report by https://www.manufacturingtodayindia.com/6019-3d-printing-market-to-reach-5177-billion-by-2026/#:~:text=The%20global%203D%20Printing%20Market,market%20in%20the%20forthcoming%20years., https://www.alliedmarketresearch.com/3d-printing-market. Boeing utilises 3D printing to manufacture components for its aircraft, resulting in reduced production costs and lead times (Singamneni et al. 2019) (Fig. 8.1).
- Digital Twin Technology: Digital twins create virtual replicas of physical assets or systems, enabling simulation, monitoring, and optimization. As far as facts are concerned, the digital twin market size is expected to reach $48.2 billion

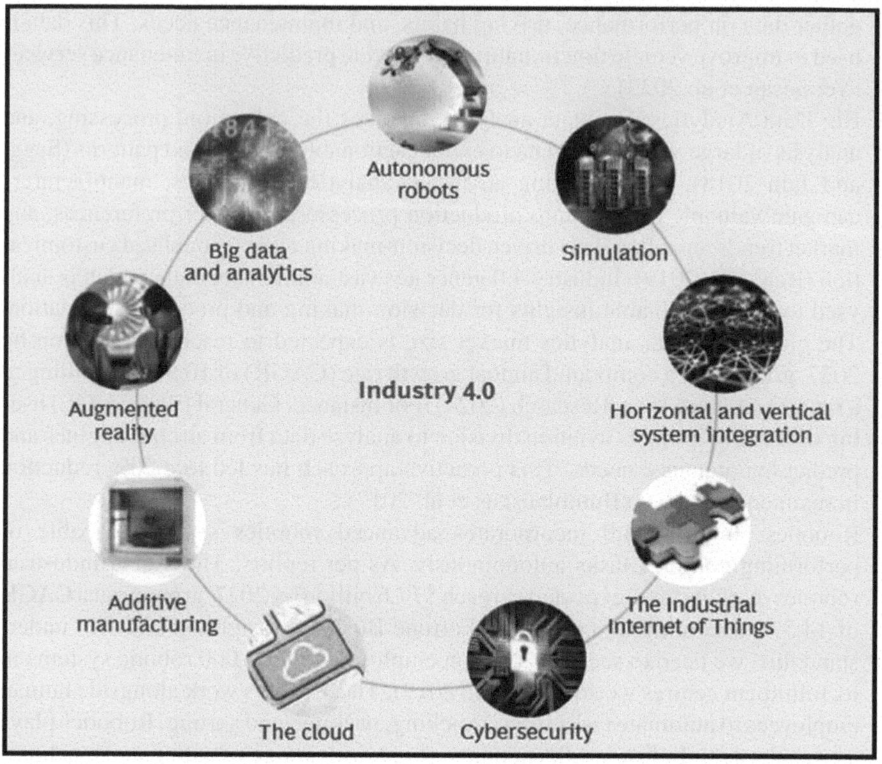

Fig. 8.1 Key technologies in Industry 4.0 (Toward Digital Twin and Simulation-Driven New Product Development—Scientific Figure on ResearchGate. Available from: https://www.researchgate.net/figure/Industry-40-key-technologies-source-BCG-Simulation-seen-as-enabler-is-foundational-in_fig2_326579729 [accessed 25 Apr, 2024])

by 2026, growing at a CAGR of 58.25%, according to a report (Staff Writer 2020). For example, Rolls-Royce utilises digital twins to simulate and optimise the performance of aircraft engines, enabling predictive maintenance and fuel efficiency improvements (Hartwell et al. 2024).

These key features of Industry 4.0 collectively enable the creation of "smart factories" and interconnected production systems that are more agile, efficient, and responsive to changing market demands. By embracing digital technologies, manufacturers can unlock new opportunities for innovation, growth, and competitiveness in an increasingly dynamic and interconnected global marketplace and setting the stage for transformation of global international realities and diplomacy.

8.3 Industry 4.0 and Its Impact on Industries

The advent of Industry 4.0 is revolutionising manufacturing processes and industries worldwide, ushering in a new era of digital transformation and technological innovation. The impact of Industry 4.0 on manufacturing and industries is profound and multifaceted, encompassing several key areas:

- Increased Efficiency: Industry 4.0 technologies, such as IoT sensors, AI-driven analytics, and robotics, enable manufacturers to streamline production processes, optimise resource allocation, and minimise waste (Jamwal et al. 2021). By harnessing real-time data and predictive analytics, manufacturers can identify inefficiencies, improve workflow management, and enhance overall operational efficiency (Omar et al. 2019).
- Flexibility and Customization: Industry 4.0 enables greater flexibility and customization in manufacturing, allowing companies to adapt quickly to changing market demands and customer preferences. Additive manufacturing technologies, such as 3D printing, enable the on-demand production of personalised products, while AI-driven automation facilitates agile production processes and rapid reconfiguration of manufacturing systems (Rüßmann et al. 2015).
- Supply Chain Optimization: Industry 4.0 facilitates the optimization of supply chains through enhanced visibility, traceability, and collaboration. IoT-enabled sensors and RFID tags enable real-time monitoring of inventory levels, shipment tracking, and supply chain logistics, reducing lead times, minimising stockouts, and improving overall supply chain efficiency (Zhang et al. 2023).
- Product Innovation and Development: Industry 4.0 fosters innovation and product development through digital design tools, simulation technologies, and rapid prototyping techniques (Tsaramirsis et al. 2022). By leveraging digital twins and virtual simulations, manufacturers can accelerate product development cycles, optimise design iterations, and bring new products to market faster and more cost-effectively (Jiao et al. 2021).
- Workforce Transformation: Industry 4.0 is reshaping the workforce and labour market, requiring new skill sets and competencies to thrive in the digital age. While automation and robotics may lead to job displacement in some areas, they also create new opportunities for skilled workers in data analytics, cybersecurity, and advanced manufacturing technologies. Education and training programmes are essential to equip the workforce with the skills needed to succeed in the era of Industry 4.0 (Marku 2024).
- Overall, the impact of Industry 4.0 on manufacturing and industries is transformative, leading to increased efficiency, flexibility, and innovation across the value chain. By embracing digital technologies and leveraging data-driven insights, manufacturers can unlock new opportunities for growth, competitiveness, and sustainability in an increasingly interconnected and dynamic global economy (Koh et al. 2019).

8.4 Industry4.0 and Global Economic Implications

Industry 4.0 is fundamentally reshaping global economic structures, trade patterns, and the competitiveness of nations. This transformation is driven by the integration of digital technologies into manufacturing and industrial processes, leading to the emergence of digital economies and the reconfiguration of traditional value chains. One significant implication of Industry 4.0 is the rise of digital economies, characterised by the proliferation of digital products, services, and platforms (Rainnie and Dean 2020). Digital technologies enable companies to create new business models, disrupt traditional industries, and capitalise on the growing demand for digital goods and services (Zaki 2019). This shift towards digitalization is fueling economic growth and innovation in sectors such as e-commerce, fintech, and digital entertainment, creating new opportunities for entrepreneurship and investment.

Industry 4.0 is leading to the reconfiguration of global value chains, as companies seek to leverage digital technologies to optimise production processes and enhance supply chain efficiency. Traditional manufacturing hubs are facing increased competition from emerging digital manufacturing centres, where advanced technologies such as 3D printing and robotics are driving production innovation and cost savings (Reynolds 2017). This reconfiguration of value chains is reshaping trade patterns and challenging established notions of comparative advantage, as countries compete to attract investment and skilled talent in the digital economy.

Industry 4.0 is influencing the competitiveness of nations by emphasising the importance of digital infrastructure, innovation ecosystems, and human capital development. Countries that invest in digital infrastructure, foster innovation, and upskill their workforce are better positioned to thrive in the era of Industry 4.0, attracting investment, talent, and technology transfer (Annunziata and Bourgeois 2018). Conversely, countries that fail to adapt to the digital transformation risk falling behind and experiencing economic stagnation.

Industry 4.0 is driving profound economic changes on a global scale, ushering in the rise of digital economies, the reconfiguration of value chains, and the reshaping of national competitiveness. To harness the opportunities presented by Industry 4.0, countries must embrace digitalization, invest in innovation, and prioritise human capital development to remain competitive in the increasingly interconnected and dynamic global economy (Andreoni et al. 2021).

8.5 Industry 4.0 and Social and Labour Market Dynamics

The advent of Industry 4.0 is having profound socio-economic implications, particularly in terms of employment, skills requirements, income inequality, and the future of work (Balliester and Elsheikhi 2018). While Industry 4.0 offers opportunities for increased productivity and innovation, it also presents challenges related to job displacement, skills mismatches, and income inequality (Tommasi et al. 2022). One of the primary concerns associated with Industry 4.0 is its impact on employment. Automation and robotics are increasingly replacing routine and repetitive tasks, leading to job displacement in certain industries and occupations (Autor 2015). While new job opportunities are emerging in fields such as data analytics, cybersecurity, and advanced manufacturing, there is a growing need for workers to acquire digital skills and adapt to changing job requirements. Additionally, Industry 4.0 is exacerbating skills requirements, as employers seek workers with proficiency in digital technologies, critical thinking, problem-solving, and adaptability (Maisiri et al. 2019). The mismatch between the skills demanded by the labour market and those possessed by workers is widening, leading to structural unemployment and underemployment. Addressing this skills gap requires investment in education and training programmes that equip workers with the digital literacy and technical skills needed to succeed in the digital economy. Income inequality is another pressing issue exacerbated by Industry 4.0. While digital technologies create opportunities for wealth generation and entrepreneurship, they also concentrate wealth and power in the hands of a few tech giants and skilled professionals. This widening gap between the wealthy elite and the rest of society can lead to social unrest, political instability, and disparities in access to opportunities and resources (Fuentes-Nieva and Galasso 2014).

Let us take a case Germany, known for its strong manufacturing base, has been at the forefront of Industry 4.0 adoption (Dachs et al. 2019). This transformation has led to increased productivity and competitiveness in the global market. However, it has also resulted in significant changes in the labour market. While some traditional manufacturing jobs have been replaced by automation, there is a growing demand for skilled workers capable of operating and maintaining advanced machinery and systems. Germany's vocational education and training programmes have been crucial in addressing this demand by providing workers with the necessary skills (Barabasch and Watt-Malcolm 2013). This transition highlights the importance of education and upskilling in adapting to the changes brought about by Industry 4.0.

Another case can be China's ambitious industrial strategy. China has embarked on an ambitious industrial strategy to become a global leader in advanced manufacturing and technology. The "Made in China 2025" initiative aims to upgrade the country's industries through innovation and the adoption of cutting-edge technologies (Akkemik and Yülek 2020). While this initiative has the potential to propel China's economy to new heights, it also raises concerns about its impact on the global labour market. China's massive manufacturing sector employs millions of workers, and the widespread adoption of automation and AI could lead to job displacement on a significant scale (Xie et al. 2021). This could have implications for international relations, as countries grapple with the challenges of managing displaced workers and potential economic disruptions.

Industry 4.0 has the potential to exacerbate existing inequalities between developed and developing countries. While advanced economies have the resources and infrastructure to embrace new technologies, many developing nations struggle to keep pace. The digital divide, characterised by disparities in access to technology and digital skills, poses challenges for inclusive economic growth and international cooperation (Riggins and Dewan 2005). Bridging this gap requires concerted efforts from governments, businesses, and international organisations to provide technical assistance, capacity building, and investment in infrastructure. Failure to address these disparities could widen the divide and contribute to social and political instability in regions already grappling with economic hardship (Bailey and De Propris 2019).

Industry 4.0 has also given rise to new forms of employment, such as the gig economy, where individuals work on a freelance or contractual basis through digital platforms (Ungureanu 2019). While this offers flexibility and opportunities for entrepreneurship, it also raises questions about job security, labour rights, and social protection (Fig. 8.2). The gig economy blurs traditional boundaries between employers and workers, making it challenging to regulate and protect workers' rights. This dynamic has implications for international relations, as governments seek to balance the need for innovation and economic growth with the protection of workers' rights and social stability.

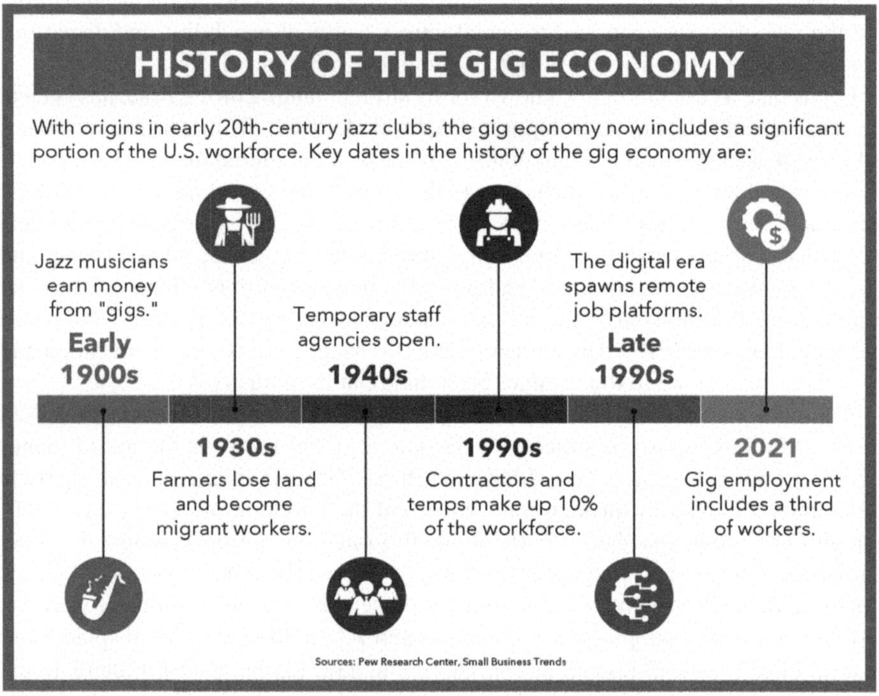

Fig. 8.2 Gig economy progression (https://online.maryville.edu/blog/what-is-the-gig-economy/)

8.6 Industry 4.0 and International Relations and Global Challenges

Industry 4.0 is reshaping international relations and diplomacy, leading to new forms of cooperation, competition, and conflict among nations. As digital technologies become increasingly integrated into manufacturing and industrial processes, countries are vying for technological leadership, market dominance, and strategic advantage in the global digital economy (Voronkova et al. 2020).

One way Industry 4.0 is shaping international relations is through cooperation and collaboration among countries to harness the benefits of digital technologies for economic development, innovation, and societal progress. Initiatives such as international research partnerships, technology transfer agreements, and joint investment projects facilitate knowledge exchange, skill development, and technology diffusion across borders, fostering global innovation ecosystems (Sozinova 2019). However, Industry 4.0 also creates competition and rivalry among countries seeking to gain a competitive edge in the digital economy. Nations are investing heavily in research and development, talent acquisition, and infrastructure development to build digital capabilities and attract investment in key strategic sectors. This competition for technological leadership and market share can lead to geopolitical tensions, trade disputes, and protectionist policies aimed at safeguarding national interests and economic competitiveness (Roberts et al. 2019). Moreover, Industry 4.0 raises concerns about data governance, cybersecurity, and intellectual property rights, which have become increasingly salient issues in international diplomacy (Culot et al. 2019). Countries are grappling with how to regulate data flows, Data privacy and protection are also critical issues in the context of Industry 4.0, as the proliferation of digital technologies generates vast amounts of data that can be exploited for various purposes (Arner et al. 2022). Ensuring robust data privacy laws and regulations is essential to protect individuals' rights to privacy and control over their personal data. Policymakers must work to establish clear guidelines and standards for data collection, storage, processing, and sharing, as well as mechanisms for accountability and enforcement to prevent data breaches and abuses.

Cybersecurity is another pressing concern in the era of Industry 4.0, as interconnected digital systems and networks are vulnerable to cyber threats and attacks (Süzen 2020). The increasing reliance on digital technologies in critical infrastructure, manufacturing processes, and everyday life heightens the risk of cyber attacks with potentially catastrophic consequences. Policymakers must invest in cybersecurity measures, such as threat detection, incident response, and information sharing, to protect against cyber threats and ensure the resilience of digital infrastructure and systems (Tiirmaa-Klaar 2016).

Moreover, ethical considerations surrounding emerging technologies, such as artificial intelligence, robotics, and biotechnology, raise complex ethical dilemmas that require careful consideration and deliberation (Boldt and Orrù 2022). Issues such as algorithmic bias, autonomous decision-making, and the impact of technology on employment and human rights demand ethical guidelines and frameworks to ensure that technological advancements are aligned with societal values and norms (Fernández Fernández 2022). Policymakers, researchers, and industry stakeholders must engage in interdisciplinary dialogue and collaboration to address these ethical concerns and promote responsible innovation in the digital age.

8.7 Geopolitical Implications

The advent of Industry 4.0 has profound geopolitical implications, reshaping the global landscape and giving rise to new dynamics of power, competition, and cooperation among nations. As digital technologies become increasingly central to economic, military, and strategic interests, countries are trying for technological dominance, influence, and control in the digital age (Khanna 2016).

One key geopolitical implication of Industry 4.0 is the emergence of tech superpowers, as countries with advanced technological capabilities seek to assert dominance and influence in the global digital economy (Diegues and Roselino 2023). Nations such as the United States, China, and the European Union are investing heavily in research and development, talent acquisition, and infrastructure development to position themselves as leaders in key strategic sectors such as artificial intelligence, quantum computing, and cybersecurity (Nouwens and Legarda 2018). This competition for technological leadership and innovation supremacy has significant implications for global power dynamics and strategic rivalries.

Industry 4.0 exacerbates digital divide issues, as countries with limited technological capabilities or access to digital infrastructure risk falling behind in the digital race (Helsper 2021). The growing disparity between tech-savvy nations and digitally disadvantaged regions widens existing inequalities and creates new challenges in terms of access to opportunities, resources, and development prospects. Bridging the digital divide requires concerted efforts to expand digital infrastructure, improve digital literacy, and promote inclusive and equitable access to technology and information.

Industry 4.0 gives rise to geopolitical tensions and conflicts arising from competition for technological dominance, control over critical digital infrastructure, and protectionist measures aimed at safeguarding national interests. Issues such as data sovereignty, intellectual property rights, and cybersecurity become flashpoints in international relations, leading to trade disputes, diplomatic tensions, and geopolitical rivalries (Bauer and Erixon 2020). Managing these tensions and promoting cooperation and dialogue are essential to prevent escalation and foster stability and peace in the digital age.

Industry 4.0 has far-reaching geopolitical implications, shaping global power dynamics, digital divide issues, and geopolitical tensions among nations (Bánkuty-Balogh 2024). Policymakers must navigate these complexities and promote cooperation, dialogue, and multilateralism to address common challenges and harness the transformative potential of digital technologies for the benefit of all.

8.8 International Collaboration and Partnerships

International collaboration and partnerships are crucial for harnessing the benefits of Industry 4.0 for global development, and innovation, and addressing common challenges. Several initiatives and examples of collaboration exist, aimed at leveraging digital technologies to tackle shared issues and promote sustainable development (Kagermann et al. 2016).

One prominent example of international collaboration is the European Union's Horizon 2020 programme, which funds research and innovation projects across various sectors, including advanced manufacturing, digitalization, and sustainable development (Pollex and Lenschow 2018). Through collaborative projects involving multiple countries and stakeholders, Horizon 2020 aims to drive technological innovation, promote knowledge exchange, and address societal challenges such as climate change, resource scarcity, and demographic shifts (Veugelers et al. 2015).

Additionally, multilateral organisations such as the World Bank and the United Nations play a vital role in fostering international collaboration and partnerships for sustainable development. Initiatives such as the UN Sustainable Development Goals (SDGs) provide a framework for global cooperation on key issues such as poverty alleviation, healthcare, education, and environmental sustainability (Morton et al. 2017). Industry 4.0 technologies, such as IoT-enabled smart cities, renewable energy systems, and digital healthcare solutions, offer innovative approaches to achieving the SDGs and advancing global development goals (Zengin et al. 2021).

Public–private partnerships (PPPs) are instrumental in driving innovation and scaling up Industry 4.0 solutions for societal benefit (Ma et al. 2022). Collaborative initiatives between governments, businesses, academia, and civil society organisations facilitate technology transfer, knowledge sharing, and capacity building, leading to the adoption of sustainable practices and the creation of inclusive economic opportunities.

Looking ahead, the future of Industry 4.0 holds immense promise for advancing human progress and sustainable development. By fostering international collaboration and partnerships, leveraging digital technologies for global development, and addressing ethical and societal concerns, we can harness the transformative potential of Industry 4.0 to build a more inclusive, equitable, and resilient world (Zhanbayev et al. 2023).

As we navigate the complex and evolving landscape of Industry 4.0 and Globalisation 4.0, it is essential to adopt a forward-looking and collaborative approach, grounded in the principles of sustainability, social responsibility, and ethical stewardship (Van Tulder and van Mil 2022). By working together across borders and sectors, we can unlock new opportunities for innovation, prosperity, and shared prosperity in the digital age.

References

Akkemik KA, Yülek M (2020) Made in China 2025" and the recent industrial policy in China. In: Designing integrated industrial policies Volume I. Routledge, pp 337–364

Andreoni A, Barnes J, Black A, Sturgeon T (2021) Digitalization, industrialization, and skills development: opportunities and challenges for middle-income countries

Anh T (2019) Artificial intelligence in e-commerce: case Amazon

Annunziata M, Bourgeois H (2018) The future of work: how G20 countries can leverage digital-industrial innovations into stronger high-quality jobs growth. Economics 12(1):20180042

Arner DW, Castellano GG, Selga EK (2022) The transnational data governance problem. Berkeley Technol Law J 37:623

Autor DH (2015) Why are there still so many jobs? The history and future of workplace automation. J Econ Perspect 29(3):3–30

Bailey D, De Propris L (2019) 6. Industry 4.0, regional disparities and transformative industrial policy. Reg Stud Policy Impact Books 1(2):67–78

Balliester T, Elsheikhi A (2018) The future of work: a literature review. ILO Research Department Working Paper 29:1–54

Bánkuty-Balogh LS (2024) The intersection of geopolitics and technological innovations: implications for the Central-European region. Doctoral dissertation, Budapesti Corvinus Egyetem

Barabasch A, Watt-Malcolm B (2013) Teacher preparation for vocational education and training in Germany: a potential model for Canada? Compare: J Comparat Int Educ 43(2):155–183

Bauer M, Erixon F (2020) Europe's quest for technology sovereignty: opportunities and pitfalls (No. 02/2020). ECIPE Occasional Paper

Boldt J, Orrù E (2022) Towards a unified list of ethical principles for emerging technologies. An analysis of four European reports on molecular biotechnology and artificial intelligence. Sustainable Futures 4, 100086

Borgia E (2014) The Internet of Things vision: key features, applications and open issues. Comput Commun 54:1–31

Bumblauskas D, Gemmill D, Igou A, Anzengruber J (2017) Smart maintenance decision support systems (SMDSS) based on corporate big data analytics. Expert Syst Appl 90:303–317

Castellani D, Lamperti F, Lavoratori K (2022) Measuring adoption of industry 4.0 technologies via international trade data: insights from European countries. J Ind Bus Econ 49(1):51–93

Chen M, Martincus CV (2022) Digital technologies and globalization: a survey of research and policy applications.

Culot G, Fattori F, Podrecca M, Sartor M (2019) Addressing industry 4.0 cybersecurity challenges. IEEE Eng Manag Rev 47(3):79–86

Dachs B, Kinkel S, Jäger A (2019) Bringing it all back home? Backshoring of manufacturing activities and the adoption of Industry 4.0 technologies. J World Bus 54(6):101017

Diegues AC, Roselino JE (2023) Industrial policy, techno-nationalism and Industry 4.0: China-USA technology war. Braz J Polit Econ 43:5–25

Fernández Fernández JL (2022) Ethical considerations regarding biases in algorithms

Fortune Business Insights (2024) The global industrial robots market size was valued at $16.78 billion in 2022 & is projected to grow from $18.19 billion in 2023 to $41.02 billion by 2030... https://www.fortunebusinessinsights.com/industry-reports/industrial-robots-market-100360 Accessed 08 April 2024

Fuentes-Nieva R, Galasso N (2014) Working for the few: political capture and economic inequality, vol 178. Oxfam

Goel R, Gupta P (2020) Robotics and industry 4.0. A roadmap to industry 4.0: smart production. In: Sharp business and sustainable development, pp 157–169

Ground View Research (2024) Data analytics market size, share & trends analysis report by type (Prescriptive Analytics, Predictive Analytics, Customer Analytics, Descriptive Analytics), By solution, by application, by region, and segment forecasts, 2023—2030. https://www.grandviewresearch.com/industry-analysis/data-analytics-market-report. Accessed 08 April 2024

Hartwell A, Montana F, Jacobs W, Kadirkamanathan V, Ameri N, Mills AR (2024) Distributed digital twins for health monitoring: resource constrained aero-engine fleet management. Aeronaut J 1–20

Helsper E (2021) The digital disconnect: the social causes and consequences of digital inequalities. The Digital Disconnect, pp 1–232

Jamwal A, Agrawal R, Sharma M, Giallanza A (2021) Industry 4.0 technologies for manufacturing sustainability: a systematic review and future research directions. Appl Sci 11(12):5725

Javaid M, Haleem A, Singh RP, Suman R (2022) Artificial intelligence applications for industry 4.0: a literature-based study. J Ind Integr Manag 7(1):83–111

Jiao R, Commuri S, Panchal J, Milisavljevic-Syed J, Allen JK, Mistree F, Schaefer D (2021) Design engineering in the age of industry 4.0. J Mech Des 143(7):070801

Kagermann H, Anderl R, Gausemeier J, Schuh G, Wahlster W (eds) (2016) Industrie 4.0 in a global context: strategies for cooperating with international partners. Herbert Utz Verlag

Khanna P (2016) Connectography: mapping the future of global civilization. Random House

Koh L, Orzes G, Jia FJ (2019) The fourth industrial revolution (Industry 4.0): technologies disruption on operations and supply chain management. Int J Oper Prod Manag 39(6/7/8):817–828

Kolny B (2021) Equipping households with durable goods in the age of the Internet of Things. Acta Scientiarum Polonorum. Oeconomia 20(3):23–32

Konar A (2018) Artificial intelligence and soft computing: behavioral and cognitive modeling of the human brain. CRC Press

Koren Y (2021) The local factory of the future for producing individualized products. The Bridge 51(1):100

Ma M, Wang N, Mu W, Zhang L (2022) The instrumentality of public-private partnerships for achieving sustainable development goals. Sustainability 14(21):13756

Maisiri W, Darwish H, Van Dyk L (2019) An investigation of industry 4.0 skills requirements. S Afr J Ind Eng 30(3):90–105

Marku M (2024) Navigating the future of work: human capital in the age of industry 4.0. Interdiscip J Res Dev 11(1):190–190

Morton S, Pencheon D, Squires N (2017) Sustainable Development Goals (SDGs), and their implementation: a national global framework for health, development and equity needs a systems approach at every level. Br Med Bull 124(1):81–90

Murr LE (2016) Frontiers of 3D printing/additive manufacturing: from human organs to aircraft fabrication. J Mater Sci Technol 32(10):987–995

Nouwens M, Legarda H (2018) Emerging technology dominance: what China's pursuit of advanced dual-use technologies means for the future of Europe's economy and defence innovation. International Institute for Strategic Studies/Mercator Institute for China Studies China Security Project 12, 9780429198533-9

Omar YM, Minoufekr M, Plapper P (2019) Business analytics in manufacturing: current trends, challenges and pathway to market leadership. Oper Res Perspecti 6:100127

Pollex J, Lenschow A (2018) Surrendering to growth? The European Union's goals for research and technology in the Horizon 2020 framework. J Clean Prod 197:1863–1871

Rainnie A, Dean M (2020) Industry 4.0 and the future of quality work in the global digital economy. Labour Ind: J Soc Econ Relat Work 30(1):16–33

Ren S, Zhang Y, Liu Y, Sakao T, Huisingh D, Almeida CM (2019) A comprehensive review of big data analytics throughout product lifecycle to support sustainable smart manufacturing: a framework, challenges and future research directions. J Clean Prod 210:1343–1365

Reynolds EB (2017) Innovation and production: advanced manufacturing technologies, trends and implications for US cities and regions. Built Environ 43(1):25–43

Riggins FJ, Dewan S (2005) The digital divide: current and future research directions. J Assoc Inf Syst 6(12):4

Roberts A, Choer Moraes H, Ferguson V (2019) Toward a geoeconomic order in international trade and investment. J Int Econ Law 22(4):655–676

Rüßmann M, Lorenz M, Gerbert P, Waldner M, Justus J, Engel P, Harnisch M (2015) Industry 4.0: the future of productivity and growth in manufacturing industries. Boston Consulting Group 9(1):54–89

Saggi MK, Jain S (2018) A survey towards an integration of big data analytics to big insights for value-creation. Inf Process Manag 54(5):758–790

Schmitz C, Tschiesner A, Jansen C, Hallerstede S, Garms F (2019) Industry 4.0: capturing value at scale in discrete manufacturing. McKinsey & Company

Singamneni S, Yifan LV, Hewitt A, Chalk R, Thomas W, Jordison D (2019) Additive manufacturing for the aircraft industry: a review. J Aeronaut Aerosp Eng 8(1):351–371

Sozinova AA (2019) Causal connections of formation of industry 4.0 from the positions of the global economy. In: Industry 4.0: industrial revolution of the 21st century, pp 131–143

Staff Writer (2020) 3D printing market to reach $51.77 billion by 2026. https://www.manufacturingtodayindia.com/6019-3d-printing-market-to-reach-5177-billion-by-2026/#:~:text=The%20global%203D%20Printing%20Market,market%20in%20the%20forthcoming%20years. Accessed 08 April 2024

Süzen AA (2020) A risk-assessment of cyber attacks and defence strategies in industry 4.0 ecosystem. Int J Comput Netw Inf Secur 14(1):1

Tiirmaa-Klaar H (2016) Building national cyber resilience and protecting critical information infrastructure. J Cyber Policy 1(1):94–106

Tommasi F, Perini M, Sartori R (2022) Multilevel comprehension for labour market inclusion: a qualitative study on experts' perspectives on Industry 4.0 competencies. Education+ Training 64(2):177–189

Tsaramirsis G, Kantaros A, Al-Darraji I, Piromalis D, Apostolopoulos C, Pavlopoulou A, ... Khan FQ (2022). A modern approach towards an industry 4.0 model: from driving technologies to management. J Sens 1–18

Ungureanu A (2019) Industry 4.0. The role of the gig economy in the industrial revolution of the 21st century. USV Ann Econ Public Adm 19(2(30)):77–84

Van Tulder R, van Mil E (2022) Principles of sustainable business: frameworks for corporate action on the SDGs. Routledge

Vermesan O, Bahr R, Falcitelli M, Brevi D, Bosi I, Dekusar A, ... Schreiner F (2022) IoT technologies for connected and automated driving applications. In: Internet of Things–The call of the edge. River Publishers, pp 255–306

Veugelers R, Cincera M, Frietsch R, Rammer C, Schubert T, Pelle A, ... Leijten J (2015) The impact of horizon 2020 on innovation in Europe. Intereconomics 50(1):4–30

Voronkova V, Punchenko O, Azhazha M (2020) Globalization and global governance in the fourth industrial revolution (industry 4.0). Humanit Stud 4(81):182–200

World Economic Forum (2016) *The fourth industrial revolution*. https://www.weforum.org/agenda/archive/fourth-industrial-revolution

Xie M, Ding L, Xia Y, Guo J, Pan J, Wang H (2021) Does artificial intelligence affect the pattern of skill demand? Evidence from Chinese manufacturing firms. Econ Model 96:295–309

Zaki M (2019) Digital transformation: harnessing digital technologies for the next generation of services. J Serv Mark 33(4):429–435

Zengin Y, Naktiyok S, Kaygın E, Kavak O, Topçuoğlu E (2021) An investigation upon Industry 4.0 and society 5.0 within the context of sustainable development goals. Sustainability 13(5):2682

Zhanbayev RA, Irfan M, Shutaleva AV, Maksimov DG, Abdykadyrkyzy R, Filiz Ş (2023) Demoethical model of sustainable development of society: a roadmap towards digital transformation. Sustainability 15(16):12478

Zhang G, Yang Y, Yang G (2023) Smart supply chain management in Industry 4.0: the review, research agenda and strategies in North America. Ann Oper Res 322(2):1075–1117

Chapter 9
Information Consumption Patterns, Fake News, and Deep Fake

Abstract The rise of digital platforms and social media has democratised the generation and flow of information, allowing for unprecedented access to information, news, and other types of content. However, it has also created an environment where misinformation can spread rapidly and deceive large audiences. This chapter discusses the characteristics of fake news, including its intentional dissemination, misleading narratives, and potential to manipulate public opinion. The chapter explores the impact of fake news and deep fakes on democratic processes, public discourse, and social cohesion. It discusses the challenges of identifying and combating misinformation, the role of social media platforms in content moderation, and the need for collaborative efforts between technology companies, policymakers, and civil society to address these issues. This chapter emphasises the importance of critical thinking, media literacy, and collaborative efforts in addressing these challenges. By promoting responsible information consumption and developing effective strategies to combat misinformation, societies can safeguard the integrity of public discourse, democratic processes, and the trustworthiness of information sources.

Keywords Information consumption · Information ecosystem · Generation · Fake news · Deep fake

9.1 Information Consumption and Patterns

The advent of the digital age has revolutionised the way individuals generate, access, consume, and interact in the information ecosystem. Digital platforms and social media have become ubiquitous, providing users with unprecedented access to a vast array of information in the form of news, opinions, and informative content (González-Bailón and Lelkes 2023). This democratisation of information has empowered individuals to engage with diverse perspectives and sources, transcending geographical and temporal boundaries (Kitchin et al. 2013).

Nielsen et al study explored the rise of digital platforms That led to the shift from traditional forms of media consumption, such as print newspapers and broadcast

S. Kumar et al., *Digital Transformation, Artificial Intelligence and Society*, Frontiers of Artificial Intelligence, Ethics and Multidisciplinary Applications,
https://doi.org/10.1007/978-981-97-5656-8_9

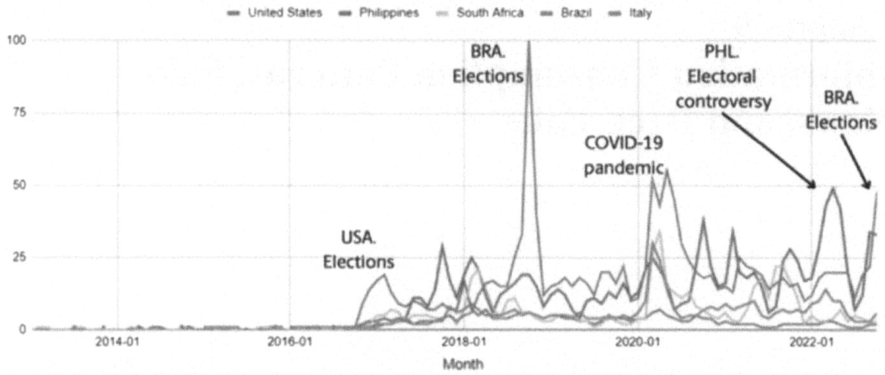

Fig. 9.1 Google Trends data reflecting online search interest for "fake news" in the last 10 years. Comparison among five different countries with the results is aggregated and normalised (https://sc.edu/study/colleges_schools/cic/initiatives/social_media_insights_lab/reports/2023/what_does_fake_news_mean.php)

television, towards online sources and social media platforms (Nielsen and Ganter 2022). These platforms offer personalised content recommendations and real-time updates, catering to individual preferences and interests (Fig. 9.1).

Moreover, the proliferation of smartphones and mobile devices has further accelerated the pace of information consumption. A report by the Pew Research Center indicates that a majority of Americans now access news through mobile devices, underscoring the growing significance of digital platforms in shaping information consumption patterns (Barthel et al. 2020).

However, alongside the benefits of increased accessibility and convenience, the digitalisation and democratisation of information due to technological and available social media platforms have also introduced new challenges and complexities (Taylor and Gibson 2017). The abundance of content available online generated by individuals makes it difficult for users to discern credible sources from misinformation. Additionally, the viral nature of social media can amplify the spread of false or misleading information, leading to the proliferation of fake news and misinformation campaigns across the world against particular countries, communities, and individuals (Dragomir 2017). In light of these developments, it is essential to critically examine how information consumption patterns have evolved in the digital age and the implications for individuals, society, and democratic processes (Papacharissi 2010). By understanding the dynamics of digital information ecosystems, stakeholders can develop strategies to promote responsible information consumption, media literacy, and digital awareness in citizens.

9.2 Understanding Fake News

Fake news refers to false or misleading information presented as legitimate news. It often seeks to deceive audiences by mimicking the style and format of credible journalism while promoting sensational or biased narratives. Fake news can take various forms, including fabricated stories, manipulated images or videos, misleading headlines, etc. A seminal study defines fake news as "news articles that are intentionally and verifiably false and could mislead readers" (Baptista and Gradim 2022). The authors highlight the deliberate intent behind the creation and dissemination of fake news, distinguishing it from unintentional errors or inaccuracies. Characteristic features of fake news include sensationalism, exaggeration, and confirmation bias. Fake news stories often exploit emotional triggers or appeal to preconceived beliefs, reinforcing existing biases and polarising opinions. Additionally, fake news may lack credible sources or corroborating evidence, relying instead on anonymous sources or fabricated quotes to lend an aura of legitimacy (Mourão and Robertson 2019) (Fig. 9.2).

In 2020, amidst the COVID-19 pandemic, fake news about supposed cures and preventive measures flooded social media platforms. For instance, false claims about drinking bleach or ingesting certain household chemicals to ward off the virus circulated widely (Leng et al. 2021). According to a study published in the American Journal of Tropical Medicine and Hygiene, misinformation regarding COVID-19 led to a significant increase in poison control calls related to exposure to household cleaners, with a reported 121% surge in calls compared to the previous year.

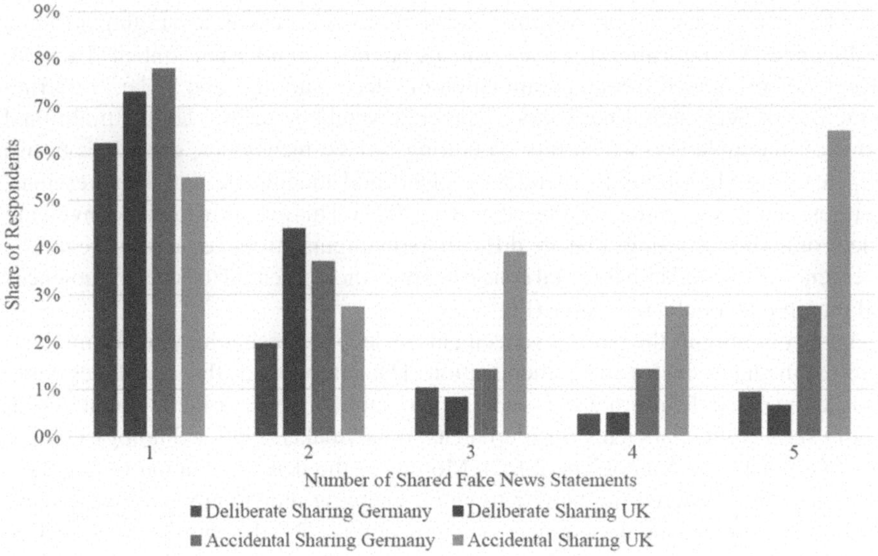

Fig. 9.2 Fake news and trends (Arin et al. 2023)

Such misinformation not only endangered public health, but also strained healthcare resources and led to unnecessary panic and harm (Cook and Brooke 2021).

The impact of fake news on political discourse and electoral processes cannot be overstated. During the 2016 U.S. presidential election, numerous false stories, such as the "Pizzagate" conspiracy theory alleging a child trafficking ring linked to a Washington, D.C. pizzeria, circulated on social media platforms (Cat 2022). According to a study by researchers at Stanford University, fabricated news stories were shared more widely and engaged more deeply on social media than legitimate news stories, potentially influencing voters' perceptions and decisions (Allcott and Gentzkow 2017). This dissemination of fake news not only eroded trust in democratic institutions, but also raised concerns about the integrity of the electoral process.

Fake news in the realm of science and technology can have far-reaching consequences, from undermining public trust in scientific research to promoting dangerous pseudoscientific beliefs (Gunderse et al. 2022). One notable example is the dissemination of false information regarding vaccines and their alleged links to autism. Despite numerous scientific studies debunking this claim, misinformation continues to circulate online, leading to vaccine hesitancy and contributing to outbreaks of preventable diseases (Chrest 2020). According to the World Health Organization (WHO), vaccine hesitancy is one of the top ten threats to global health, highlighting the detrimental impact of fake news on public health efforts and scientific progress.

9.3 Understanding Deep Fakes

Deep Fakes represent a more advanced form of misinformation, leveraging artificial intelligence (AI) algorithms to create realistic but false audiovisual content. The term "deepfake" originated from a combination of "deep learning" and "fake," referring to the use of deep neural networks to generate synthetic media. Unlike traditional forms of manipulation, which rely on editing or CGI techniques, deepfakes utilise deep learning algorithms to seamlessly blend and manipulate facial expressions, gestures, and speech patterns (Whittaker et al. 2021). This results in highly convincing videos or audio recordings that are difficult to distinguish from genuine content. The emergence of deepfakes has raised concerns about their potential to deceive audiences and manipulate public discourse (Fig. 9.3).

A study highlights the rapid advancements in deepfake technology and its implications for media forensics and authentication. The author warns that deepfakes could be used to spread disinformation, impersonate public figures, or incite social unrest, posing significant challenges for journalists, policymakers, and technology companies (Kalpokas and Kalpokiene 2022). Moreover, the democratisation of deepfake technology has lowered the barrier to entry, enabling individuals with basic technical skills to create and disseminate synthetic media. This decentralised production model makes it increasingly difficult to detect and mitigate the spread of deep fakes, exacerbating the challenges of combating misinformation in the digital age.

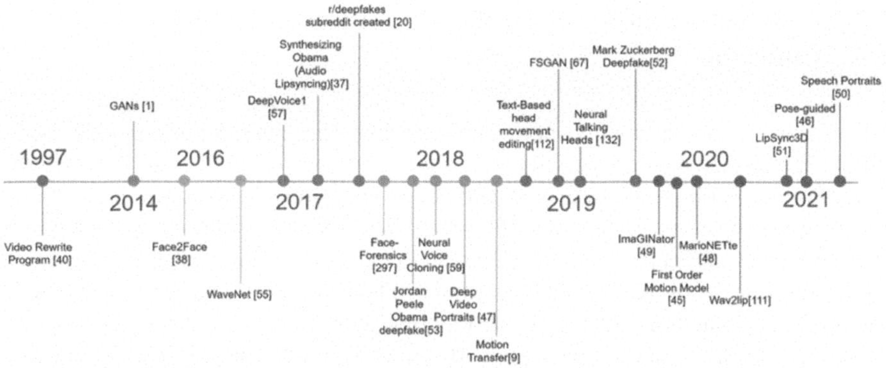

Fig. 9.3 Timeline of the evolution of deepfakes (Deepfakes generation and detection: state-of-the-art, open challenges, countermeasures, and way forward—Scientific Figure on ResearchGate. Available from: https://www.researchgate.net/figure/Timeline-of-the-evolution-of-Deepfakes_fig3_361086563 [accessed 25 Apr, 2024])

9.4 Fake Information Impact on Democratic Processes

The proliferation of fake news and deep fakes has profound implications for democratic processes, including elections, public discourse, and civic engagement. By manipulating public opinion and undermining trust in institutions, misinformation can erode the foundations of democracy and compromise the integrity of electoral outcomes (Loveless 2020). Research by Guess et al. (2019) suggests that exposure to fake news during the 2016 U.S. presidential election was associated with increased belief in false information and decreased support for democratic norms. The authors argue that the spread of misinformation through social media platforms can distort voter perceptions and undermine the legitimacy of democratic institutions. Similarly, the rise of deepfakes introduces new challenges for electoral integrity and political discourse. A report by the Atlantic Council's Digital Forensic Research Lab (DFRLab) warns that deep fakes could be used to fabricate compromising videos or smear campaigns against political candidates, leading to voter manipulation and electoral interference (Venkataramakrishnan 2020).

Furthermore, the erosion of trust in media sources and public institutions exacerbates social polarisation and undermines social cohesion. A study found that trust in traditional media and government institutions has declined globally, driven in part by the proliferation of misinformation and declining confidence in information sources (Flew 2021). Fake news and deep fakes pose significant challenges to democratic processes and social cohesion. By exploiting vulnerabilities in digital information ecosystems, misinformation can manipulate public opinion, distort reality, and undermine trust in institutions. Addressing these challenges requires collaborative efforts from technology companies, policymakers, civil society organisations, and the public to promote media literacy, combat misinformation, and safeguard the integrity of democratic governance (Marda and Milan 2018).

9.5 Fake Information in Public Discourse and Social Cohesion

Misinformation, including fake news and deep fakes, has far-reaching societal implications that extend beyond individual instances of deception. One of the most significant impacts is on public discourse and social cohesion (Al-Khazraji et al. 2023). Misinformation has the potential to distort public discourse by influencing the narratives that shape collective understanding and decision-making processes. Research highlights how exposure to misinformation can lead to the formation of false beliefs and attitudes, which in turn can polarise public opinion and exacerbate social divisions (Spohr 2017). By amplifying partisan viewpoints and reinforcing existing biases, misinformation undermines the foundation of informed public discourse essential for democratic governance. Moreover, misinformation erodes trust in media sources and undermines the credibility of journalistic institutions. A study found that a significant portion of the public has little confidence in the accuracy of news sources, with partisan differences exacerbating perceptions of media bias and unreliability (Hinsley 2021). This erosion of trust further fragments society, hindering efforts to foster dialogue and consensus-building. The spread of misinformation also poses challenges to social cohesion by fostering distrust and division within communities (Uslaner 2012). A study published in Science by Vosoughi et al. (2018) found that false news spreads faster and more extensively than true news on social media platforms, creating echo chambers and reinforcing ideological divides.

The effects of misinformation on public discourse and social cohesion are profound and multifaceted. By distorting reality, fueling polarisation, and eroding trust, misinformation undermines the foundations of democratic governance and social cohesion (Mondini 2023). Addressing these challenges requires concerted efforts to promote media literacy, critical thinking, and responsible information consumption.

9.6 Challenges of Identifying and Combating Misinformation

Identifying and combating misinformation presents numerous technical and ethical challenges, compounded by the evolving nature of digital information ecosystems and the rapid advancement of deepfake technology (Whittaker et al. 2023). One of the primary challenges is the sheer volume and velocity of information circulating online, making it difficult to discern credible sources from misinformation (Sharma et al. 2019). More specifically, Misinformation/Fake News/Deep Fake can spread rapidly through social media and online platforms, often achieving virality before it can be adequately addressed. By the time false information is identified, it may have already reached a wide audience, making it challenging to contain its impact. Individuals may be predisposed to believe and share information that aligns with their existing beliefs or biases, regardless of its accuracy. This confirmation bias makes it difficult to correct misinformation, as people may reject contradictory evidence and cling to false narratives (Moravec et al. 2022). The proliferation of advanced technologies, such as deepfakes and AI-generated content, complicates the task of discerning between authentic and manipulated media (Wagner and Blewer 2019). Deepfake videos, for example, can convincingly depict individuals saying or doing things they never actually did, making it harder to distinguish fact from fiction (Masood et al. 2023). Social media algorithms often prioritise content based on user's preferences and engagement history, creating echo chambers where individuals are exposed primarily to information that reinforces their viewpoints. This selective exposure can perpetuate the spread of misinformation within closed networks, further entrenching false beliefs. The majority of people lack the critical thinking skills necessary to evaluate information critically and discern credible sources from unreliable ones (Soon and Goh 2018). Without proper media literacy education, individuals may fall prey to misinformation and inadvertently contribute to its dissemination. Bad actors, including foreign governments, political operatives, and extremist groups, actively seek to sow discord and manipulate public opinion through disinformation campaigns. These campaigns often exploit societal divisions and vulnerabilities in online platforms to amplify false narratives and undermine trust in institutions (Kupriienko 2019).

Automated content moderation systems, such as algorithms and machine learning models, play a crucial role in both generating, detecting and flagging suspicious content (Gongane et al. 2022). However, these systems are not infallible and often struggle to distinguish between genuine content and sophisticated forms of manipulation, such as deep fakes. Moreover, the decentralised nature of online platforms and the anonymity afforded to users make it challenging to hold perpetrators of misinformation accountable (Nsude et al. 2021). A study published in Nature Communications by Shao et al. (2018) highlights the role of malicious actors in exploiting social media platforms to disseminate false information and manipulate public opinion, underscoring the need for robust strategies to combat misinformation (Bradshaw and Howard 2018). Ethical considerations also complicate efforts to combat misinformation, particularly regarding freedom of expression and censorship. Balancing the need to protect against harmful content with respect for individual rights and freedoms poses complex ethical dilemmas for policymakers and technology companies alike. Additionally, misinformation campaigns often target vulnerable populations, exploiting cognitive biases and psychological vulnerabilities to amplify the spread of false information (Scheufele and Krause 2019). A study found that individuals with lower cognitive abilities are more susceptible to believing false information, highlighting the importance of targeted interventions to promote media literacy and critical thinking skills (Guess et al. 2020). The challenges of identifying and combating misinformation are multifaceted and require a comprehensive approach that integrates technological solutions with ethical considerations and educational initiatives.

9.7 Social Media Platforms and Misinformation

Social media platforms play a central role in shaping the dissemination and amplification of misinformation due to their vast user bases and algorithmic recommendation systems. These platforms enable the rapid spread of content through virality and engagement metrics, often prioritising sensational or provocative content over accuracy and reliability (Mwangi 2023). A study found that social media algorithms prioritise content based on user engagement, leading to the formation of filter bubbles and echo chambers where individuals are exposed to information that aligns with their existing beliefs (Kitchens et al. 2020). Moreover, the business model of social media platforms, which relies on advertising revenue driven by user engagement, incentivizes the spread of clickbait and sensational content. This creates fertile ground for the proliferation of fake news and misinformation campaigns orchestrated by malicious actors seeking to exploit the platform's reach and influence. In response to growing concerns about misinformation, social media platforms have implemented various content moderation policies and fact-checking initiatives. However, the effectiveness of these measures remains limited by challenges such as algorithmic bias, scalability, and the rapid evolution of disinformation tactics (Caled and Silva 2022). Furthermore, the role of social media platforms in regulating content raises complex ethical and legal questions regarding freedom of expression, censorship, and platform accountability. Balancing the need to protect against harmful content with respect for individual rights and democratic principles requires nuanced policy frameworks and collaborative efforts between stakeholders (Helberger et al. 2018). Overall, the role of social media platforms in facilitating the spread of misinformation underscores the need for robust content moderation policies, transparent algorithms, and greater accountability mechanisms to mitigate the impact of fake news and safeguard the integrity of public discourse.

9.8 Addressing Misinformation and Challenges

9.8.1 Need for Collaborative Efforts

Addressing the root causes of misinformation requires collaborative efforts between technology companies, policymakers, civil society organisations, and academic institutions (Koulolias et al. 2018). No single actor can address the complex and multifaceted challenges posed by misinformation alone. Technology companies have a responsibility to design platforms and algorithms that prioritise accuracy, transparency, and user safety (Gradoń et al. 2021). This includes investing in research and development of AI-powered content moderation tools, implementing transparent policies for content removal and user data protection, and fostering partnerships with fact-checking organisations and academic researchers. Policymakers play a crucial role in shaping regulatory frameworks that promote accountability, transparency, and ethical standards in the digital sphere. This may involve enacting legislation to combat disinformation, establishing independent oversight bodies to monitor platform practices, and fostering international cooperation to address global challenges posed by misinformation (Marsden et al. 2020). Civil society organisations and grassroots initiatives play a vital role in raising awareness, promoting media literacy, and empowering individuals to critically evaluate information sources and discern credible content from misinformation. Educational initiatives targeting vulnerable populations, such as students, seniors, and marginalised communities, can help build resilience against misinformation and foster a culture of digital citizenship (Harris and Johns 2021). Academic institutions and research institutions have a responsibility to conduct research, generate evidence, and develop best practices for combating misinformation (Gradoń et al. 2021). Interdisciplinary collaborations between researchers in fields such as computer science, communication studies, psychology, and political science can yield insights into the underlying mechanisms of misinformation and inform evidence-based interventions. Addressing the challenges of misinformation requires collaborative efforts from all stakeholders, including technology companies, policymakers, civil society organisations, and academic institutions (Gradoń et al 2021). By working together to promote media literacy, transparency, and accountability, we can mitigate the impact of fake news and deep fakes and safeguard the integrity of public discourse and democratic processes.

9.8.2 Promoting Media Literacy and Critical Thinking

Media literacy education and critical thinking skills are indispensable tools in the fight against misinformation. By empowering individuals to critically evaluate information sources and discern credible content from misinformation, media literacy fosters a culture of informed citizenship and responsible information consumption (Bulger and Davison 2018). A study emphasises the importance of media literacy education in equipping individuals with the skills and knowledge to navigate the complexities of the digital information landscape (Kellner and Share 2019). Media literacy encompasses a range of competencies, including the ability to evaluate sources, analyse content for bias and credibility, and recognise persuasive techniques used in media messaging (Bulger and Davison 2018). Furthermore, critical thinking skills play a central role in media literacy education by encouraging individuals to question assumptions, challenge narratives, and seek evidence-based explanations. Research by Wineburg and McGrew (2017) highlights the effectiveness of critical thinking interventions in improving students' ability to discern credible information and distinguish between fact and opinion (McGrew 2020). Incorporating media literacy education into formal curricula and lifelong learning initiatives is essential to building a resilient society capable of resisting the influence of misinformation (Jolls and Johnsen 2017). Educational institutions, community organisations, and media literacy advocates play a vital role in promoting media literacy skills and fostering a culture of critical inquiry and discernment.

9.8.3 Technological Solutions and Innovations

Emerging technological solutions offer promising avenues for combating misinformation and detecting fraudulent content. AI-powered fact-checking tools and deepfake detection algorithms represent innovative approaches to identifying and mitigating the spread of false information. AI-powered fact-checking tools leverage machine learning algorithms to analyse the credibility of news articles and verify factual claims (Unver 2023). Platforms such as Google's Fact Check Explorer and Facebook's Fact-Checking Program use AI algorithms to identify misinformation and flag questionable content for further review by human fact-checkers (Školkay and Filin 2019). Similarly, deepfake detection algorithms employ advanced image and video analysis techniques to identify manipulated media and synthetic content. Research demonstrates the effectiveness of deep learning algorithms in detecting deep fakes by analysing subtle visual artefacts and inconsistencies in facial expressions and speech patterns (Nguyen et al. 2022) (Fig. 9.4).

Moreover, collaborations between tech companies, academic researchers, and civil society organisations are driving innovation in misinformation detection and mitigation. Initiatives such as the Deepfake Detection Challenge organised by Facebook, Microsoft, and academic partners aim to spur the development of robust

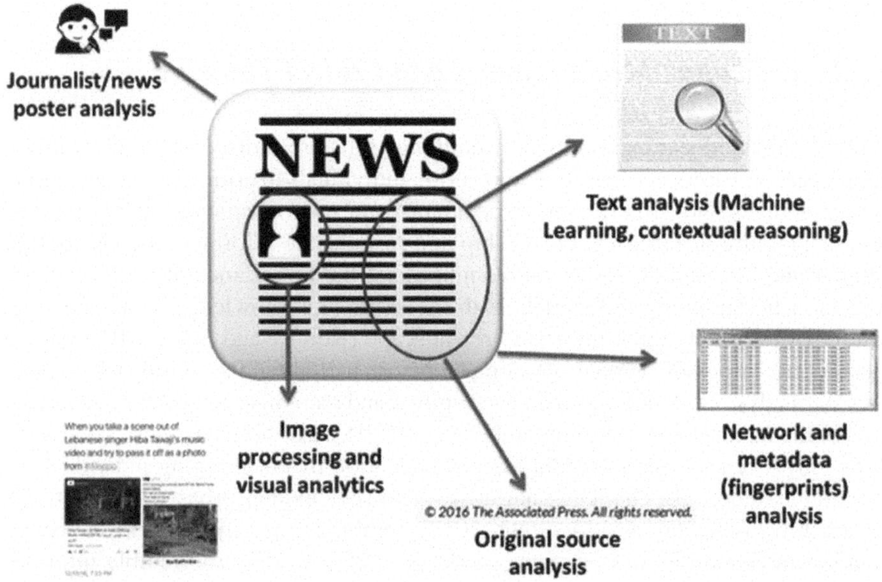

Fig. 9.4 Technological solutions and innovations for fake news mitigation (Choraś, M., Giełczyk, A., Demestichas, K., Puchalski, D., Kozik, R. (2018). Pattern Recognition Solutions for Fake News Detection. In: Saeed, K., Homenda, W. (eds) Computer Information Systems and Industrial Management. CISIM 2018. Lecture Notes in Computer Science, vol 11,127. Springer, Cham. https://doi.org/10.1007/978-3-319-99954-8_12)

deep fake detection algorithms and promote open collaboration in addressing the challenges posed by synthetic media (Leibowicz et al. 2021).

While technological solutions hold promise in combating misinformation, they are not without limitations. The rapid evolution of misinformation tactics and the proliferation of sophisticated deepfake technology pose ongoing challenges for detection and mitigation efforts. Moreover, ethical considerations surrounding privacy, bias, and algorithmic transparency must be carefully addressed to ensure the responsible deployment of AI-powered solutions.

9.8.4 Transparency and Accountability

Transparency and accountability are essential principles in content moderation practices, ensuring that platforms uphold ethical standards, respect user rights, and maintain trust with their audiences (Tworek et al. 2020). Clear policies and mechanisms for user reporting and appeals are fundamental to promoting transparency and accountability in content moderation. Platforms should establish transparent guidelines and standards for acceptable content and community behaviour, clearly outlining prohibited activities such as hate speech, harassment, and misinformation (Pavleska et al. 2018). These guidelines should be accessible to users and regularly updated to reflect evolving societal norms and legal standards. Additionally, platforms should implement robust mechanisms for user reporting and content moderation, enabling users to flag inappropriate or misleading content for review by platform moderators (Gorwa et al. 2020). Timely responses to user reports and transparent communication about moderation decisions are critical to maintaining user trust and confidence in platform integrity. Furthermore, platforms should provide avenues for user appeals and recourse in cases where content moderation decisions are disputed. Fair and impartial adjudication processes, coupled with transparent communication channels, promote accountability and ensure that users have recourse to challenge unjust or arbitrary moderation actions (Amsler et al. 2020). Moreover, platforms should be transparent about their data practices, including how user data is collected, used, and protected. Clear privacy policies and opt-in consent mechanisms empower users to make informed choices about their data and hold platforms accountable for responsible data stewardship (Wong et al. 2022). Transparency and accountability are essential pillars of responsible content moderation practices, promoting trust, fairness, and integrity in digital platforms. By upholding these principles, platforms can foster a safe and inclusive online environment conducive to healthy public discourse and democratic engagement (Fig. 9.5).

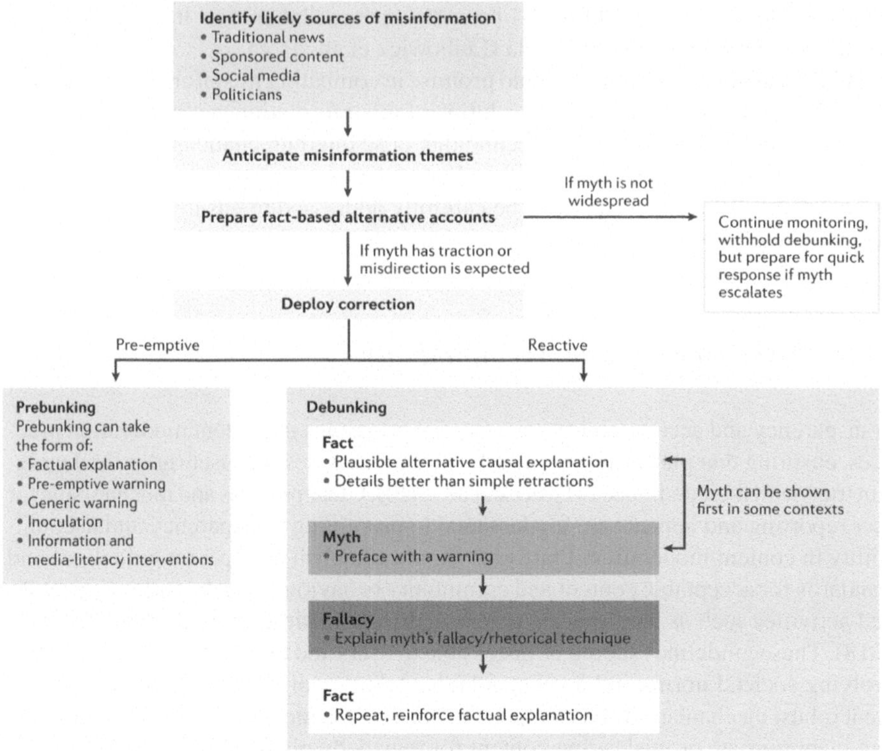

Fig. 9.5 Handling misinformation and fake news (https://www.nature.com/articles/s44159-021-00006-y/figures/6)

9.9 Conclusion and Call to Action

The proliferation of misinformation, including fake news and deep fakes, poses significant challenges to the integrity of public discourse, democratic governance, and social cohesion (Pawelec 2022). Addressing these challenges requires collective action and a commitment to promoting responsible information consumption, media literacy, and critical thinking skills. Throughout this chapter, we have explored the various dimensions of misinformation, from its defining characteristics to its societal impacts and the challenges of combating it. We have examined the role of digital platforms, the importance of technological innovations, and the need for transparency and accountability in content moderation practices. As we navigate the complexities of the digital age, we must remain vigilant and proactive in combating misinformation. This requires collaborative efforts from all stakeholders, including technology companies, policymakers, civil society organisations, and individual users. We must invest in media literacy education, critical thinking skills, and technological solutions to empower individuals to discern credible information from misinformation

(Pavleska et al. 2018). We must hold digital platforms accountable for upholding ethical standards, transparency, and user trust. We must foster a culture of responsible information consumption and civic engagement that values truth, integrity, and democratic principles. In conclusion, it is important to call upon stakeholders to join forces in the fight against misinformation. By promoting collaboration, innovation, and accountability, we can safeguard the integrity of public discourse, democratic processes, and the trustworthiness of information sources in the digital age (Armstrong 2005). Together, let us build a future where truth prevails, informed citizens thrive, and democratic ideals endure.

References

Al-Khazraji SH, Saleh HH, Khalid AI, Mishkhal IA (2023) Impact of deepfake technology on social media: detection, misinformation and societal implications. Eurasia Proc Sci Technol Eng Math 23:429–441

Allcott H, Gentzkow M (2017) Social media and fake news in the 2016 election. J Econ Perspect 31(2):211–236

Amsler LB, Martinez J, Smith SE (2020) Dispute system design: preventing, managing, and resolving conflict. Stanford University Press

Arin KP, Mazrekaj D, Thum M (2023) Ability of detecting and willingness to share fake news. Sci Rep 13(1):7298

Armstrong E (2005) Integrity, transparency and accountability in public administration: recent trends, regional and international developments and emerging issues. United Nations, Department of Economic and Social Affairs 1(10):1–10

Baptista JP, Gradim A (2022) A working definition of fake news. Encyclopedia 2(1)

Barthel M, Mitchell A, Asare-Marfo D, Kennedy C, Worden K (2020) Measuring news consumption in a digital era. Pew Research Center, Washington, DC

Bradshaw S, Howard PN (2018) Challenging truth and trust: a global inventory of organized social media manipulation. Comput Propaganda Project 1:1–26

Bulger M, Davison P (2018) The promises, challenges, and futures of media literacy

Caled D, Silva MJ (2022) Digital media and misinformation: an outlook on multidisciplinary strategies against manipulation. J Comput Soc Sci 5(1):123–159

Cat MJ (2022) QAnon & the# pizzagates of hell: unreal tales of occult child abuse by the CIA. TrineDay

Chrest B (2020) Understanding and quantifying anti-vaccine misinformation online: a critical report and social media analysis about Emeritus Professor Timothy Noakes

Cook MA, Brooke N (2021) Event-based surveillance of poisonings and potentially hazardous exposures over 12 months of the COVID-19 pandemic. Int J Environ Res Public Health 18(21):11133

Dragomir AM (2017) The fake news phenomenon in the social media era. Strategic Impact 65:54–65

Flew T (2021) The global trust deficit disorder: a communications perspective on trust in the time of global pandemics. J Commun 71(2):163–186

Gongane VU, Munot MV, Anuse AD (2022) Detection and moderation of detrimental content on social media platforms: current status and future directions. Soc Netw Anal Min 12(1):129

González-Bailón S, Lelkes Y (2023) Do social media undermine social cohesion? A critical review. Soc Issues Policy Rev 17(1):155–180

Gorwa R, Binns R, Katzenbach C (2020) Algorithmic content moderation: technical and political challenges in the automation of platform governance. Big Data Soc 7(1):2053951719897945

Gradoń KT, Hołyst JA, Moy WR, Sienkiewicz J, Suchecki K (2021) Countering misinformation: a multidisciplinary approach. Big Data Soc 8(1):20539517211013850

Guess AM, Lerner M, Lyons B, Montgomery JM, Nyhan B, Reifler J, Sircar N (2020) A digital media literacy intervention increases discernment between mainstream and false news in the United States and India. Proc Natl Acad Sci 117(27):15536–15545

Gundersen T, Alinejad D, Branch TY, Duffy B, Hewlett K, Holst C, ... Baghramian M (2022) A new dark age? Truth, trust, and environmental science. Annual Rev Environ Resour 47:5–29

Harris A, Johns A (2021) Youth, social cohesion and digital life: from risk and resilience to a global digital citizenship approach. J Sociol 57(2):394–411

Helberger N, Pierson J, Poell T (2018) Governing online platforms: from contested to cooperative responsibility. Inf Soc 34(1):1–14

Hinsley A (2021) Cued up: how audience demographics influence reliance on news cues, confirmation bias and confidence in identifying misinformation. Int Symp Online J 11(1):89–109

Jolls T, Johnsen M (2017) Media literacy: a foundational skill for democracy in the 21st century. Hastings Law J 69:1379

Kalpokas I, Kalpokiene J (2022) Deepfakes: a realistic assessment of potentials, risks, and policy regulation. Springer Nature

Kellner D, Share J (2019) The critical media literacy guide: engaging media and transforming education. In: The critical media literacy guide. Brill

Kitchens B, Johnson SL, Gray P (2020) Understanding echo chambers and filter bubbles: the impact of social media on diversification and partisan shifts in news consumption. MIS Q 44(4)

Kitchin R, Linehan D, O'Callaghan C, Lawton P (2013) Public geographies through social media. Dialog Human Geogr 3(1):56–72

Koulolias V, Jonathan GM, Fernandez M, Sotirchos D (2018) Combating misinformation: an ecosystem in co-creation. OECD Publishing

Kupriienko M (2019) Influencing public opinion in social media. trolling and disinformation strategies. Doctoral dissertation, Vytautas Magnus University

Leibowicz CR, McGregor S, Ovadya A (2021, July) The deepfake detection dilemma: a multistakeholder exploration of adversarial dynamics in synthetic media. In: Proceedings of the 2021 AAAI/ACM conference on AI, ethics, and society, pp 736–744

Leng Y, Zhai Y, Sun S, Wu Y, Selzer J, Strover S, ... Ding Y (2021) Misinformation during the COVID-19 outbreak in China: cultural, social and political entanglements. IEEE Trans Big Data 7(1):69–80

Loveless M (2020) Information and democracy: fake news as an emotional weapon. In: Democracy and fake news. Routledge, pp 64–76

Marda V, Milan S (2018) Wisdom of the crowd: multistakeholder perspectives on the fake news debate. Internet Policy Review series, Annenberg School of Communication

Marsden C, Meyer T, Brown I (2020) Platform values and democratic elections: how can the law regulate digital disinformation? Comput Law Secur Rev 36:105373

Masood M, Nawaz M, Malik KM, Javed A, Irtaza A, Malik H (2023) Deepfakes generation and detection: state-of-the-art, open challenges, countermeasures, and way forward. Appl Intell 53(4):3974–4026

McGrew S (2020) Learning to evaluate: an intervention in civic online reasoning. Comput Educ 145:103711

Mondini F (2023) Unveiling the threat: the cognitive mechanisms behind disinformation's influence on democratic systems

Moravec PL, Kim A, Dennis AR, Minas RK (2022) Do you really know if it's true? How asking users to rate stories affects belief in fake news on social media. Inf Syst Res 33(3):887–907

Mourão RR, Robertson CT (2019) Fake news as discursive integration: an analysis of sites that publish false, misleading, hyperpartisan and sensational information. J Stud 20(14):2077–2095

Mwangi E (2023) Technology and fake news: shaping social, political, and economic perspectives. Polit Econ Perspect

Nguyen TT, Nguyen QVH, Nguyen DT, Nguyen DT, Huynh-The T, Nahavandi S, ... Nguyen CM (2022) Deep learning for deepfakes creation and detection: a survey. Comput Vision Image Understand 223:103525
Nielsen RK, Ganter SA (2022) The power of platforms: shaping media and society, vol 16, No 2. Oxford University Press
Nsude I, Ogbodo JN, Nwamini S (2021) Creating and fighting fake news: artificial intelligence as a double-edged sword. Artif Intell Media 47
Papacharissi Z (2010) A private sphere: democracy in a digital age. Polity
Pavleska T, Školkay A, Zankova B, Ribeiro N, Bechmann A (2018) Performance analysis of fact-checking organizations and initiatives in Europe: a critical overview of online platforms fighting fake news. Soc Media Converg 29:1–28
Pawelec M (2022) Deepfakes and democracy (theory): how synthetic audio-visual media for disinformation and hate speech threaten core democratic functions. Dig Soc 1(2):19
Scheufele DA, Krause NM (2019) Science audiences, misinformation, and fake news. Proc Natl Acad Sci 116(16):7662–7669
Sharma K, Qian F, Jiang H, Ruchansky N, Zhang M, Liu Y (2019) Combating fake news: a survey on identification and mitigation techniques. ACM Trans Intell Syst Technol (TIST) 10(3):1–42
Školkay A, Filin J (2019) A comparison of fake news detecting and fact-checking AI based solutions. Studia Medioznawcze 4:365–383
Soon C, Goh S (2018) Fake news, false information and more: countering human biases. Institute of Policy Studies (IPS) Working Papers 31
Spohr D (2017) Fake news and ideological polarization: filter bubbles and selective exposure on social media. Bus Inf Rev 34(3):150–160
Taylor J, Gibson LK (2017) Digitisation, digital interaction and social media: embedded barriers to democratic heritage. Int J Herit Stud 23(5):408–420
Tworek H, Fathaigh RÓ, Bruggeman L, Tenove C (2020) Dispute resolution and content moderation: fair, accountable, independent. Algorithms
Unver A (2023) Emerging technologies and automated fact-checking: tools, techniques and algorithms. Techniques and Algorithms, August 29
Uslaner EM (2012) Segregation and mistrust: diversity, isolation, and social cohesion. Cambridge University Press
Venkataramakrishnan S (2020) After deep fakes, a new frontier of AI trickery: fake faces. https://www.ft.com/content/b50d22ec-db98-4891-86da-af34f06d1cb1
Vosoughi S, Roy D, Aral S (2018) The spread of true and false news online. science 359(6380):1146–1151
Wagner TL, Blewer A (2019) "The word real is no longer real": deepfakes, gender, and the challenges of ai-altered video. Open Inf Sci 3(1):32–46
Whittaker L, Letheren K, Mulcahy R (2021) The rise of deepfakes: a conceptual framework and research agenda for marketing. Aust Mark J 29(3):204–214
Whittaker L, Mulcahy R, Letheren K, Kietzmann J, Russell-Bennett R (2023) Mapping the deepfake landscape for innovation: a multidisciplinary systematic review and future research agenda. Technovation 125:102784
Wong J, Henderson T, Ball K (2022) Data protection for the common good: developing a framework for a data protection-focused data commons. Data Policy 4:e3

Chapter 10
Artificial Intelligence and Climate Change Mitigation

Abstract This chapter explores the intersection of artificial intelligence (AI) and the challenges of climate change and its monitoring and mitigation. It examines how AI technologies can be leveraged to address the complex challenges posed by climate change and accelerate efforts towards sustainable and low-carbon solutions. Climate change is one of the most pressing global challenges, requiring urgent action to reduce greenhouse gas emissions, adapt to changing conditions, and transition to a sustainable future. This chapter discusses how AI can play a transformative role in these endeavours. It explores applications of AI in various aspects of climate change mitigation, including energy systems, transportation, agriculture, urban planning, and natural resource management. Furthermore, the chapter explores the role of AI in climate modelling, prediction, and decision-making. It discusses how AI algorithms and machine learning techniques can analyse vast amounts of climate data, enhance weather forecasting, and support informed decision-making in climate change adaptation and mitigation strategies.

Keywords Climate change · Artificial intelligence · Climate actions · Mitigation · Algorithms · Accountability

10.1 Introduction

The twenty-first century presents humanity with unprecedented challenges, chief among them being climate change. The rapid increase in greenhouse gas emissions, primarily from human activities such as burning fossil fuels and deforestation, has led to rising global temperatures, leading to extreme weather events, and disruptions to ecosystems worldwide (Shivanna 2022). Addressing climate change has become an urgent imperative for the international community, necessitating innovative solutions and concerted efforts across various sectors by the global community (Kinley et al. 2021).

Climate change, driven predominantly by human activities, presents a formidable challenge to the planet's ecosystems and human societies (Steffen et al. 2011). The

S. Kumar et al., *Digital Transformation, Artificial Intelligence and Society*, Frontiers of Artificial Intelligence, Ethics and Multidisciplinary Applications,
https://doi.org/10.1007/978-981-97-5656-8_10

primary driver of climate change is the emission of greenhouse gases (GHGs) such as carbon dioxide (CO_2), methane (CH_4) and nitrous oxide (N_2O) from burning fossil fuels, industrial processes, deforestation, and agricultural practices (Kumar 2018). Since the Industrial Revolution, atmospheric CO_2 levels have risen by over 40%, primarily due to human activities like burning coal, oil, and natural gas for energy (Yoro and Daramola 2020). Deforestation exacerbates the issue by reducing the Earth's capacity to absorb CO_2 (Bala et al. 2007). Moreover, industrial processes like cement production and chemical manufacturing emit GHGs directly into the atmosphere. Agriculture contributes significantly to GHG emissions through livestock farming, which produces methane, and rice cultivation, which generates methane through anaerobic decomposition (Verge et al. 2007). The consequences of climate change are already evident, with rising temperatures causing more frequent and intense heat waves, altered precipitation patterns, and shifts in weather extremes. Melting ice caps and glaciers contribute to rising sea levels, threatening coastal communities worldwide (Singh and Singh 2012). For instance, Greenland's ice sheet lost an average of 279 billion metric tonnes of ice per year between 2000 and 2019 (Bian et al. 2019). Coral reefs which are crucial for marine biodiversity and coastal protection, face bleaching and degradation due to ocean warming and acidification. These impacts underscore the urgent need for ambitious global action to mitigate greenhouse gas emissions, transition to renewable energy sources, and adapt to the changing climate to ensure a sustainable future for generations to come (Kılkış et al. 2022) (Fig. 10.1).

The urgency of addressing climate change cannot be overstated. The Intergovernmental Panel on Climate Change (IPCC) has issued stark warnings about the consequences of inaction, highlighting the need for immediate and decisive measures to reduce greenhouse gas emissions and mitigate the impacts of climate change (Kinley

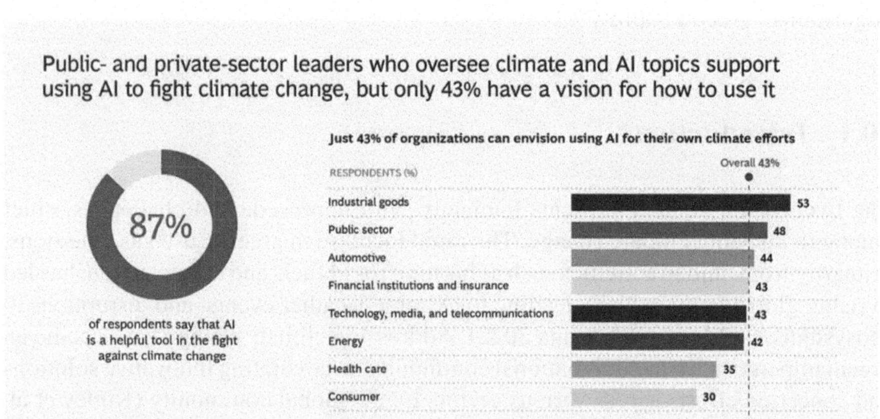

Fig. 10.1 Fighting climate change using AI (https://www.forbes.com/sites/markminevich/2022/07/08/how-to-fight-climate-change-using-ai/?sh=665acf12a838)

et al. 2021). Rising sea levels, biodiversity loss, food and water scarcity, and more frequent and severe weather events are among the many challenges humanity faces in a warming world.

At the heart of this global challenge of climate change lies the intersection of artificial intelligence (AI) and climate change mitigation (Cowls et al. 2023). AI, with its capacity to process vast amounts of data, identify patterns, and make predictions, offers a powerful toolkit for tackling climate-related problems. From optimising energy systems to revolutionising transportation and agriculture, AI holds immense potential to accelerate efforts towards a sustainable, low-carbon future (Stein 2020).

Global communities and stakeholders need to explore how the latest technological advancements such as digital technologies and AI can be harnessed as a transformative tool in the fight against climate change. By leveraging AI technologies, we can enhance our understanding of climate dynamics, develop innovative solutions, and implement effective strategies to mitigate and adapt to the changing climate (Cowls et al. 2023). From optimising energy systems to revolutionising transportation and agriculture, AI has the potential to revolutionise how we address climate change challenges (Fig. 10.1).

10.2 Artificial Intelligence and Climate Change Mitigation

Artificial Intelligence (AI) holds tremendous potential in climate change mitigation efforts across various sectors. Through its ability to analyse vast amounts of data, recognise patterns, and make predictions, AI offers innovative solutions to address the complexities of climate change. Here's how AI can significantly contribute to mitigation efforts. By harnessing the power of AI, we can enhance renewable energy deployment, improve energy efficiency, optimise carbon capture and storage, promote sustainable agriculture, and protect forests (Dauvergne 2020). These AI-driven interventions not only contribute to emissions reductions, but also foster economic growth, enhance resilience, and create a more sustainable future for generations to come.

10.2.1 Artificial Intelligence and Climate Actions in Energy Systems

The energy sector can play a critical role in climate change mitigation, as the majority of greenhouse gas emissions originate from energy production and consumption (Owusu and Asumadu-Sarkodie 2016). AI offers promising solutions to optimise energy systems, improve efficiency, and integrate renewable energy sources into the grid (Ahmad et al. 2021). One example of AI's impact on energy systems is the development of smart grids. Smart grids leverage AI algorithms to analyse real-time data on energy supply and demand, enabling more efficient distribution and utilisation of electricity (Ahmad et al. 2022a, b). By optimising grid operations, reducing wastage, and balancing supply and demand, smart grids contribute to lower emissions and increased reliability of energy supply. Furthermore, AI-driven demand-side management (DSM) programmes enable utilities to incentivize consumers to shift their electricity usage to off-peak hours, reducing the need for fossil fuel-based peaker plants and lowering overall emissions (Alasseri et al. 2017). These programmes use machine learning algorithms to analyse consumption patterns and offer personalised recommendations to consumers, encouraging energy conservation and efficiency (Fig. 10.2).

Renewable energy integration is another area where AI is making significant strides. AI algorithms are being used to forecast renewable energy production, such as wind and solar power, with greater accuracy, enabling grid operators to better anticipate fluctuations in supply and adjust accordingly (Şerban and Lytras 2020). Additionally, AI-driven predictive maintenance techniques help optimise the performance of renewable energy infrastructure, such as wind turbines and solar panels, reducing downtime and increasing overall efficiency. Research published highlights the potential of AI to revolutionise energy systems and accelerate the transition to a low-carbon future (Ahmad et al. 2021). The study demonstrates how AI algorithms can optimise the operation of power plants, improve energy efficiency in buildings, and facilitate the integration of renewable energy sources into the grid, ultimately reducing greenhouse gas emissions and mitigating climate change (Fig. 10.2).

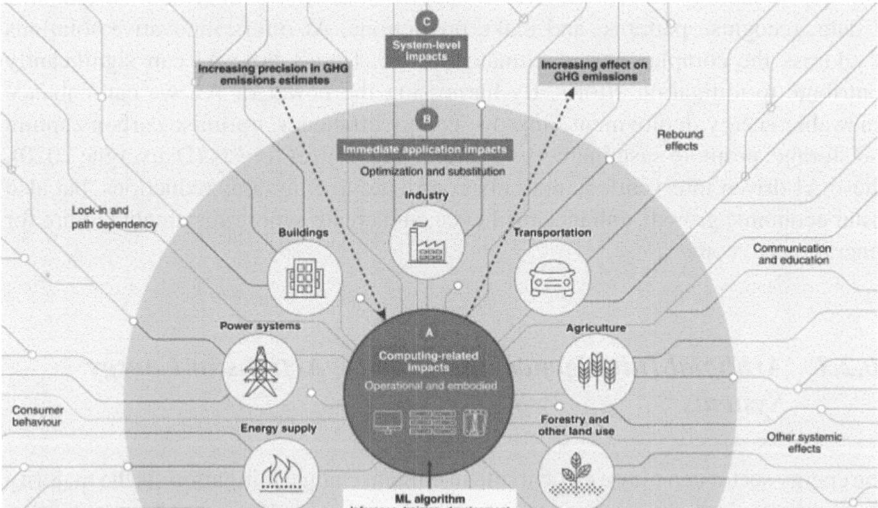

Fig. 10.2 Framework for assessing the GHG emissions impacts of ML (Kaack et al. 2022)

10.2.2 Artificial Intelligence and Climate Actions in Transportation

Transportation is another major contributor to greenhouse gas emissions, accounting for a significant portion of global carbon dioxide emissions. AI technologies offer opportunities to improve transportation efficiency, reduce emissions, and promote sustainable mobility solutions. One area where AI is making significant strides is in the development of electric and autonomous vehicles. Electric vehicles (EVs) powered by AI-driven battery management systems offer a cleaner alternative to traditional internal combustion engine vehicles, reducing emissions and dependence on fossil fuels (Hu et al. 2024). Moreover, AI algorithms are enabling the development of autonomous vehicles that optimise route planning, reduce traffic congestion, and minimise energy consumption, further contributing to emissions reductions (Abduljabbar et al. 2019). Traffic management is another area where AI is making a difference. AI-driven traffic management systems analyse real-time traffic data to optimise signal timings, manage congestion, and reduce fuel consumption. By dynamically adjusting traffic flow and prioritising alternative modes of transportation, such as public transit and cycling, these systems help reduce emissions and improve air quality in urban areas (de la Torre et al. 2021). Logistics optimization is also benefiting from AI technologies. AI algorithms optimise freight transportation routes, minimise empty miles, and reduce fuel consumption in logistics operations (Chung 2021). By streamlining supply chains and reducing inefficiencies, AI-driven logistics solutions contribute to lower emissions and reduced environmental impact. A study published highlights the potential of AI to transform transportation systems and mitigate climate change (Dikshit et al. 2023). The research demonstrates how AI-driven traffic management systems can reduce emissions by up to 20% in urban areas through improved signal timing and congestion management (Dikshit et al. 2023). Additionally, the study shows how AI-enabled logistics optimization can significantly reduce fuel consumption and emissions in freight transportation.

10.2.3 Artificial Intelligence and Climate Actions in Agriculture

Agriculture is a significant contributor to greenhouse gas emissions and is highly vulnerable to the impacts of climate change. AI technologies offer promising solutions to enhance agricultural productivity while minimising environmental impacts and promoting sustainability. Precision farming is one area where AI is revolutionising agriculture (Javaid et al. 2023). AI-driven precision farming techniques analyse data from satellites, drones, and sensors to monitor soil conditions, optimise irrigation, and tailor crop management practices to specific field conditions (Shaikh et al. 2022). By reducing inputs such as water, fertilisers, and pesticides, precision farming practices help minimise environmental impact and improve resource efficiency. Crop monitoring is another application of AI in agriculture. AI algorithms analyse satellite imagery and other remote sensing data to monitor crop health, detect pests and diseases, and predict yield levels with greater accuracy (Javaid et al. 2023). By providing early warnings of potential threats to crops, such as pests, diseases, or adverse weather conditions, AI-driven crop monitoring systems enable farmers to take proactive measures to protect their crops and minimise losses. Resource-efficient agriculture practices are also benefiting from AI technologies. AI-driven decision support systems help farmers make informed decisions about crop selection, planting schedules, and input optimization, maximising yields while minimising resource use and environmental impact (Javaid et al. 2023). By optimising resource allocation and reducing waste, these systems contribute to more sustainable agricultural practices and mitigate climate change. A study demonstrates the potential of AI-driven precision farming techniques to improve resource efficiency and reduce environmental impact (Shaikh et al. 2022). The research shows how AI algorithms can optimise irrigation scheduling, reduce fertiliser use, and increase crop yields, resulting in significant reductions in water consumption, greenhouse gas emissions, and environmental pollution. AI technologies hold immense promise in addressing climate change challenges across various sectors, from energy systems and transportation to agriculture and beyond. By leveraging AI's capabilities to analyse data, optimise processes, and inform decision-making, we can accelerate efforts towards a sustainable, low-carbon future. However, realising this potential requires collaboration between policymakers, researchers, industry stakeholders, and civil society to overcome challenges and ensure equitable access to AI technologies for climate change mitigation (Akter 2024) (Fig. 10.3).

10.2.4 Artificial Intelligence and Climate Actions in Urban Planning

Urbanisation is rapidly transforming the landscape of our planet, with more than half of the global population now residing in cities. As urban areas continue to grow, so do the challenges associated with sustainability and climate change (Satterthwaite 2009). AI offers innovative solutions to assist in designing sustainable cities and mitigating urban heat islands, which are areas with significantly higher temperatures than their rural counterparts due to human activities and infrastructure (Yigitcanlar et al. 2020). AI-driven urban design tools utilise algorithms to optimise city layouts, building designs, and green spaces to maximise energy efficiency and minimise environmental impact. For example, machine learning algorithms can analyse data on urban morphology, land use patterns, and climatic conditions to inform the placement of parks, green roofs, and other vegetation to mitigate heat island effects and improve air quality (Kafy et al. 2022). Transportation planning is another area where AI can make a significant impact on urban sustainability. AI algorithms analyse

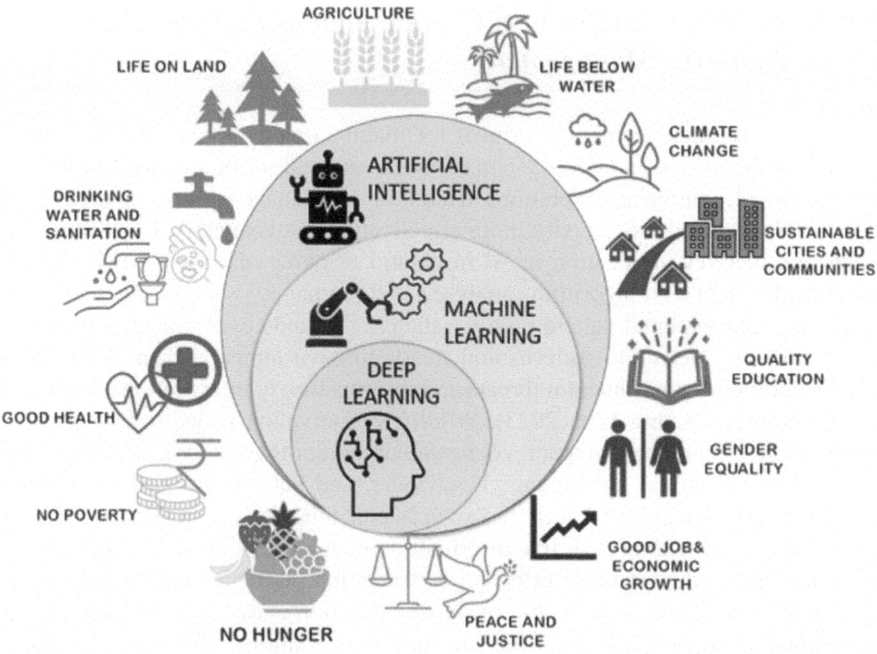

Fig. 10.3 Application of artificial intelligence in environmental sustainability and climate change (Kumari and Pandey 2023). Application of artificial intelligence in environmental sustainability and climate change. In Visualization techniques for climate change with machine learning and artificial intelligence (pp. 293–316). Elsevier

traffic patterns, commuting behaviours, and public transit usage to optimise transportation systems, reduce congestion, and promote the use of low-carbon modes of transportation such as walking, cycling, and public transit (Lv and Shang 2023). By facilitating more efficient transportation networks, AI contributes to reducing greenhouse gas emissions and improving urban livability. Energy-efficient building management is essential for reducing energy consumption and mitigating the heat island effect in urban areas (Ortega-Fernández et al. 2020). AI-powered building management systems utilise sensors and data analytics to optimise heating, cooling, and lighting systems based on occupancy patterns, weather conditions, and energy prices. By dynamically adjusting building operations in real time, these systems improve energy efficiency, reduce carbon emissions, and enhance occupant comfort and well-being (Šujanová et al. 2019). Research demonstrates the potential of AI-driven urban design tools to improve the sustainability and resilience of cities (Bibri et al. 2024). The study showcases how AI algorithms can optimise the placement of green infrastructure, such as parks and green roofs, to reduce the urban heat island effect and enhance urban biodiversity. Additionally, the research highlights how AI-enabled transportation planning can reduce traffic congestion and emissions, leading to more sustainable and livable urban environments (Abd El-Hameed 2020).

10.2.5 Artificial Intelligence, Climate Actions in Natural Resource Management

Natural resource management is critical for maintaining ecosystem health, biodiversity, and the provision of ecosystem services essential for human well-being. AI technologies offer innovative solutions to monitor and manage natural resources such as water, forests, and biodiversity more effectively and sustainably. Environmental monitoring is a key application of AI in natural resource management (Lozo and Onishchenko 2021). AI algorithms analyse satellite imagery, sensor data, and other sources of environmental data to monitor changes in land cover, water quality, and air pollution. By detecting patterns and trends in environmental data, AI enables early detection of environmental threats and informs timely interventions to protect natural resources (Liang et al. 2023). Wildlife conservation is another area where AI can make a significant impact. AI-powered camera traps and acoustic sensors analyse data on animal movements, behaviours, and habitats to monitor wildlife populations and detect illegal activities such as poaching and deforestation (Chisom et al. 2024). By providing real-time information on wildlife populations and threats, AI technologies support more effective conservation strategies and contribute to preserving biodiversity. Sustainable resource extraction is essential for minimising environmental impacts and ensuring the long-term viability of natural resource-dependent industries (Lozo and Onishchenko 2021). AI algorithms analyse geological data, remote sensing imagery, and operational data to optimise resource extraction processes, reduce waste, and minimise environmental footprint. By improving efficiency and reducing environmental impacts, AI technologies contribute to more sustainable resource management practices. A study highlights the potential of AI technologies to enhance natural resource management and biodiversity conservation (Silvestro et al. 2022). The research demonstrates how AI-driven environmental monitoring systems can detect changes in land cover and habitat fragmentation, enabling proactive conservation measures to protect biodiversity hotspots. Additionally, the study showcases how AI-powered resource extraction optimization techniques can reduce ecological disturbance and minimise environmental impacts in natural resource extraction industries.

10.2.6 Artificial Intelligence, Climate Actions, Climate Modelling, and Prediction

Accurate climate modelling and prediction are essential for understanding the impacts of climate change, assessing risks, and informing adaptation and mitigation strategies. AI algorithms offer innovative approaches to improve the accuracy and predictive capabilities of climate models, weather forecasting systems, and risk assessment tools (Huntingford et al. 2019). Climate models simulate the complex interactions between the atmosphere, oceans, land surface, and ice cover to project future climate conditions under different scenarios of greenhouse gas emissions. AI techniques such as machine learning can enhance climate models by improving their representation of physical processes, reducing computational costs, and incorporating new sources of data such as satellite observations and paleoclimate records (Monteleoni et al. 2013). Weather forecasting systems rely on numerical models to predict short-term weather conditions and extreme weather events. AI algorithms can improve the accuracy and lead time of weather forecasts by analysing vast amounts of observational data, identifying patterns, and making predictions based on historical weather patterns and atmospheric dynamics (Huntingford et al. 2019). By providing more accurate and timely weather forecasts, AI technologies help communities and governments prepare for and respond to extreme weather events such as hurricanes, heat waves, and floods. Risk assessment tools are essential for evaluating the potential impacts of climate change on human societies, ecosystems, and economies. AI techniques such as probabilistic modelling and scenario analysis enable researchers to quantify uncertainties, assess risks, and identify adaptation and mitigation strategies to reduce vulnerability and enhance resilience to climate change impacts (Gallina et al. 2016). By integrating AI-driven risk assessment tools into decision-making processes, policymakers can make more informed decisions and prioritise actions to minimise climate risks and protect vulnerable communities and ecosystems. Research demonstrates the potential of AI algorithms to improve climate modelling accuracy and predictive capabilities (Huntingford et al. 2019). The study shows how machine learning techniques can enhance the representation of cloud processes in climate models, leading to more accurate projections of future climate conditions. Additionally, the research highlights how AI-driven weather forecasting systems can improve the accuracy of short-term weather forecasts, enabling more effective preparedness and response measures for extreme weather events (Gupta et al. 2022).

10.2.7 Artificial Intelligence and Informed Decision-Making in Climate Actions

In the realm of climate change mitigation, informed decision-making is crucial for policymakers, businesses, and communities to effectively address the complex challenges posed by a changing climate. AI technologies offer powerful tools to support decision-makers by analysing data, identifying trends, and predicting outcomes related to climate change impacts and mitigation strategies. AI-powered decision support systems leverage advanced analytics and machine learning algorithms to process large volumes of data from diverse sources, including climate models, satellite observations, socioeconomic indicators, and stakeholder feedback (Nishant et al.

2020). These systems provide decision-makers with actionable insights and recommendations to inform policy development, investment decisions, and resource allocation for climate change mitigation efforts. Scenario analysis tools enable decision-makers to explore various future scenarios of climate change impacts and mitigation strategies and evaluate their potential outcomes and trade-offs. AI algorithms analyse complex interactions between different factors, such as greenhouse gas emissions, economic development, and technological innovation, to assess the effectiveness of different mitigation pathways and inform long-term planning and decision-making, (Nishant et al. 2020). Risk management frameworks integrate AI-driven risk assessment tools with decision support systems to identify and prioritise climate risks, evaluate their potential impacts on human societies, ecosystems, and economies, and develop strategies to manage and reduce risks. By quantifying uncertainties and evaluating the likelihood and severity of different climate-related risks, these frameworks enable decision-makers to allocate resources effectively and implement adaptive measures to enhance resilience to climate change impacts (Nishant et al. 2020). For example, the Climate Risk Atlas developed by the World Bank utilises AI algorithms to assess climate risks and vulnerabilities at a global scale, providing decision-makers with valuable insights to inform adaptation planning and investment decisions (Parker et al. 2019). Similarly, the Climate Action Tracker uses AI-driven scenario analysis tools to evaluate the impact of different climate mitigation policies and commitments on global temperature rise, helping policymakers set ambitious targets and track progress towards achieving them (Fig. 10.4).

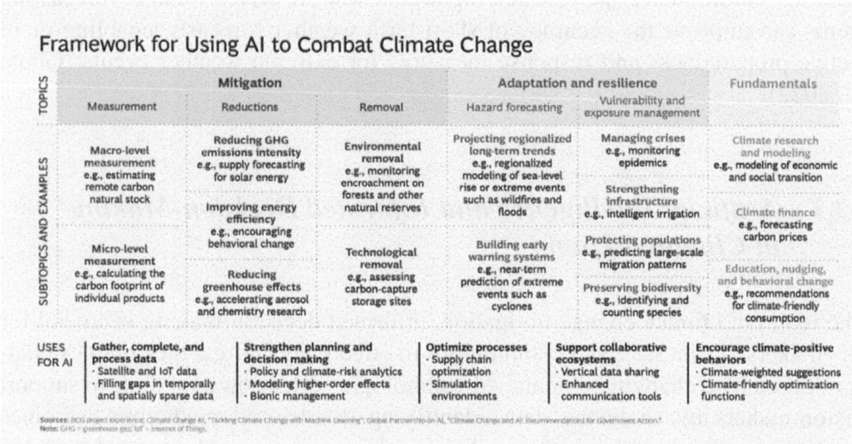

Fig. 10.4 Framework for using AI to combat climate change (https://www.bcg.com/publications/2022/how-ai-can-help-climate-change)

10.3 Challenges and Ethical Considerations and Future Directions

Despite the promise of AI technologies in climate change mitigation, their use also raises significant challenges and ethical considerations that must be addressed to ensure their responsible and equitable deployment. One major challenge is data privacy and security (Ahmad et al. 2022a, b). AI systems rely on vast amounts of data, including sensitive information about individuals, communities, and ecosystems. Ensuring the privacy and security of this data is essential to prevent unauthorised access, misuse, and exploitation, especially in the context of climate-related risks and vulnerabilities (Biden 2023). Equitable access to AI technologies is essential to ensure that all stakeholders, including marginalised communities and developing countries, can benefit from their potential to address climate change challenges (Yigitcanlar et al. 2021). However, disparities in access to technology, digital literacy, and financial resources may exacerbate existing inequalities and hinder efforts to build climate resilience and adaptation capacity. Additionally, the rapid pace of technological innovation and deployment raises concerns about the potential unintended consequences of AI technologies for climate change mitigation (Biden 2023). Anticipating and mitigating these risks requires ongoing monitoring, evaluation, and adaptation of AI systems to ensure their effectiveness, safety, and ethical integrity.

Looking ahead, the future of AI for climate change mitigation holds immense promise but also presents significant challenges and uncertainties. Continued research and collaboration are essential to unlock the full potential of AI technologies and address the complex challenges of climate change in a rapidly changing world. Future developments in AI for climate change mitigation may include advances in data analytics, machine learning algorithms, and computational modelling techniques to improve the accuracy, scalability, and accessibility of climate-related information and decision support tools (Huntingford et al. 2019). Additionally, interdisciplinary research and innovation are needed to integrate AI technologies with other approaches, such as remote sensing, citizen science, and participatory decision-making, to enhance climate resilience and adaptation efforts (Leal Filho et al. 2022).

AI has the potential to revolutionise how we address climate change challenges by providing decision-makers with the tools and insights needed to make informed decisions, allocate resources effectively, and implement adaptive measures to build climate resilience and sustainability. However, realising this potential requires proactive efforts to address challenges and ethical considerations associated with the use of AI in climate change mitigation, while also ensuring equitable access and benefits for all stakeholders. By harnessing the transformative power of AI technologies and fostering collaboration across disciplines and sectors, we can accelerate progress towards a more sustainable and resilient future for all.

References

Abd El-Hameed AK (2020, November) Artificial intelligence shaping sustainable cities for climate change mitigation: a review of literature. In: Architecture and urbanism: a smart outlook: proceedings of the 3rd international conference on architecture and urban planning, Cairo, Egypt. Springer International Publishing, Cham, pp 483–495

Abduljabbar R, Dia H, Liyanage S, Bagloee SA (2019) Applications of artificial intelligence in transport: an overview. Sustainability 11(1):189

Ahmad K, Maabreh M, Ghaly M, Khan K, Qadir J, Al-Fuqaha A (2022a) Developing future human-centered smart cities: critical analysis of smart city security, data management, and ethical challenges. Comput Sci Rev 43:100452

Ahmad T, Madonski R, Zhang D, Huang C, Mujeeb A (2022b) Data-driven probabilistic machine learning in sustainable smart energy/smart energy systems: key developments, challenges, and future research opportunities in the context of smart grid paradigm. Renew Sustain Energy Rev 160:112128

Ahmad T, Zhang D, Huang C, Zhang H, Dai N, Song Y, Chen H (2021) Artificial intelligence in sustainable energy industry: status Quo, challenges and opportunities. J Clean Prod 289:125834

Akter S (2024) Harnessing technology for environmental sustainability: utilizing AI to Tackle global ecological challenges. J Artif Intell General Sci (JAIGS) 2(1):49–57. ISSN: 3006-4023

Alasseri R, Tripathi A, Rao TJ, Sreekanth KJ (2017) A review on implementation strategies for demand side management (DSM) in Kuwait through incentive-based demand response programs. Renew Sustain Energy Rev 77:617–635

Bala G, Caldeira K, Wickett M, Phillips TJ, Lobell DB, Delire C, Mirin A (2007) Combined climate and carbon-cycle effects of large-scale deforestation. Proc Natl Acad Sci 104(16):6550–6555

Bian Y, Yue J, Gao W, Li Z, Lu D, Xiang Y, Chen J (2019) Analysis of the spatiotemporal changes of ice sheet mass and driving factors in Greenland. Remote Sens 11(7):862

Bibri SE, Krogstie J, Kaboli A, Alahi A (2024) Smarter eco-cities and their leading-edge artificial intelligence of things solutions for environmental sustainability: a comprehensive systematic review. Environ Sci Ecotechnol 19:100330

Biden JR (2023) Executive order on the safe, secure, and trustworthy development and use of artificial intelligence

Chisom ON, Biu PW, Umoh AA, Obaedo BO, Adegbite AO, Abatan A (2024) Reviewing the role of AI in environmental monitoring and conservation: a data-driven revolution for our planet. World J Adv Res Rev 21(1):161–171

Chung SH (2021) Applications of smart technologies in logistics and transport: a review. Transport Res Part E: Logist Transport Rev 153:102455

Cowls J, Tsamados A, Taddeo M, Floridi L (2023) The AI gambit: leveraging artificial intelligence to combat climate change—opportunities, challenges, and recommendations. Ai & Society 1–25

Dauvergne P (2020) AI in the wild: sustainability in the age of artificial intelligence. MIT Press

de la Torre R, Corlu CG, Faulin J, Onggo BS, Juan AA (2021) Simulation, optimization, and machine learning in sustainable transportation systems: models and applications. Sustainability 13(3):1551

Dikshit S, Atiq A, Shahid M, Dwivedi V, Thusu A (2023) The use of artificial intelligence to optimize the routing of vehicles and reduce traffic congestion in urban areas. EAI Endorsed Transactions on Energy Web, 10

Gallina V, Torresan S, Critto A, Sperotto A, Glade T, Marcomini A (2016) A review of multi-risk methodologies for natural hazards: consequences and challenges for a climate change impact assessment. J Environ Manag 168:123–132

Gupta S, Modgil S, Kumar A, Sivarajah U, Irani Z (2022) Artificial intelligence and cloud-based collaborative platforms for managing disaster, extreme weather and emergency operations. Int J Prod Econ 254:108642

Hu J, Lin Y, Li J, Hou Z, Chu L, Zhao D, ... Zhang Y (2024) Performance analysis of AI-based energy management in electric vehicles: a case study on classic reinforcement learning. Energy Convers Manag 300:117964

Huntingford C, Jeffers ES, Bonsall MB, Christensen HM, Lees T, Yang H (2019) Machine learning and artificial intelligence to aid climate change research and preparedness. Environ Res Lett 14(12):124007

Javaid M, Haleem A, Khan IH, Suman R (2023) Understanding the potential applications of artificial intelligence in the agriculture sector. Adv Agrochem 2(1):15–30

Kaack LH, Donti PL, Strubell E et al (2022) Aligning artificial intelligence with climate change mitigation. Nat Clim Chang 12:518–527. https://doi.org/10.1038/s41558-022-01377-7)

Kafy AA, Saha M, Rahaman ZA, Rahman MT, Liu D, Fattah MA, ... Ahasan MAK (2022) Predicting the impacts of land use/land cover changes on seasonal urban thermal characteristics using machine learning algorithms. Build Environ 217:109066

Kılkış Ş, Krajačić G, Duić N, Rosen MA (2022) Effective mitigation of climate change with sustainable development of energy, water and environment systems. Energy Convers Manag 269:116146

Kinley R, Cutajar MZ, de Boer Y, Figueres C (2021) Beyond good intentions, to urgent action: former UNFCCC leaders take stock of thirty years of international climate change negotiations. Climate Policy 21(5):593–603

Kumar A (2018) Global warming, climate change and greenhouse gas mitigation. In: Biofuels: greenhouse gas mitigation and global warming: next generation biofuels and role of biotechnology, pp 1–16

Leal Filho W, Wall T, Mucova SAR, Nagy GJ, Balogun AL, Luetz JM, ... Gandhi O (2022) Deploying artificial intelligence for climate change adaptation. Technol Forecast Soc Change 180:121662

Liang L, Daniels J, Bailey C, Hu L, Phillips R, South J (2023) Integrating low-cost sensor monitoring, satellite mapping, and geospatial artificial intelligence for intra-urban air pollution predictions. Environ Pollut 331:121832

Lozo O, Onishchenko O (2021) The potential role of artificial intelligence in combating climate change and natural resources management: political, legal and ethical challenges. J Nat Resour 4(3):111–131

Lv Z, Shang W (2023) Impacts of intelligent transportation systems on energy conservation and emission reduction of transport systems: a comprehensive review. Green Technol Sustain 1(1):100002

Monteleoni C, Schmidt GA, Alexander FJ, Niculescu-Mizil A, Steinhaeuser K, Tippett M, ... Tedesco M (2013) Climate informatics (No. GSFC-E-DAA-TN19114). CRC Press

Nishant R, Kennedy M, Corbett J (2020) Artificial intelligence for sustainability: challenges, opportunities, and a research agenda. Int J Inf Manag 53:102104

Ortega-Fernández A, Martín-Rojas R, García-Morales VJ (2020) Artificial intelligence in the urban environment: Smart cities as models for developing innovation and sustainability. Sustainability 12(19):7860

Owusu PA, Asumadu-Sarkodie S (2016) A review of renewable energy sources, sustainability issues and climate change mitigation. Cogent Eng 3(1):1167990

Parker L, Bourgoin C, Martinez-Valle A, Läderach P (2019) Vulnerability of the agricultural sector to climate change: the development of a pan-tropical climate risk vulnerability assessment to inform sub-national decision making. PLoS ONE 14(3):e0213641

Satterthwaite D (2009) The implications of population growth and urbanization for climate change. Environ Urban 21(2):545–567

Şerban AC, Lytras MD (2020) Artificial intelligence for smart renewable energy sector in Europe—smart energy infrastructures for next generation smart cities. IEEE Access 8:77364–77377

Shaikh TA, Rasool T, Lone FR (2022) Towards leveraging the role of machine learning and artificial intelligence in precision agriculture and smart farming. Comput Electron Agric 198:107119

Shivanna KR (2022) Climate change and its impact on biodiversity and human welfare. Proc Indian Natl Sci Acad 88(2):160–171

Silvestro D, Goria S, Sterner T, Antonelli A (2022) Improving biodiversity protection through artificial intelligence. Nat Sustain 5(5):415–424

Singh BR, Singh O (2012) Study of impacts of global warming on climate change: rise in sea level and disaster frequency. In: Global warming—impacts and future perspective, pp 94–118

Steffen W, Persson Å, Deutsch L, Zalasiewicz J, Williams M, Richardson K, ... Svedin U (2011) The Anthropocene: from global change to planetary stewardship. Ambio 40:739–761

Stein AL (2020) Artificial intelligence and climate change. Yale J Reg 37:890

Šujanová P, Rychtáriková M, Sotto Mayor T, Hyder A (2019) A healthy, energy-efficient and comfortable indoor environment, a review. Energies 12(8):1414

Verge XPC, De Kimpe C, Desjardins RL (2007) Agricultural production, greenhouse gas emissions and mitigation potential. Agric Meteorol 142(2–4):255–269

Yigitcanlar T, Kankanamge N, Regona M, Ruiz Maldonado A, Rowan B, Ryu A, ... Li RYM (2020) Artificial intelligence technologies and related urban planning and development concepts: how are they perceived and utilized in Australia? J Open Innov: Technol, Market, Complex 6(4):187

Yigitcanlar T, Mehmood R, Corchado JM (2021) Green artificial intelligence: towards an efficient, sustainable and equitable technology for smart cities and futures. Sustainability 13(16):8952

Yoro KO, Daramola MO (2020) CO_2 emission sources, greenhouse gases, and the global warming effect. In: Advances in carbon capture. Woodhead Publishing, pp 3–28

Chapter 11
Digital Revolution, Artificial Intelligence, and Ethical Challenges

Abstract This chapter delves into the ethical challenges posed by the digital revolution driven by digital transformation, artificial intelligence (AI) technologies, and intelligent algorithms. It explores the core ethical and socio-economic issues of ethical nature and implications arising from the widespread adoption of digital technologies and AI systems in this rapidly evolving landscape. This chapter discusses issues such as job displacements, data and privacy issues, intellectual property issues, data ownership and misuse, algorithmic discrimination, and bias with case studies and real-world examples. It emphasises the importance of addressing these challenges to ensure the responsible development and deployment of digital technologies and AI systems. By fostering a culture of ethics, collaboration, and stakeholder engagement, society can harness the potential of digital technologies and AI systems while ensuring they align with human values, promote fairness, and contribute to the betterment of individuals and communities.

Keywords Digital revolution · Ethical challenges · Algorithmic bias · Data and privacy issues · Job displacements · Discrimination

11.1 Digital Revolution and Artificial Intelligence

The digital revolution stands as one of the most transformative periods in human history, reshaping nearly every aspect of society through the widespread adoption and integration of digital technologies (Allam 2019). This profound shift has touched various facets of human life, including the economy, education, healthcare, and communication, fundamentally altering how individuals interact with information and with each other. At its core, the digital revolution is defined by the digitization and virtualization of information, processes, and interactions, resulting in unprecedented levels of connectivity, efficiency, and innovation (Curley and Salmelin 2017).

In the contemporary digital landscape, technology serves as a double-edged sword, offering unprecedented opportunities for advancement while simultaneously presenting complex ethical dilemmas (Akram 2023). One of the foremost ethical

S. Kumar et al., *Digital Transformation, Artificial Intelligence and Society*, Frontiers of Artificial Intelligence, Ethics and Multidisciplinary Applications,
https://doi.org/10.1007/978-981-97-5656-8_11

concerns revolves around the issue of privacy and data protection. In the era of big data, massive amounts of personal information are routinely collected, stored, and analysed by tech companies for various purposes, including targeted advertising and algorithmic decision-making (Vassakis et al. 2018). The Cambridge Analytica scandal serves as a poignant example of this ethical quandary, wherein the personal data of millions of Facebook users were harvested without their consent for political profiling and manipulation (Heawood 2018). This breach not only underscored the importance of robust data protection regulations, but also highlighted the potential risks associated with the unchecked accumulation of personal information in the digital realm. Furthermore, the proliferation of artificial intelligence (AI) algorithms has raised concerns regarding algorithmic bias and fairness. These algorithms, often trained on biased datasets or reflecting societal prejudices, can perpetuate and exacerbate existing disparities and discrimination (Pessach and Shmueli 2023). For instance, facial recognition technology has shown higher error rates for women and people of colour, leading to concerns about its deployment in law enforcement and surveillance (Bacchini and Lorusso 2019). Similarly, predictive algorithms used in various domains, such as criminal justice and finance, have been found to exhibit racial biases, resulting in unfair outcomes and reinforcing systemic inequalities (Huq 2018). Addressing algorithmic bias requires not only technical solutions, but also broader societal awareness and regulatory measures to ensure fairness and accountability in algorithmic decision-making processes (Lepri et al. 2018) (Fig. 11.1).

Fig. 11.1 Humans implementation of ethical AI design (https://www.weforum.org/agenda/2021/12/ai-artificial-intelligence-robots/)

11.2 Understanding Digital Ethics and Its Component

Digital ethics comprises various components that guide the responsible use of technology, particularly in the context of digital technologies artificial intelligence (AI), and emerging digital technologies. Here are some key components of digital ethics along with examples:

- Privacy and Data Protection: Privacy refers to individuals' rights to control access to their personal information. Data protection involves safeguarding sensitive data from unauthorised access, use, or disclosure (King and Raja 2012). Digital ethics emphasises the importance of respecting individuals' privacy rights and implementing robust data protection measures to prevent data breaches and unauthorised data collection. For instance, end-to-end encryption in messaging apps like Signal and WhatsApp ensures that only the sender and recipient can access the contents of their messages, protecting user privacy (Rösler et al. 2018).
- Transparency and Accountability: Transparency entails openness and honesty in disclosing information about the use of technology, including how data is collected, stored, and processed. Accountability involves holding individuals and organisations responsible for their actions and decisions related to technology use (Turilli and Floridi 2009). Digital ethics advocates for transparency and accountability to build trust among stakeholders and ensure ethical behaviour in technological development and deployment. For example, Companies should disclose how they collect, use, and share user data through transparent privacy policies and terms of service agreements (Felzmann et al. 2020).
- Fairness and Bias Mitigation: Fairness concerns ensuring equal treatment and opportunities for all individuals, regardless of their background or characteristics. Bias mitigation involves identifying and addressing biases that may exist in technological systems, particularly AI algorithms (Mehrabi et al. 2021). Digital ethics promotes fairness and bias mitigation to prevent discrimination and ensure equitable outcomes in technology-mediated interactions and decision-making processes. For instance, auditing algorithms for bias and conducting regular assessments to ensure fairness in hiring practices, loan approvals, and criminal justice sentencing (Ashokan and Haas 2021).
- Inclusivity and Accessibility: Inclusivity involves designing technology to be accessible and usable by individuals with diverse abilities, backgrounds, and needs. Accessibility focuses on removing barriers to participation and ensuring equal access to digital resources and services (Gilbert 2019). Digital ethics advocates for inclusivity and accessibility to promote social inclusion and empower marginalised communities in the digital age (Sanders and Scanlon 2021). Designing digital products and services to be inclusive and accessible to individuals with disabilities. For example, web accessibility standards such as the Web Content Accessibility Guidelines (WCAG) ensure that websites and digital content are usable by people with visual, auditory, motor, and cognitive disabilities (Caldwell et al. 2008).

- User Empowerment and Consent: User empowerment entails empowering individuals to make informed choices about their use of technology and control over their data. Consent involves obtaining explicit permission from individuals before collecting, processing, or sharing their personal information (Tene and Polonetsky 2012). Digital ethics emphasises the importance of user empowerment and consent to respect individuals' autonomy and promote ethical practices in technology use. It also provides users with meaningful control over their data through consent mechanisms and privacy settings. For instance, allowing users to opt out of data collection and targeted advertising or providing clear and easily accessible options to delete their accounts and data (Dhotre et al. 2018).
- Ethical AI Development and Deployment: Ethical AI development involves designing and deploying AI systems that align with ethical principles, such as fairness, transparency, and accountability (Sanderson et al. 2023). It encompasses ethical considerations throughout the AI lifecycle, from data collection and algorithm design to deployment and evaluation (Burr and Leslie 2023). Digital ethics advocates for ethical AI development and deployment to mitigate potential risks and ensure beneficial outcomes for society. For instance, organisations like the Global Partnership on AI and the IEEE Global Initiative for Ethical Considerations in AI and Autonomous Systems provide ethical guidelines and best practices for AI research and development (Shahriari and Shahriari 2017).
- Digital Citizenship and Education: Digital citizenship refers to the responsible and ethical use of technology, including respecting others' rights and contributing positively to digital communities (Oxley 2011). Digital education involves promoting digital literacy and ethical awareness to empower individuals to navigate the digital world safely and ethically. Digital ethics emphasises the importance of digital citizenship and education to foster a culture of responsible technology use mitigate harmful behaviours online and promote digital literacy and responsible digital citizenship through education and awareness programmes (Frau-Meigs et al. 2017). For instance, teaching students critical thinking skills, online safety practices, and ethical considerations in technology use to navigate the digital landscape responsibly.

These components of digital ethics serve as guiding principles for individuals, organisations, and policymakers to navigate the complex ethical challenges posed by digital technologies and artificial intelligence. By incorporating ethical considerations into the design, development, and use of technology, stakeholders can ensure that digital innovations are aligned with ethical values and contribute positively to society (Fig. 11.2).

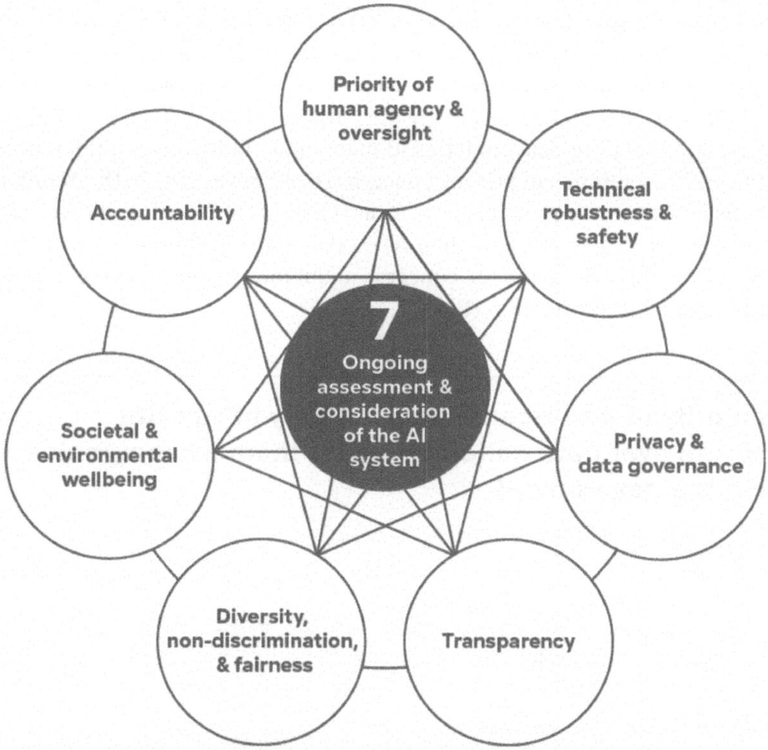

Fig. 11.2 Digital and AI ethics components (https://data.europa.eu/doi/10.2759/856513/ https://comma-soft.com/en/blog/digital-ethics-what-does-it-mean/)

11.3 Ethical Challenges in the Digital Age

The digital age has brought about unprecedented convenience and connectivity, but it has also raised significant ethical challenges that must be addressed to ensure the responsible development and deployment of digital technologies. Among the foremost ethical concerns are issues related to privacy, data misuse, algorithmic bias, and the socio-economic impacts of automation and AI adoption.

11.3.1 Privacy Concerns and Challenges

Privacy concerns loom large in an era where personal data has become a valuable commodity for corporations and governments. The collection, storage, and utilisation of personal data raise questions about individual privacy rights, consent, and data ownership. From social media platforms harvesting user data for targeted advertising to governments surveilling citizens for national security purposes, the pervasive collection of personal data has sparked debates about the balance between privacy and innovation (Westerlund et al. 2021). For example, In 2018, Cambridge Analytica, a political consulting firm, harvested the personal data of millions of Facebook users without their consent for political advertising purposes. This scandal shed light on the risks of using AI and big data analytics to manipulate individuals' preferences and behaviours, raising significant privacy concerns (Boldyreva et al. 2018). Similarly, in Smart home devices, such as Amazon Echo and Google Home, AI systems constantly collect audio recordings to improve their AI models and algorithms (Sepasgozar et al. 2020). However, this raises privacy concerns about the storage and potential misuse of sensitive personal information (Fig. 11.3).

Majority of Americans feel as if they have little control over data collected about them by companies and the government

% of U.S. adults who say ...

		Companies	The government
Lack of control	They have very little/no control over the data __ collect(s)	81%	84%
Risks outweigh benefits	Potential risks of __ collecting data about them outweigh the benefits	81%	66%
Concern over data use	They are very/somewhat concerned about how __ use(s) the data collected	79%	64%
Lack of understanding about data use	They have very little/no understanding about what __ do/does with the data collected	59%	78%

Note: Those who did not give an answer or who gave other responses are not shown.
Source: Survey conducted June 3-17, 2019.
"Americans and Privacy: Concerned, Confused and Feeling Lack of Control Over Their Personal Information"

PEW RESEARCH CENTER

Fig. 11.3 Trends of concern on privacy and data protection (https://www.pewresearch.org/internet/2019/11/15/americans-and-privacy-concerned-confused-and-feeling-lack-of-control-over-their-personal-information/)

11.3.2 Security and Misuse Risk

Data misuse and security risks pose significant ethical dilemmas in the digital age, as evidenced by the prevalence of data breaches, cyberattacks, and the unauthorised use of data for surveillance or manipulation. The unauthorised access, theft, or exploitation of sensitive data can have far-reaching consequences for individuals, organisations, and society as a whole, eroding trust and undermining the integrity of digital systems and services (Saraswat and Meel 2022). For example, the development of autonomous weapons systems, also known as lethal autonomous weapons (LAWs), raises profound ethical questions about the use of AI in warfare (Pedron and Cruz 2020). These systems can select and engage targets without human intervention, leading to concerns about accountability and the potential for mass atrocities. The United Nations has been discussing the ethical implications of autonomous weapons, with some countries calling for a ban on their development and deployment to prevent the erosion of human control over lethal force (Fig. 11.4).

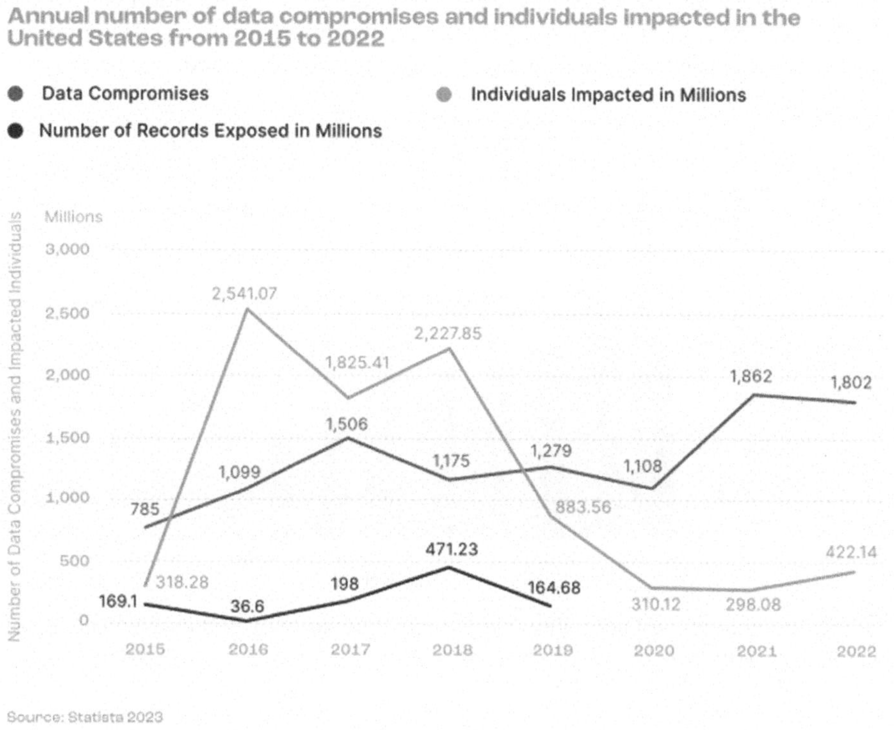

Fig. 11.4 Trends of cyber crime in US (https://seon.io/resources/global-cybercrime-report/)

11.3.3 Artificial Systems Biases and Discrimination

Algorithmic bias and discrimination have become growing concerns as AI technologies play an increasingly influential role in decision-making processes. Biases encoded in AI algorithms, whether due to biased training data or human biases embedded in machine learning models, can lead to discriminatory outcomes in areas such as hiring, lending, criminal justice, and healthcare (Fig. 11.5). For example, In 2018, Amazon scrapped an AI recruitment tool after discovering it was biased against women engineers (Kodiyan 2019). The system was trained on resumes submitted to the company over a ten-year period, which were predominantly from men. As a result, the AI model learned to favour male candidates over female candidates, reflecting and exacerbating the existing gender bias in the tech industry. Another example has been in Facial recognition systems that have also shown biases, with studies revealing higher error rates for women and people of colour. For instance, in 2019, a study by the National Institute of Standards and Technology (NIST) found that some facial recognition algorithms misidentified African American and Asian faces up to 100 times more than Caucasian faces (Grother et al. 2019). Addressing algorithmic bias requires careful attention to data quality, model fairness, and algorithmic transparency to ensure equitable and inclusive outcomes for all individuals.

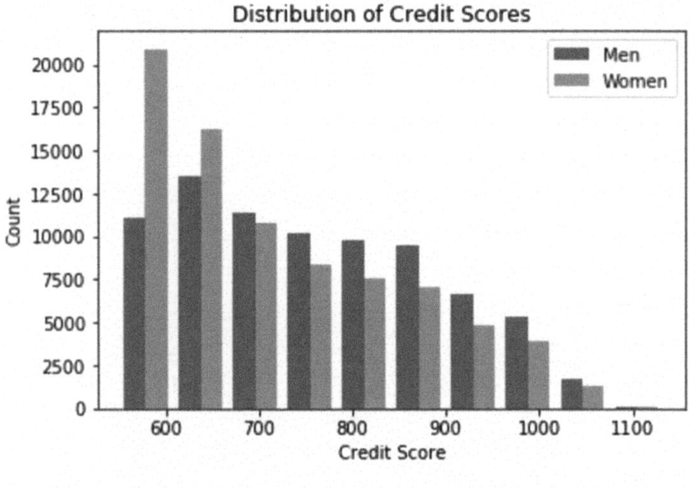

Fig. 11.5 Fairness in machine learning and building an unbiased credit score (https://medium.com/@pranavp802/fairness-in-machine-learning-building-an-unbiased-credit-score-9931ceb9f017) Accessed on 26th April 2024

11.3.4 Unemployment and Job Risk

AI-driven job displacement raises profound ethical and socio-economic questions about the future of work and the distribution of wealth and opportunity in society. Automation and AI adoption have the potential to disrupt traditional industries, leading to job loss, skill mismatch, and income inequality (Deschacht 2021). While AI technologies offer opportunities for increased productivity and innovation, they also pose challenges for workers whose jobs are vulnerable to automation. Addressing the ethical implications of AI-driven job displacement requires proactive measures to support workers through retraining programmes, lifelong learning initiatives, and social safety nets to ensure a just transition to the digital economy (Chen 2018). The rise of automation driven by AI technologies has led to concerns about job displacement and widening economic inequality. For example, the introduction of autonomous vehicles threatens to disrupt the livelihoods of millions of truck drivers worldwide. In the financial sector, AI-powered algorithms are increasingly used for tasks such as trading, risk assessment, and fraud detection, potentially replacing human workers and exacerbating job insecurity.

AI technology has undoubtedly brought about significant changes in the job market, raising concerns about unemployment and job displacement. According to a study conducted by the Brookings Institution, around 25% of U.S. jobs are at high risk of automation, with lower-wage roles facing the greatest jeopardy (Ghimire et al. 2020). The report highlights that tasks such as manual labour in predictable environments and routine data processing are particularly susceptible to automation (Fig. 11.6). Moreover, a survey by the World Economic Forum suggests that by 2025, AI and automation could potentially displace 85 million jobs globally in customer service, manufacturing, and administrative roles. These figures underscore the magnitude of the challenge posed by AI-driven unemployment (Willcocks 2020).

However, it's essential to recognise that the impact of AI on employment is nuanced and multifaceted. While certain jobs may be at risk of automation, AI also creates new opportunities and roles. For example, the same Brookings report suggests that the adoption of AI could create demand for new jobs in areas such as healthcare, technology, and creative industries. Roles like AI trainers, data analysts, and cybersecurity experts are expected to see growth as organisations adapt to AI technologies. Additionally, a study by PwC estimates that AI could contribute up to $15.7 trillion to the global economy by 2030, potentially leading to the creation of millions of new jobs in AI-related fields (Belkacemi 2022).

Nevertheless, the transition to an AI-driven economy poses challenges for workers and policymakers alike. There is a pressing need for upskilling and reskilling programmes to equip the workforce with the necessary skills to thrive in a digital age. Governments and businesses must collaborate to invest in education and training initiatives that prepare individuals for the jobs of the future. Moreover, policies need to be developed to ensure that the benefits of AI are distributed equitably and that vulnerable populations are not left behind. By addressing these issues proactively,

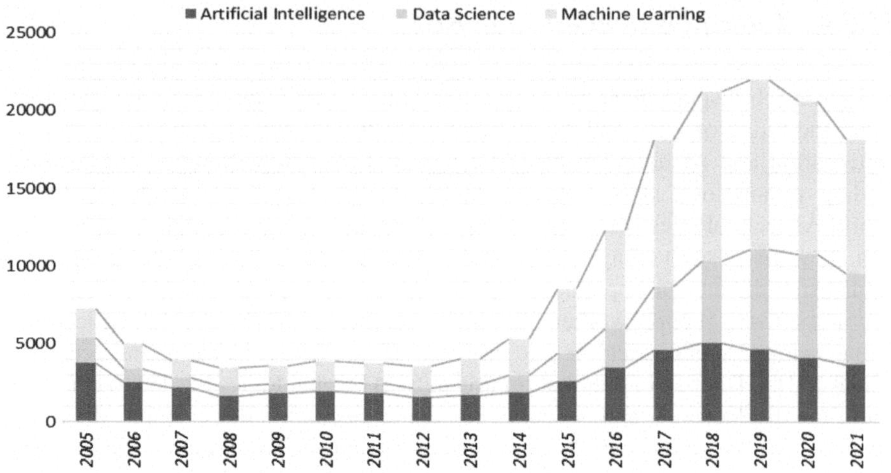

Fig. 11.6 Automation and unemployment trends due to AI technology (Guliyev 2023)

societies can harness the transformative potential of AI while mitigating its impact on unemployment and ensuring inclusive economic growth.

11.3.5 Algorithmic Accountability and Transparency

Algorithmic accountability and transparency are crucial ethical considerations in the digital age, particularly concerning the use of AI and machine learning algorithms. These concepts entail ensuring that algorithms are fair, transparent, and accountable for their decisions and outcomes. For example, Mortgage Lending Algorithms In the financial sector, algorithms are commonly (Lee and Floridi 2021) used to assess creditworthiness and determine loan approval for mortgage applicants. However, concerns have been raised about the potential biases inherent in these algorithms, which may lead to discriminatory lending practices. Suppose a mortgage lending algorithm is trained on historical data that reflects existing biases in lending practices, such as favouring applicants from certain demographic groups or neighbourhoods (Fu et al. 2020). Without proper mitigation strategies, the algorithm may inadvertently perpetuate these biases, leading to unfair outcomes for marginalised communities. Algorithmic transparency is essential in this scenario to understand how the algorithm makes lending decisions and identify any biases or disparities. However, many financial institutions may consider their algorithms proprietary and thus resist disclosing their inner workings. Algorithmic accountability becomes crucial to ensure that lenders are held responsible for the fairness and equity of their algorithms (Bruckner 2018). If a lending algorithm is found to systematically disadvantage certain groups, financial regulators or consumer advocacy groups can intervene to demand transparency, audit the algorithm, and implement corrective measures to mitigate bias and ensure fair lending practices (Fig. 11.7). In 2019, Apple came under scrutiny when it was revealed that its credit card algorithm offered higher credit limits to men than to women with similar creditworthiness (Ben-Ishai and Bedford 2021). This incident highlighted the importance of algorithmic transparency and accountability in ensuring fair and equitable outcomes. Social media platforms like Facebook and Twitter face criticism for their opaque algorithms, which can amplify misinformation, polarisation, and harmful content (Stark et al. 2020). Calls for greater transparency and oversight have intensified in recent years to address these issues.

The ethical challenges posed by the digital age are multifaceted and complex, encompassing issues related to privacy, data misuse, algorithmic bias, and socio-economic impacts. Addressing these challenges requires a holistic approach that balances innovation with ethical considerations, fosters transparency and accountability, and prioritises the well-being and dignity of individuals and communities. Through collaborative efforts across academia, industry, government, and civil society, we can navigate the ethical complexities of the digital age and harness the transformative potential of digital technologies for the benefit of all.

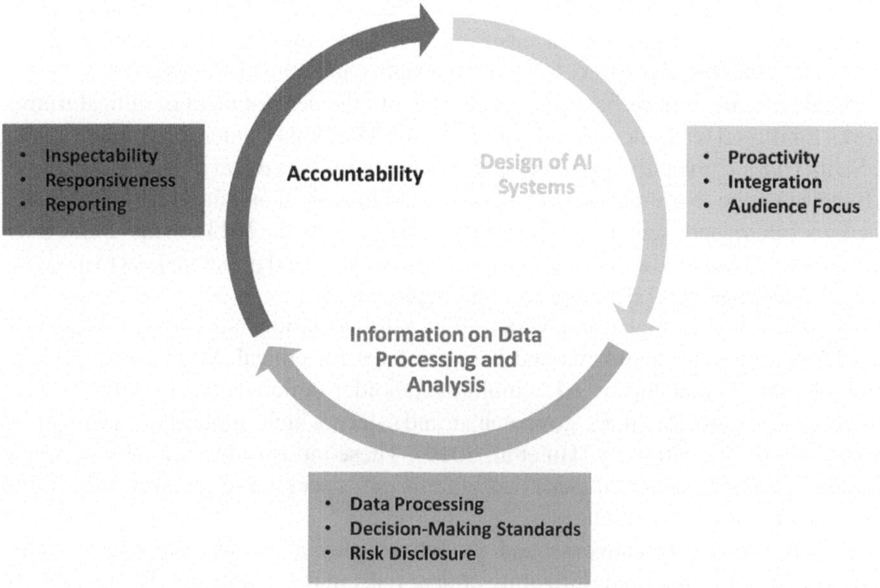

Fig. 11.7 Design for accountability and transparency (Felzmann et al. 2020)

11.4 Ethical Frameworks and Guidelines

In response to the ethical challenges posed by the digital age, various organisations, academia, and industry leaders have proposed ethical frameworks and guidelines to guide the responsible development and deployment of digital technologies and AI systems. These frameworks emphasise principles such as fairness, transparency, accountability, and inclusivity to ensure that technological advancements align with human values and promote the well-being of individuals and communities. One prominent example of an ethical framework is the IEEE Global Initiative on Ethics of Autonomous and Intelligent Systems, which outlines a set of principles for the ethical design and deployment of AI technologies (Leikas et al. 2019). These principles include transparency, accountability, awareness of bias, data privacy, and respect for human rights. By adhering to these principles, developers and stakeholders can mitigate ethical risks and promote trust in AI systems. Similarly, the European Commission has proposed ethical guidelines for trustworthy AI, emphasising principles such as human agency and oversight, technical robustness and safety, privacy and data governance, transparency, diversity, non-discrimination, fairness, and societal and environmental well-being (Hickman and Petrin 2021). These guidelines provide a comprehensive framework for ensuring that AI technologies are developed and used in a manner that respects fundamental rights and ethical values.

Academic institutions have also contributed to the development of ethical frameworks for digital technologies. For example, the Markkula Center for Applied Ethics at Santa Clara University has developed a framework for ethical decision-making in AI and machine learning, which emphasises values such as fairness, transparency, accountability, and social responsibility (Flahaux et al. 2023). This framework provides practical guidance for developers, researchers, and policymakers to navigate ethical dilemmas in AI development and deployment.

In addition to formal frameworks, industry associations and consortiums have developed voluntary standards and best practices for ethical AI development. For example, the Partnership on AI, a multi-stakeholder initiative, has established a set of best practices for AI ethics, governance, and safety, which emphasise transparency, fairness, and accountability (Hu et al. 2019). These industry-led initiatives provide valuable guidance for companies and organisations seeking to integrate ethics into their AI strategies and practices.

Overall, ethical frameworks and guidelines play a crucial role in promoting responsible innovation and mitigating ethical risks in the digital age. By adhering to principles such as fairness, transparency, accountability, and inclusivity, developers, policymakers, and stakeholders can ensure that digital technologies and AI systems serve the common good and contribute to a more equitable and sustainable future.

11.5 Strategies for Ethical AI Development and Deployment

Integrating ethics into the AI lifecycle is essential for addressing ethical challenges and ensuring the responsible development and deployment of AI technologies. This requires a multifaceted approach that encompasses ethical design principles, bias mitigation techniques, and algorithmic transparency measures, as well as interdisciplinary collaboration between technologists, ethicists, policymakers, and stakeholders (Khanna and Srivastava 2020).

One strategy for ethical AI development is to incorporate ethical considerations into the design process from the outset. This involves identifying potential ethical risks and trade-offs associated with AI applications and integrating mechanisms for ethical decision-making and oversight into the design process. For example, developers can use tools such as ethical impact assessments to evaluate the potential social, cultural, and ethical implications of AI systems and make informed design choices that prioritise ethical values and principles (Sanderson et al. 2023) (Fig. 11.8).

Another strategy is to employ bias mitigation techniques to address the inherent biases in AI algorithms. This involves identifying and mitigating biases in training data, algorithms, and decision-making processes to ensure fair and equitable outcomes for all individuals. For example, developers can use techniques such

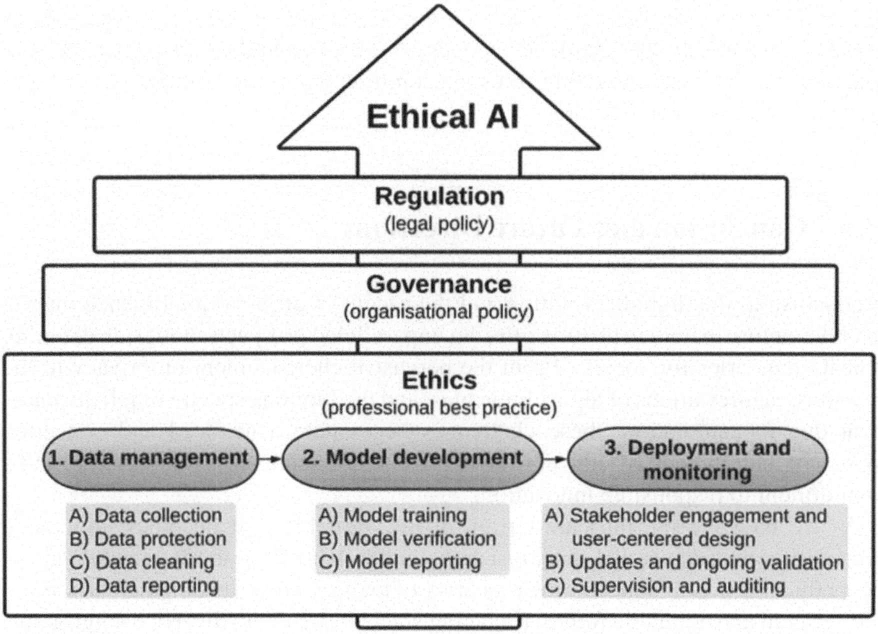

Fig. 11.8 Ethical AI development (https://pub.aimind.so/ethical-considerations-in-ai-and-data-science-navigating-the-complex-landscape-c5809f3584f6) Accessed on 26 April 2026

as data preprocessing, algorithmic auditing, and fairness-aware machine learning to detect and mitigate biases in AI systems and promote fairness and inclusivity (González-Sendino et al. 2023).

Algorithmic transparency is also critical for ensuring accountability and trust in AI systems. This involves making AI algorithms and decision-making processes transparent and understandable to users, stakeholders, and regulators. For example, developers can use techniques such as explainable AI to provide insights into how AI systems make decisions and enable users to understand, challenge, and verify the outcomes of AI-driven decisions. By promoting transparency and accountability, developers can build trust and confidence in AI systems and mitigate concerns about opacity and algorithmic black boxes.

Interdisciplinary collaboration is essential for identifying and mitigating ethical risks associated with AI technologies. This involves bringing together technologists, ethicists, policymakers, and stakeholders to engage in dialogue, share expertise, and develop solutions to ethical challenges. For example, interdisciplinary research centres and initiatives can facilitate collaboration between diverse stakeholders and foster a culture of ethical innovation and responsible AI development (Taylor et al. 2018). By fostering collaboration and dialogue, stakeholders can work together to address ethical concerns and promote the responsible use of AI technologies for the benefit of society.

Integrating ethics into the AI lifecycle requires a holistic approach that encompasses ethical design principles, bias mitigation techniques, algorithmic transparency measures, and interdisciplinary collaboration. By prioritising ethical considerations and engaging stakeholders in the design, development, and deployment of AI technologies, we can ensure that AI serves the common good and contributes to a more equitable and sustainable future.

11.6 Conclusion and Future Directions

In conclusion, the digital revolution and the ascent of artificial intelligence mark a pivotal juncture in human history, offering unparalleled prospects alongside daunting ethical quandaries for society. From the pervasive encroachment on privacy to the insidious manifestations of algorithmic bias, and the looming spectre of job displacement due to automation, these challenges necessitate a nuanced and concerted approach, underpinned by ethical frameworks, interdisciplinary collaboration, and a commitment to responsible innovation.

As we navigate the intricate terrain of the digital age, it becomes imperative to prioritise continuous dialogue, research, and collaboration to effectively address these ethical concerns and steer the trajectory of technological development towards a more ethical and equitable future. Engaging stakeholders from diverse backgrounds, including academia, industry, government, and civil society, is paramount in fostering a shared understanding of the ethical implications of digital technologies and AI systems.

Furthermore, ongoing research and inquiry are indispensable in elucidating the multifaceted dimensions of ethical challenges in the digital age and devising robust solutions to mitigate potential harms. Interdisciplinary collaboration between technologists, ethicists, policymakers, and stakeholders can foster innovative approaches to addressing ethical concerns while balancing the imperatives of technological advancement and societal well-being.

Moreover, fostering a culture of responsible innovation requires a commitment to ethical principles and values, including transparency, fairness, accountability, and inclusivity. By embedding these principles into the design, development, and deployment of digital technologies and AI systems, stakeholders can cultivate trust and confidence among users and stakeholders, thereby enhancing the societal acceptance and adoption of transformative technologies.

Looking ahead, it is essential to remain vigilant and proactive in anticipating and addressing emerging ethical challenges in the rapidly evolving landscape of digital technologies and AI systems. As technology continues to advance at an unprecedented pace, it is incumbent upon us to remain cognizant of the ethical implications of our innovations and to uphold the fundamental rights and dignity of individuals and communities.

In summary, the digital revolution and the rise of artificial intelligence offer immense promise for human progress and prosperity, but they also pose profound ethical challenges that demand careful consideration and concerted action. By fostering a culture of ethical responsibility, collaboration, and innovation, we can harness the transformative potential of digital technologies and AI systems while ensuring that they serve the collective good and contribute to a more equitable and sustainable future.

References

Akram A (2023) The impact of social media on communication and relationships: a double-Edged Sword. Policy Res J 1(1):15–24

Allam Z (2019) Cities and the digital revolution: aligning technology and humanity. Springer Nature

Ashokan A, Haas C (2021) Fairness metrics and bias mitigation strategies for rating predictions. Inf Process Manag 58(5):102646

Bacchini F, Lorusso L (2019) Race, again: how face recognition technology reinforces racial discrimination. J Inf Commun Ethics Soc 17(3):321–335

Belkacemi S (2022) Artificial Intelligence "AI" and its impact on the global economy. J Financ Account Manag Stud 9(2)

Ben-Ishai S, Bedford M (2021) AI, consumer credit, and discrimination: a comparative look at Canada and the United States. Corp Bus Law J 2:271

Boldyreva EL, Grishina NY, Duisembina Y, Boldyreva E L, Grishina N Y (2018) Cambridge analytica: ethics and online manipulation with decision-making process. Eur Proc Soc Behav Sci 51

Bruckner MA (2018) The promise and perils of algorithmic lenders' use of big data. Chi.-Kent Law Rev 93:3

Burr C, Leslie D (2023) Ethical assurance: a practical approach to the responsible design, development, and deployment of data-driven technologies. AI Ethics 3(1):73–98

Caldwell B, Cooper M, Reid LG, Vanderheiden G, Chisholm W, Slatin J, White J (2008) Web content accessibility guidelines (WCAG) 2.0. WWW Consortium (W3C) 290(1–34):5–12
Chen M (2018) The global impact of artificial intelligence on job markets. Int J Transcontinental Discov 5(1):7–13. ISSN: 3006-628X
Curley M, Salmelin B (2017) Open innovation 2.0: the new mode of digital innovation for prosperity and sustainability. Springer
Deschacht N (2021) The digital revolution and the labour economics of automation: a review. Robonomics: J Autom Econ 1:8–8
Dhotre PS, Olesen H, Khajuria S (2018) User privacy and empowerment: trends, challenges, and opportunities. In: Intelligent computing and information and communication: proceedings of 2nd international conference, ICICC 2017. Springer Singapore, pp 291–304
Felzmann H, Fosch-Villaronga E, Lutz C, Tamò-Larrieux A (2020) Towards transparency by design for artificial intelligence. Sci Eng Ethics 26(6):3333–3361
Flahaux JR, Green BP, Skeet AG (2023) Ethics in the age of disruptive technologies: an operational roadmap. Markkula Center for Applied Ethics, ITEC, and Santa Clara University
Frau-Meigs D, O'Neill B, Soriani A, Tomé V (2017) Digital citizenship education: Volume 1: Overview and new perspectives
Fu R, Huang Y, Singh PV (2020) Ai and algorithmic bias: source, detection, mitigation and implications. Detection, Mitigation and Implications, July 26
Ghimire R, Skinner J, Carnathan M (2020) Who perceived automation as a threat to their jobs in metro Atlanta: results from the 2019 Metro Atlanta speaks survey. Technol Soc 63:101368
Gilbert RM (2019) Inclusive design for a digital world: designing with accessibility in mind. Apress
González-Sendino R, Serrano E, Bajo J, Novais P (2023) A review of bias and fairness in artificial intelligence
Grother P, Ngan M, Hanaoka K (2019) Face recognition vendor test (FVRT): Part 3, demographic effects. National Institute of Standards and Technology, Gaithersburg, MD
Guliyev H (2023) Artificial intelligence and unemployment in high-tech developed countries: new insights from dynamic panel data model. Res Glob 7, 100140
Heawood J (2018) Pseudo-public political speech: democratic implications of the Cambridge Analytica scandal. Inf Polity 23(4):429–434
Hickman E, Petrin M (2021) Trustworthy AI and corporate governance: the EU's ethics guidelines for trustworthy artificial intelligence from a company law perspective. Eur Bus Organiz Law Rev 22:593–625
Hu X, Neupane B, Echaiz LF, Sibal P, Rivera Lam M (2019) Steering AI and advanced ICTs for knowledge societies: a rights, openness, access, and multi-stakeholder perspective. UNESCO Publishing
Huq AZ (2018) Racial equity in algorithmic criminal justice. Duke Law J 68:1043
Khanna S, Srivastava S (2020) Patient-centric ethical frameworks for privacy, transparency, and bias awareness in deep learning-based medical systems. Appl Res Artif Intell Cloud Comput 3(1):16–35
King NJ, Raja VT (2012) Protecting the privacy and security of sensitive customer data in the cloud. Comput Law Secur Rev 28(3):308–319
Kodiyan AA (2019) An overview of ethical issues in using AI systems in hiring with a case study of Amazon's AI-based hiring tool. Researchgate Preprint 1–19
Lee MSA, Floridi L (2021) Algorithmic fairness in mortgage lending: from absolute conditions to relational trade-offs. Mind Mach 31(1):165–191
Leikas J, Koivisto R, Gotcheva N (2019) Ethical framework for designing autonomous intelligent systems. J Open Innov: Technol, Market, Complex 5(1):18
Lepri B, Oliver N, Letouzé E, Pentland A, Vinck P (2018) Fair, transparent, and accountable algorithmic decision-making processes: the premise, the proposed solutions, and the open challenges. Philos Technol 31(4):611–627
Mehrabi N, Morstatter F, Saxena N, Lerman K, Galstyan A (2021) A survey on bias and fairness in machine learning. ACM Comput Surv (CSUR) 54(6):1–35

Oxley C (2011) Digital citizenship: developing an ethical and responsible online culture. Access 25(3):5–9
Pedron SM, da Cruz JDA (2020) The future of wars: Artificial intelligence (AI) and lethal autonomous weapon systems (laws). Int J Secur Stud 2(1):2
Pessach D, Shmueli E (2023) Algorithmic fairness. In: Machine learning for data science handbook: data mining and knowledge discovery handbook. Springer International Publishing, Cham, pp 867–886
Rösler P, Mainka C, Schwenk J (2018, April) More is less: on the end-to-end security of group chats in signal, whatsapp, and threema. In: 2018 IEEE European symposium on security and privacy (EuroS&P). IEEE, pp 415–429
Sanders CK, Scanlon E (2021) The digital divide is a human rights issue: advancing social inclusion through social work advocacy. J Hum Rights Soc Work 6(2):130–143
Sanderson C, Douglas D, Lu Q, Schleiger E, Whittle J, Lacey J, ... Hansen D (2023) AI ethics principles in practice: perspectives of designers and developers. IEEE Trans Technol Soc
Saraswat AK, Meel V (2022) Protecting data in the 21st century: challenges, strategies and future prospects. Inf Technol Ind 10(2):26–35
Sepasgozar S, Karimi R, Farahzadi L, Moezzi F, Shirowzhan S, Ebrahimzadeh S M, ... Aye L (2020) A systematic content review of artificial intelligence and the internet of things applications in smart home. Appl Sci 10(9):3074
Shahriari K, Shahriari M (2017, July) IEEE standard review—Ethically aligned design: a vision for prioritizing human wellbeing with artificial intelligence and autonomous systems. In: 2017 IEEE Canada international humanitarian technology conference (IHTC). IEEE, pp 197–201
Stark B, Stegmann D, Magin M, Jürgens P (2020) Are algorithms a threat to democracy? The rise of intermediaries: a challenge for public discourse. Algorithm Watch 26
Taylor S, Boniface M, Pickering B, Anderson M, Danks D, Følstad A, ... Woollard F (2018) Responsible AI–Key themes, concerns & recommendations for European research and innovation
Tene O, Polonetsky J (2012) Big data for all: privacy and user control in the age of analytics. Nw J Tech Intell Prop 11:239
Turilli M, Floridi L (2009) The ethics of information transparency. Ethics Inf Technol 11:105–112
Vassakis K, Petrakis E, Kopanakis I (2018) Big data analytics: applications, prospects and challenges. In: Mobile big data: a roadmap from models to technologies, pp 3–20
Westerlund M, Isabelle DA, Leminen S (2021) The acceptance of digital surveillance in an age of big data. Technol Innov Manag Rev 11(3):32–44
Willcocks L (2020) Robo-Apocalypse cancelled? Reframing the automation and future of work debate. J Inf Technol 35(4):286–302

Chapter 12
Way Forward—Moving Towards Responsible Artificial Intelligence

Abstract This chapter explores and suggests ways and directions for the sustainable use of technology for the benefit of society. It discusses the imperative of moving towards the responsible adoption of digital transformation and artificial intelligence (AI) and highlights the mechanism to address the ethical considerations, challenges, and strategies associated with the responsible deployment of AI systems. It emphasises the need to align AI development with ethical principles, societal values, and human well-being. Responsible AI ensures that AI systems are fair, transparent, accountable, and respectful of human rights and privacy. It emphasises the importance of addressing these ethical concerns to build trust and foster the responsible adoption of AI technologies.

Keywords Responsible artificial intelligence · Digital transformation · Digital welfare · Handling ethical issues · Policies and framework · Way forward

12.1 Understanding Ethical and Responsible Digital Technology

Responsible and ethical use and adoption of digital technology involve recognising the importance of incorporating ethical considerations into each stage of problem-solving using technology such as conceptualization, formulation, requirement gathering and analysis, design, development, and fair use of technology (Weber-Lewerenz 2021). The digital age and information age have brought about significant concerns and challenges for individuals, society, and governments across the world which need thorough exploration of apprehensions related to privacy (Milanovic 2015). Privacy including data breaches, unauthorised surveillance, and the exploitation of personal information by tech companies have become prevalent issues. For example, the Cambridge Analytica scandal in 2018 involved the unauthorised harvesting of millions of Facebook users' data for political targeting purposes and manipulating their behaviour to exercise the choice in a particular direction (Hu 2020). Ethical and responsible digital technology is needed to ensure that users' privacy rights

S. Kumar et al., *Digital Transformation, Artificial Intelligence and Society*, Frontiers of Artificial Intelligence, Ethics and Multidisciplinary Applications,
https://doi.org/10.1007/978-981-97-5656-8_12

are respected and protected. Similarly, AI Algorithms used in various applications, such as hiring, lending, and predictive policing, can perpetuate and exacerbate biases present in society. For instance, biased algorithms in hiring processes may lead to discrimination against certain demographic groups (Packin and Lev-Aretz 2018). Ethical and responsible digital technology is necessary to address algorithmic bias and promote fairness and equity. This involves auditing algorithms for bias, diversifying datasets, and designing algorithms that prioritise fairness and transparency (Mensah 2023).

Despite the widespread adoption of digital technology, there are still significant disparities in access and usage, particularly among marginalised communities. The digital divide exacerbates existing inequalities in education, employment, and economic opportunities. Ethical and responsible digital technology is essential for bridging the digital divide and ensuring that technology is accessible to all (Yu 2002). This includes initiatives to provide affordable internet access, improve digital literacy programmes, and design inclusive technologies that accommodate diverse needs and abilities. The increasing adoption of artificial intelligence and automation raises ethical concerns related to accountability, transparency, and job displacement. Biassed algorithms, autonomous weapons systems, and the potential for mass unemployment are among the ethical challenges associated with AI and automation. Ethical and responsible digital technology is essential for ensuring that AI and automation are developed and deployed in ways that prioritise human well-being and societal benefit (Stahl 2021). This includes ethical guidelines for AI development, mechanisms for accountability and oversight, and policies to mitigate the negative impact on employment (Ashok et al. 2022).

12.2 Understanding Responsible Artificial Intelligence

In the quest for ethical AI development, the definition of "responsible AI" serves as the cornerstone. Responsible AI embodies a set of principles and practices that prioritise ethical considerations, societal well-being, and human values throughout the lifecycle of AI systems (Cheng et al. 2021). At its core, responsible AI seeks to ensure that AI technologies are developed and deployed in a manner that upholds fairness, transparency, accountability, and respect for human rights and dignity. One crucial aspect of defining responsible AI is addressing the concept of bias and fairness (Fig. 12.1). AI algorithms, fueled by vast amounts of data, have the potential to perpetuate or even exacerbate societal biases present in the data (Schwartz et al. 2022). This bias can manifest in various forms, including racial, gender, or socioeconomic biases, leading to discriminatory outcomes in AI-driven decision-making processes. Responsible AI development necessitates proactive measures to mitigate bias and promote fairness, thereby safeguarding against the amplification of societal inequalities (Cheng et al. 2021).

Furthermore, ethical AI development entails prioritising transparency and interpretability in AI systems. The inherent complexity of AI algorithms often renders

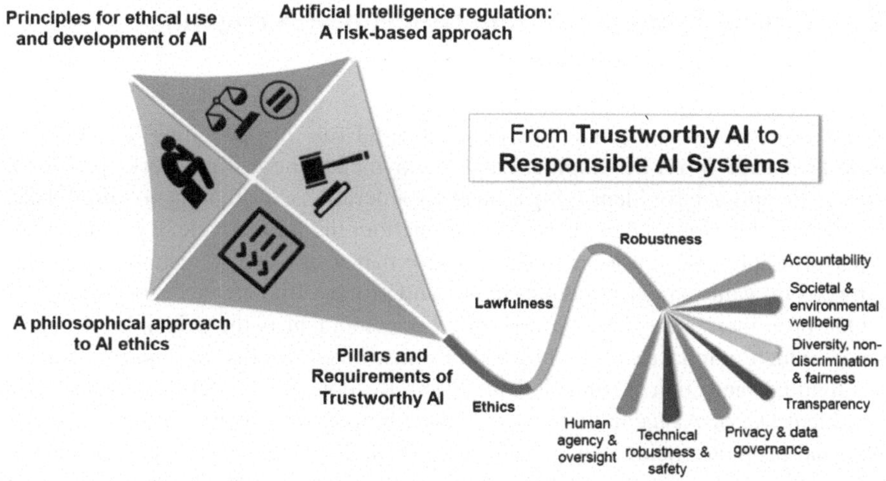

Fig. 12.1 Responsible AI (RAI) (https://www.linkedin.com/pulse/responsible-ai-rai-imperative-artificial-intelligence-mark-kovarski-iwsxc/)

them opaque, making it challenging to understand how decisions are made or to detect potential biases. This lack of transparency not only undermines trust in AI systems, but also poses risks of unintended consequences or ethical violations. By prioritising transparency and interpretability, responsible AI developers can empower end-users to comprehend AI-driven decisions and hold AI systems accountable for their actions (Radanliev et al. 2024).

To illustrate, a study highlighted the prevalence of gender and racial biases in facial recognition algorithms, underscoring the need for responsible AI development to address algorithmic biases (Sharma and Graydon 2021). Additionally, research emphasised the importance of transparency and interpretability in AI systems, advocating for the adoption of ethical principles to enhance the accountability of AI technologies (Williams et al. 2022).

Defining responsible AI requires a holistic approach that integrates ethical principles, societal values, and human rights into the development and deployment of AI systems. By prioritising fairness, transparency, and accountability, responsible AI development can help mitigate ethical risks and foster trust in AI technologies, ultimately contributing to a more equitable and inclusive society.

12.3 Ethical Frameworks and Guidelines: Navigating the Moral Landscape of AI

Ethical frameworks and guidelines play a pivotal role in navigating the complex moral landscape of AI development and deployment. These frameworks provide a structured approach for identifying ethical considerations, evaluating potential risks, and guiding decision-making processes throughout the AI lifecycle. By adhering to ethical principles, organisations and developers can ensure that AI technologies align with societal values, respect human rights, and promote the greater good.

One prominent ethical framework in AI development is the principle of beneficence, which emphasises the obligation to maximise benefits and minimise harm to individuals and society (Floridi et al. 2018). Responsible AI developers prioritise the ethical use of AI technologies to enhance human well-being, mitigate societal risks, and promote social justice (Sanderson et al. 2023). By applying the principle of beneficence, developers can mitigate the potential negative consequences of AI deployment and maximise its positive impact on society.

Moreover, ethical guidelines serve as a roadmap for ethical AI development, offering practical recommendations for addressing specific ethical concerns and dilemmas. For example, guidelines such as the IEEE Global Initiative on Ethics of Autonomous and Intelligent Systems provide a comprehensive framework for incorporating ethical considerations into AI design, development, and deployment (Michael et al. 2020). These guidelines cover a wide range of topics, including transparency, accountability, fairness, privacy, and human rights, offering valuable insights for responsible AI development.

Furthermore, ethical frameworks facilitate ethical decision-making in AI development by guiding developers through complex ethical dilemmas and trade-offs. For instance, the utilitarian approach to ethics advocates for maximising overall societal welfare, even if it entails sacrificing individual interests or preferences. By applying utilitarian principles, responsible AI developers can prioritise societal benefits while mitigating potential harms, thereby promoting ethical outcomes in AI deployment.

To illustrate, the European Commission's High-Level Expert Group on Artificial Intelligence (AI HLEG) developed ethical guidelines for trustworthy AI, emphasising principles such as human agency and oversight, technical robustness and safety, privacy and data governance, transparency, diversity, non-discrimination, societal and environmental well-being, and accountability (Smuha 2019). These guidelines provide a comprehensive framework for promoting responsible and ethical AI development in Europe and beyond.

12.4 Strategies for Promoting Responsible AI Adoption

Ethical design principles are essential for embedding ethics into the AI development lifecycle, ensuring that ethical considerations are integrated from the outset and throughout the entire process. By incorporating ethical principles into the design, development, deployment, and maintenance of AI systems, organisations can proactively address ethical concerns and promote responsible AI adoption (Burr and Leslie 2023). One key aspect of ethical design principles is the concept of privacy by design, which advocates for incorporating privacy protections into AI systems from the initial design phase. This involves implementing privacy-enhancing technologies, such as data anonymization and encryption, to safeguard individuals' privacy rights and mitigate the risks of unauthorised access or misuse of personal data. By prioritising privacy by design, organisations can demonstrate their commitment to ethical AI development and foster trust among users (Shen and Pearson 2011). Additionally, ethical design principles emphasise the importance of fairness and transparency in AI algorithms and decision-making processes. By designing AI systems to be fair and transparent, organisations can mitigate the risks of algorithmic bias and discrimination, thereby promoting inclusivity and equity. Techniques such as algorithmic auditing and fairness-aware machine learning can help identify and address biases in AI models, ensuring that they produce equitable outcomes across diverse demographic groups. Furthermore, ethical design principles encourage interdisciplinary collaboration and stakeholder engagement throughout the AI development lifecycle (Burr and Leslie 2023). By involving ethicists, social scientists, policymakers, and other stakeholders in the design process, organisations can gain diverse perspectives and insights into the ethical implications of AI technologies. This collaborative approach fosters a more comprehensive understanding of ethical issues and enables developers to make informed decisions that prioritise societal values and human rights. To illustrate, the concept of "AI ethics by design" emphasises the integration of ethical considerations into the design and development of AI systems, advocating for the adoption of ethical design principles to promote responsible AI adoption (Floridi and Cowls 2022) (Fig. 12.2).

Similarly, research highlights the importance of incorporating fairness, transparency, and accountability into AI systems from the outset, underscoring the need for ethical design principles to address ethical concerns in AI development. Ethical design principles therefore play a crucial role in promoting responsible AI adoption by embedding ethics into the AI development lifecycle (Díaz-Rodríguez et al. 2023). By prioritising privacy, fairness, transparency, and interdisciplinary collaboration, organisations can develop AI systems that uphold ethical principles, respect human rights, and contribute to the greater good.

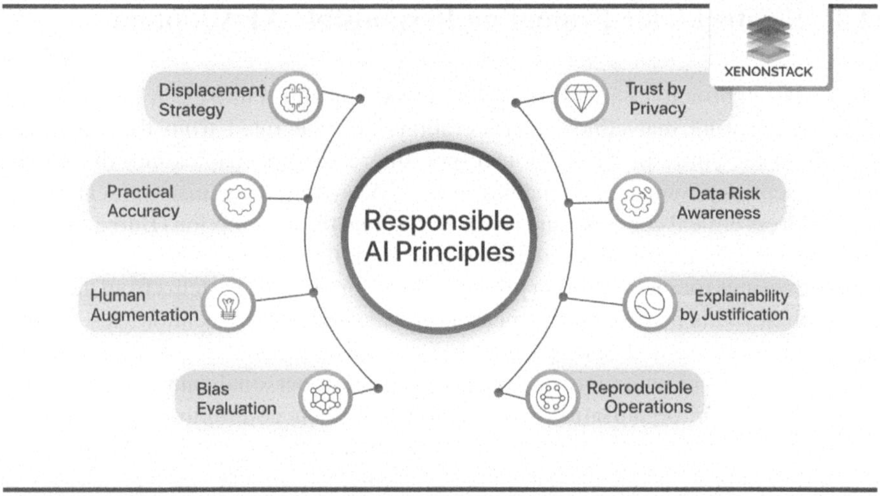

Fig. 12.2 Responsible AI strategy (https://www.xenonstack.com/blog/responsible-ai-principles/) Accessed on April 26, 2026

12.5 Regulatory Frameworks and Legal Compliance: Shaping Policies for Ethical AI Governance

Regulatory frameworks and legal compliance are instrumental in shaping policies for ethical AI governance, providing the necessary guidelines and oversight mechanisms to ensure that AI technologies are developed and deployed responsibly and ethically. As AI technologies continue to evolve and permeate various sectors of society, regulatory frameworks play a crucial role in safeguarding against potential risks and abuses while promoting the ethical and responsible use of AI (Oladoyinbo et al. 2024). One key aspect of regulatory frameworks is establishing clear guidelines and standards for ethical AI development and deployment. Regulatory bodies can develop principles, guidelines, and certification schemes that outline the ethical principles and requirements for AI systems, such as transparency, accountability, fairness, and privacy. By setting clear expectations and standards, regulatory frameworks guide organisations and developers to comply with ethical norms and best practices in AI governance. Additionally, regulatory frameworks can incorporate mechanisms for oversight and enforcement to ensure compliance with ethical standards and legal requirements. This may include conducting audits, inspections, and assessments of AI systems to evaluate their adherence to ethical principles and identify potential risks or violations (Shneiderman 2020). By enforcing regulatory compliance, authorities can hold organisations and developers accountable for ethical lapses or violations in AI development and deployment. Furthermore, regulatory frameworks can foster international collaboration and harmonisation to address ethical challenges and promote consistency in AI governance across borders. By collaborating

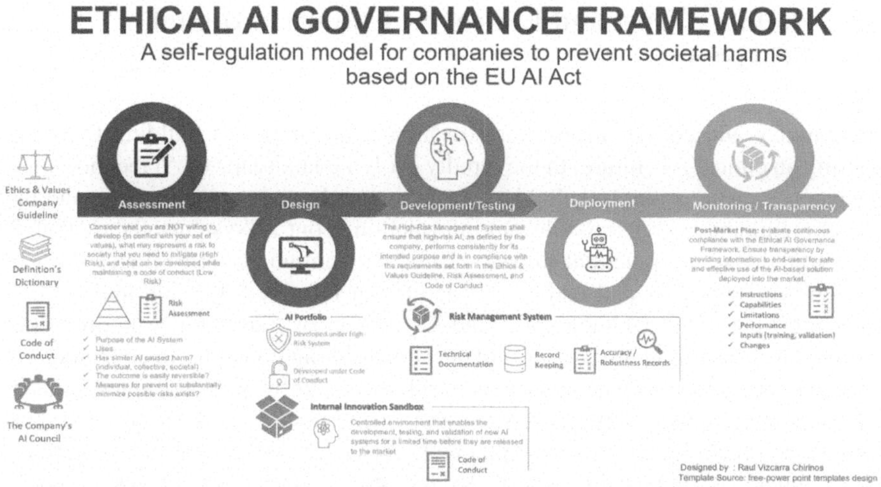

Fig. 12.3 Ethical AI governance framework (https://medium.com/latinxinai/navigating-muddy-waters-a-framework-for-ethical-ai-governance-inspired-by-the-eu-ai-act-3d6339ba364)

with other countries and international organisations, regulatory bodies can share best practices, exchange information, and coordinate efforts to address global challenges, such as algorithmic bias, data protection, and AI-driven surveillance. This collaborative approach helps ensure that regulatory frameworks are effective, responsive, and adaptable to the evolving landscape of AI technologies. To illustrate, the European Union's General Data Protection Regulation (GDPR) incorporates provisions related to AI and automated decision-making, imposing requirements for transparency, fairness, and accountability in the use of AI systems (Sartor and Lagioia 2020) (Fig. 12.3).

Similarly, the United States Federal Trade Commission (FTC) has issued guidelines for AI and algorithmic decision-making, emphasising the importance of transparency, consumer protection, and non-discrimination in AI governance (Slaughter et al. 2020). Regulatory frameworks and legal compliance play a critical role in shaping policies for ethical AI governance, providing the necessary guidelines, oversight mechanisms, and enforcement measures to ensure that AI technologies are developed and deployed responsibly and ethically. By establishing clear standards, promoting compliance, and fostering international collaboration, regulatory frameworks contribute to the advancement of ethical AI adoption and the protection of human rights and societal values (Cihon 2019).

12.6 Building Trust and Ethical AI Culture in Digital Ecosystem

Transparency and communication are essential components in building trust and fostering an ethical AI culture. In the rapidly evolving landscape of AI technologies, transparency ensures that stakeholders, including end-users, policymakers, and the general public, have access to relevant information about AI systems, their capabilities, limitations, and potential impacts. Effective communication bridges the gap between AI developers and end-users, facilitating informed decision-making and enhancing trust in AI technologies. One key aspect of transparency is providing clear explanations of AI algorithms and decision-making processes to end-users. AI developers should strive to demystify the black box of AI by offering explanations in understandable terms, enabling users to comprehend how AI systems arrive at their conclusions. Techniques such as explainable AI (XAI) and model interpretability help elucidate the inner workings of AI algorithms, empowering users to assess the reliability and fairness of AI-driven decisions Moreover, transparent communication involves disclosing potential risks, limitations, and biases associated with AI systems upfront (Dwivedi et al. 2023). By acknowledging the uncertainties and ethical dilemmas inherent in AI technologies, developers can manage expectations and foster realistic perceptions among end-users. Transparency also entails providing avenues for feedback, grievance redressal, and accountability, enabling stakeholders to raise concerns and hold AI developers accountable for ethical lapses or unintended consequences. Furthermore, transparent communication extends beyond technical aspects to encompass broader ethical considerations, such as privacy, data security, and societal impact. AI developers should engage in proactive dialogue with stakeholders to address ethical concerns, solicit feedback, and incorporate diverse perspectives into AI development processes. By fostering transparency and open communication, organisations can build trust, enhance accountability, and promote responsible AI adoption. To illustrate, initiatives such as the AI Transparency and Ethics Toolkit developed by the Partnership on AI provide resources and guidelines for promoting transparency and ethical communication in AI development and deployment (Jobin et al. 2019). Similarly, research studies highlight the importance of transparent communication in building trust and fostering ethical AI cultures, emphasising the need for clear explanations and disclosure of AI systems' decision-making processes (Robinson 2020).

Stakeholders need to actively work to identify and mitigate biases in AI algorithms and data. This may involve diverse representation in data collection, algorithmic audits, and ongoing monitoring for bias. Stakeholders also need to promote the inclusion of design by involving diverse stakeholders in the design and development process to ensure that AI systems are inclusive and considerate of various perspectives and needs. Data Privacy and Security must also be prioritised for the protection of user data and ensure that AI systems comply with relevant privacy regulations. There are need for continuous learning and improvement that fosters a culture of continuous learning and improvement, where AI systems are regularly evaluated and updated to reflect evolving ethical standards and best practices (Shneiderman 2020). Interdisciplinary training in the Ethics framework needs to be explored and provide training to developers, data scientists, and other stakeholders on ethical considerations in AI development and deployment. This helps raise awareness of potential ethical issues and empowers individuals to make ethical decisions. Government public institutions and educational institutions must engage with communities affected by AI technologies to understand their concerns and priorities and incorporate their feedback into the development and deployment process to ensure that AI systems align with societal values and norms (Nam and Pardo 2011). Technology regulators keep putting regulatory compliance stay informed about relevant regulations and guidelines governing AI technologies, and ensure compliance with legal and ethical standards. All stakeholders and communities must promote open dialogue encouraging open dialogue and collaboration among stakeholders, including industry leaders, policymakers, researchers, and advocacy groups, to address ethical challenges and develop shared solutions.

12.7 Education and Awareness: Empowering Stakeholders with Ethical AI Literacy

Education and awareness can play a crucial role in empowering stakeholders with ethical AI literacy, enabling them to navigate the ethical complexities of AI technologies and make informed decisions. In an increasingly AI-driven world, it is essential to equip individuals, organisations, policymakers, and communities with the knowledge, skills, and awareness necessary to understand the ethical implications of AI and promote responsible AI adoption (Mikalef et al. 2022).

One key aspect of ethical AI literacy is promoting awareness of ethical principles, values, and guidelines governing AI development and deployment. Educational initiatives, training programmes, and awareness campaigns can raise awareness about ethical considerations such as fairness, transparency, accountability, privacy, and human rights in the context of AI technologies (Ng et al. 2021). By fostering a culture of ethical awareness, organisations can empower stakeholders to recognise and address ethical dilemmas in AI applications.

Moreover, ethical AI literacy involves providing stakeholders with the knowledge and skills to critically evaluate AI technologies and their potential impacts on individuals and society (Zhang et al. 2023). This includes understanding the technical aspects of AI algorithms, recognising biases and limitations in AI systems, and assessing the ethical implications of AI-driven decisions. By promoting critical thinking and ethical reasoning, education initiatives enable stakeholders to engage in informed discussions, advocate for ethical practices, and hold AI developers accountable for responsible AI deployment.

Furthermore, ethical AI literacy extends beyond technical proficiency to encompass broader societal implications and ethical dilemmas related to AI technologies. Educational programmes should incorporate interdisciplinary perspectives from fields such as philosophy, sociology, law, and ethics to provide a holistic understanding of the ethical challenges posed by AI. By fostering interdisciplinary dialogue and collaboration, stakeholders can develop a nuanced understanding of AI ethics and contribute to the development of ethical AI solutions.

To illustrate, educational initiatives such as AI ethics courses, workshops, and online resources offered by universities, professional organisations, and civil society groups aim to promote ethical AI literacy among diverse stakeholders. Similarly, research studies, emphasise the importance of ethical education and awareness in shaping responsible AI cultures, advocating for interdisciplinary approaches to AI ethics education (Saad 2023).

Education and awareness are essential for empowering stakeholders with ethical AI literacy, enabling them to understand, evaluate, and navigate the ethical complexities of AI technologies. By promoting awareness of ethical principles, fostering critical thinking, and encouraging interdisciplinary dialogue, education initiatives contribute to the development of responsible AI cultures and the promotion of ethical AI adoption.

12.8 Ethical AI in Emerging Markets: Addressing Global Disparities in AI Development

The advancement and adoption of AI technologies have the potential to exacerbate global disparities in AI development, access, and impact, raising ethical concerns about equity, inclusivity, and social justice. Ethical AI in emerging markets focuses on addressing these disparities and ensuring that AI technologies contribute to positive societal outcomes for all individuals and communities, regardless of geographical location or socio-economic status (Roche et al. 2023).

One key challenge in ethical AI development is addressing data biases and inequalities in emerging markets, where data may be scarce, unrepresentative, or biased towards certain demographic groups. AI systems trained on biased or limited data may perpetuate existing inequalities and reinforce societal biases, leading to unfair outcomes and exacerbating disparities. Ethical AI research focuses on developing strategies for mitigating data biases, enhancing data diversity, and promoting inclusive representation in AI datasets to ensure that AI technologies are equitable and inclusive (Roshanaei 2024).

Moreover, ethical AI in emerging markets entails promoting responsible AI adoption and capacity building among diverse stakeholders, including governments, businesses, civil society organisations, and local communities. This involves providing training, resources, and support for AI literacy, skill development, and technology transfer to empower emerging markets to leverage AI technologies for social and economic development. By promoting inclusive participation and collaboration, ethical AI initiatives foster local ownership and sustainability in AI deployment.

Furthermore, ethical AI in emerging markets emphasises the importance of cultural sensitivity and contextual relevance in AI development and deployment. AI technologies should be tailored to the specific needs, preferences, and cultural contexts of diverse communities, respecting local values, norms, and traditions (Robinson 2020). This involves engaging with local stakeholders, understanding their priorities and concerns, and co-designing AI solutions that address their unique challenges and aspirations.

To illustrate, initiatives such as the AI for Good Foundation and the Global AI Ethics Consortium focus on promoting ethical AI adoption and capacity building in emerging markets, advocating for inclusive and sustainable approaches to AI development (Cihon 2019). Similarly, research studies highlight the importance of addressing global disparities in AI development and promoting ethical AI initiatives that prioritise equity, inclusivity, and social justice (Roche et al. 2023).

In summary, ethical AI in emerging markets addresses the ethical challenges and opportunities associated with AI development, access, and impact in diverse geographical and socioeconomic contexts. By promoting inclusive participation, capacity building, and cultural sensitivity, ethical AI initiatives empower emerging markets to harness the potential of AI technologies for positive societal outcomes and contribute to global efforts towards ethical and responsible AI adoption.

12.9 Ethical Leadership in AI Innovation: Role of Industry Leaders, Academia, and Policy Makers

Ethical leadership plays a pivotal role in shaping the trajectory of AI innovation, guiding the development and deployment of AI technologies responsibly and ethically. Industry leaders, academia, and policymakers have a shared responsibility to uphold ethical principles, promote transparency, and foster trust in AI technologies, thereby ensuring that AI innovation serves the greater good and advances human well-being.

One key aspect of ethical leadership in AI innovation is promoting ethical culture and values within organisations and institutions. Industry leaders, including technology companies and research institutions, have a responsibility to cultivate a culture of ethics, integrity, and accountability in AI development and deployment. This involves establishing ethical guidelines, training programmes, and mechanisms for ethical oversight to ensure that AI technologies adhere to ethical principles and respect human rights.

Moreover, ethical leadership entails advocating for responsible AI policies and regulations that prioritise ethical considerations, such as fairness, transparency, and accountability. Policymakers and regulatory bodies play a crucial role in shaping the legal and regulatory framework for AI governance, ensuring that AI technologies are developed and deployed in a manner that upholds societal values and protects human rights (de Almeida et al. 2021). By enacting legislation, guidelines, and standards for ethical AI, policymakers can promote trust, foster innovation, and mitigate risks associated with AI deployment.

Furthermore, ethical leadership involves fostering collaboration and knowledge sharing among industry, academia, and civil society to address ethical challenges and promote best practices in AI development and deployment. Interdisciplinary collaboration enables diverse perspectives and expertise to inform AI innovation, leading to more robust and ethical AI solutions. By fostering a culture of collaboration and openness, ethical leaders can harness the collective wisdom and creativity of stakeholders to address complex ethical dilemmas in AI (Hastuti 2023).

To illustrate, initiatives such as the Partnership on AI and the AI Ethics Guidelines Global Network bring together industry leaders, academic researchers, and policymakers to develop ethical guidelines and standards for AI governance (Abbas 2023). Similarly, research studies, highlight the importance of ethical leadership in shaping responsible AI innovation, advocating for proactive measures to address ethical challenges and promote ethical AI adoption.

In summary, ethical leadership in AI innovation involves promoting ethical culture and values, advocating for responsible policies and regulations, and fostering collaboration among stakeholders to address ethical challenges and promote responsible AI adoption (Abbas 2023). By upholding ethical principles, industry leaders, academia, and policymakers can guide AI innovation towards ethical and socially responsible outcomes, thereby advancing human well-being and societal progress.

12.10 Conclusion: Navigating the Path Towards Responsible AI

The journey towards responsible artificial intelligence (AI) is a complex and multifaceted endeavour that requires collective action, unwavering commitment, and continuous adaptation. Throughout this chapter, we have explored the imperative of moving towards responsible AI adoption, addressing ethical considerations, challenges, and strategies associated with the development and deployment of AI technologies.

At the heart of responsible AI lies a commitment to ethical principles, societal values, and human well-being. Responsible AI development entails ensuring that AI systems embody traits of fairness, transparency, accountability, and respect for human rights and privacy. By prioritising these ethical imperatives, organisations and developers can mitigate the risks of algorithmic bias, promote inclusivity, and foster trust in AI technologies, thereby contributing to a more equitable and just society (Dwivedi et al. 2021).

However, the path towards responsible AI is not without its challenges. Bias and fairness in AI algorithms, transparency, and interpretability in AI decision-making, and accountability and liability in AI-driven actions are among the key challenges that must be addressed to realise the full potential of AI while minimising its risks and negative impacts. Moreover, as AI technologies continue to evolve and advance, emerging trends such as autonomous systems, deep learning, and artificial general intelligence present new ethical considerations that demand proactive attention and ethical foresight.

In navigating these challenges, stakeholders must embrace proactive strategies for promoting responsible AI adoption. Ethical design principles, regulatory frameworks, stakeholder engagement, transparency, education, and ethical leadership all play critical roles in shaping the trajectory of AI innovation towards ethical and socially responsible outcomes. By integrating these strategies into AI development and deployment processes, stakeholders can build trust, enhance accountability, and foster a culture of responsible AI adoption.

Looking towards the future, the responsible adoption of AI technologies will require ongoing collaboration, innovation, and adaptation. Emerging trends in ethical AI, including the ethical implications of advanced AI technologies and AI in emerging markets, present both opportunities and challenges that demand interdisciplinary collaboration, ethical leadership, and global cooperation (Dwivedi et al. 2021). By addressing global disparities in AI development, promoting inclusivity, and prioritising ethical considerations, stakeholders can ensure that AI technologies contribute to positive societal outcomes and advance human well-being on a global scale.

In conclusion, the imperative of moving towards responsible artificial intelligence is clear. By aligning AI development with ethical principles, societal values, and human rights, stakeholders can mitigate ethical risks, foster trust, and harness the transformative potential of AI for the greater good. As we navigate the complexities of AI innovation, let us remain steadfast in our commitment to responsible AI adoption, guided by the principles of fairness, transparency, accountability, and respect for human dignity (Dwivedi et al. 2021). Together, we can build a future where AI technologies empower individuals, strengthen communities, and contribute to a more just and sustainable world.

References

Abbas T (2023) Ethical implications of AI in modern education: balancing innovation and responsibility. Soc Sci Spectr 2(1):51–57

Ashok M, Madan R, Joha A, Sivarajah U (2022) Ethical framework for artificial intelligence and digital technologies. Int J Inf Manag 62:102433

Burr C, Leslie D (2023) Ethical assurance: a practical approach to the responsible design, development, and deployment of data-driven technologies. AI Ethics 3(1):73–98

Cheng L, Varshney KR, Liu H (2021) Socially responsible ai algorithms: Issues, purposes, and challenges. J Artif Intell Res 71:1137–1181

Cihon P (2019) Standards for AI governance: international standards to enable global coordination in AI research & development. Future of Humanity Institute. University of Oxford, pp 340–342 de Almeida PGR, dos Santos CD, Farias JS (2021) Artificial intelligence regulation: a framework for governance. Ethics Inf Technol 23(3):505–525

Díaz-Rodríguez N, Del Ser J, Coeckelbergh M, de Prado ML, Herrera-Viedma E, Herrera F (2023) Connecting the dots in trustworthy artificial intelligence: from AI principles, ethics, and key requirements to responsible AI systems and regulation. Inf Fusion 99:101896

Dwivedi R, Dave D, Naik H, Singhal S, Omer R, Patel P, ... Ranjan R (2023) Explainable AI (XAI): core ideas, techniques, and solutions. ACM Comput Surv 55(9):1–33

Dwivedi YK, Hughes L, Ismagilova E, Aarts G, Coombs C, Crick T, ... Williams MD (2021) Artificial Intelligence (AI): multidisciplinary perspectives on emerging challenges, opportunities, and agenda for research, practice and policy. Int J Inf Manag 57:101994

Floridi L, Cowls J (2022) A unified framework of five principles for AI in society. In: Machine learning and the city: applications in architecture and urban design, pp 535–545

Floridi L, Cowls, J, Beltrametti M, Chatila R, Chazerand P, Dignum V, ... Vayena E (2018) AI4People—an ethical framework for a good AI society: opportunities, risks, principles, and recommendations. Minds Mach 28:689–707

Hastuti R (2023) Ethical considerations in the age of artificial intelligence: balancing innovation and social values. West Sci Soc Human Stud 1(02):76–87

Hu M (2020) Cambridge analytica's black box. Big Data Soc 7(2):2053951720938091

Jobin A, Ienca M, Vayena E (2019) The global landscape of AI ethics guidelines. Nat Mach Intell 1(9):389–399

Mensah GB (2023) Artificial intelligence and ethics: a comprehensive review of bias mitigation, transparency, and accountability in AI systems.

Michael K, Abbas R, Roussos G, Scornavacca E, Fosso-Wamba S (2020) Ethics in AI and autonomous system applications design. IEEE Trans Technol Soc 1(3):114–127

Mikalef P, Conboy K, Lundström JE, Popovič A (2022) Thinking responsibly about responsible AI and 'the dark side of AI. Eur J Inf Syst 31(3):257–268

Milanovic M (2015) Human rights treaties and foreign surveillance: privacy in the digital age. Harv Int Law J 56:81

Nam T, Pardo TA (2011, June) Conceptualizing a smart city with dimensions of technology, people, and institutions. In: Proceedings of the 12th annual international digital government research conference: digital government innovation in challenging, pp 282–291

Ng DTK, Leung JKL, Chu SKW, Qiao MS (2021) Conceptualizing AI literacy: an exploratory review. Comput Educ: Artif Intell 2:100041

Oladoyinbo TO, Olabanji SO, Olaniyi OO, Adebiyi OO, Okunleye OJ, Ismaila Alao A (2024) Exploring the challenges of artificial intelligence in data integrity and its influence on social dynamics. Asian J Adv Res Reports 18(2):1–23

Packin NG, Lev-Aretz Y (2018) Learning algorithms and discrimination. In: Research handbook on the law of artificial intelligence. Edward Elgar Publishing, pp 88–113

Radanliev P, Santos O, Brandon-Jones A, Joinson A (2024) Ethics and responsible AI deployment. Front Artif Intell 7:1377011

Robinson SC (2020) Trust, transparency, and openness: How inclusion of cultural values shapes Nordic national public policy strategies for artificial intelligence (AI). Technol Soc 63:101421

Roche C, Wall PJ, Lewis D (2023) Ethics and diversity in artificial intelligence policies, strategies and initiatives. AI Ethics 3(4):1095–1115

Roshanaei M (2024) Towards best practices for mitigating artificial intelligence implicit bias in shaping diversity, inclusion and equity in higher education. Educ Inf Technol 1–26

Saad M (2023) Educating for AI ethics: integrating moral reasoning in artificial intelligence curricula. Soc Sci Spectr 2(1):58–64

Sanderson C, Douglas D, Lu Q, Schleiger E, Whittle J, Lacey J, ... Hansen D (2023) AI ethics principles in practice: Perspectives of designers and developers. IEEE Trans Technol Soc

Sartor G, Lagioia F (2020) The impact of the General Data Protection Regulation (GDPR) on artificial intelligence

Schwartz R, Schwartz R, Vassilev A, Greene K, Perine L, Burt A, Hall P (2022) Towards a standard for identifying and managing bias in artificial intelligence, vol 3. US Department of Commerce, National Institute of Standards and Technology

Sharma S, Graydon MS (2021) Social bias in AI and its implications

Shen Y, Pearson S (2011) Privacy-enhancing technologies: a review. Hewlet Packard Development Company. https://bit.ly/3cfpAKz

Shneiderman B (2020) Bridging the gap between ethics and practice: guidelines for reliable, safe, and trustworthy human-centered AI systems. ACM Trans Interact Intell Syst (TiiS) 10(4):1–31

Slaughter RK, Kopec J, Batal M (2020) Algorithms and economic justice: a taxonomy of harms and a path forward for the federal trade commission. Yale J Law Technol 23:1

Smuha NA (2019) The EU approach to ethics guidelines for trustworthy artificial intelligence. Comput Law Rev Int 20(4):97–106

Stahl BC (2021) Artificial intelligence for a better future: an ecosystem perspective on the ethics of AI and emerging digital technologies. Springer Nature, p 124

Weber-Lewerenz B (2021) Corporate digital responsibility (CDR) in construction engineering—ethical guidelines for the application of digital transformation and artificial intelligence (AI) in user practice. SN Appl Sci 3:1–25

Williams R, Cloete R, Cobbe J, Cottrill C, Edwards P, Markovic M, ... Pang W (2022) From transparency to accountability of intelligent systems: moving beyond aspirations. Data Policy 4:e7

Yu PK (2002) Bridging the digital divide: equality in the information age. Cardozo Arts Entertain Law J 20:1

Zhang H, Lee I, Ali S, DiPaola D, Cheng Y, Breazeal C (2023) Integrating ethics and career futures with technical learning to promote AI literacy for middle school students: an exploratory study. Int J Artif Intell Educ 33(2):290–324

SPRINGER NATURE

GPSR Compliance

The European Union's (EU) General Product Safety Regulation (GPSR) is a set of rules that requires consumer products to be safe and our obligations to ensure this.

If you have any concerns about our products, you can contact us on ProductSafety@springernature.com

In case Publisher is established outside the EU, the EU authorized representative is:

Springer Nature Customer Service Center GmbH
Europaplatz 3
69115 Heidelberg, Germany

The manufacturer's authorised representative in the EU is Springer Nature Customer Service Centre GmbH, Europaplatz 3, 69115 Heidelberg, Germany. If you have any concerns regarding our products, please contact ProductSafety@springernature.com

Printed and bound by CPI Group (UK) Ltd, Croydon, CR0 4YY
06/10/2026
02228459-0001